Advanced Introduction to Entrepreneurship

D1494143

Elgar Advanced Introductions are stimulating and thoughtful introductions to major fields in the social sciences and law, expertly written by some of the world's leading scholars. Designed to be accessible yet rigorous, they offer concise and lucid surveys of the substantive and policy issues associated with discrete subject areas.

The aims of the series are two-fold: to pinpoint essential principles of a particular field, and to offer insights that stimulate critical thinking. By distilling the vast and often technical corpus of information on the subject into a concise and meaningful form, the books serve as accessible introductions for undergraduate and graduate students coming to the subject for the first time. Importantly, they also develop well-informed, nuanced critiques of the field that will challenge and extend the understanding of advanced students, scholars and policy-makers.

Titles in the series include:

International Political Economy
Benjamin J. Cohen

The Austrian School of Economics
Randall G. Holcombe

Cultural Economics
Ruth Towse

Law and Development
Michael J. Trebilcock and Mariana Mota Prado

International Conflict and Security Law
Nigel D. White

Comparative Constitutional Law
Mark Tushnet

International Human Rights Law
Dinah L. Shelton

Entrepreneurship
Robert D. Hisrich

Advanced Introduction to

Entrepreneurship

ROBERT D. HISRICH

*Garvin Professor of Global Entrepreneurship
and Director, Walker Center for Global
Entrepreneurship, Thunderbird School of
Global Management, USA*

Elgar Advanced Introductions

Edward Elgar
Cheltenham, UK • Northampton, MA, USA

Published by
Edward Elgar Publishing Limited
The Lypiatts
15 Lansdown Road
Cheltenham
Glos GL50 2JA
UK

Edward Elgar Publishing, Inc.
William Pratt House
9 Dewey Court
Northampton
Massachusetts 01060
USA

A catalogue record for this book
is available from the British Library

Library of Congress Control Number: 2014938769

MIX
Paper from
responsible sources
FSC
www.fsc.org   FSC® C013056

ISBN 978 1 78254 615 3 (cased)
ISBN 978 1 78254 617 7 (paperback)
ISBN 978 1 78254 616 0 (eBook)

Typeset by Servis Filmsetting Ltd, Stockport, Cheshire
Printed and bound in Great Britain by T.J. International Ltd, Padstow

Contents

Preface

Being an entrepreneur and creating value by establishing a new organization plays an important role in profit and non-profit organizations; medicine, religion, science and the arts; and in the growth and prosperity of regions and nations. Large-scale outcomes in each of these areas can have quite humble beginnings: the entrepreneurial opportunity begins at the nexus of an enterprising individual solving a need that provides the basis for a lucrative opportunity.

For entrepreneurs to flourish and for new organizations to be created, four elements are required: an infrastructure that is supportive; an idea with unique value propositions; capital to get started and grow; and an entrepreneur to work toward making the venture a reality. While this sounds simple, it is not. Laws and tax structures are not always encouraging, not all ideas are viable in a given market, capital is often not readily available for risky start-up opportunities and, of course, the right person has to be the driving force behind it all. Thinking of entrepreneurship in this way, it is no wonder strong business ventures do not emerge overnight. Traits needed include: being a visionary; being able to fail; persistence; being a team player; and commitment. For the entrepreneur today who starts their own enterprise, the experience is filled with enthusiasm, frustration, anxiety and hard work. There is a high failure rate due to such things as poor sales, too high costs, lack of capital, hypercompetition or lack of skills or managerial ability. Even though the financial, social and emotional risk can be high, so can be the rewards.

This book – *Advanced Introduction to Entrepreneurship* – provides insights into the person as well as the venture creation process. To provide this understanding, the book is divided into 14 chapters that can be grouped into four parts.

Part 1, Overview of the Entrepreneur, consisting of the first three chapters, focuses on the person – the entrepreneur, corporate entrepreneur, government entrepreneur and social entrepreneur. Their characteristics, motivations and decision making process are developed, providing an understanding of the individual who creates the new venture.

Part 2, Innovation and the Idea, focuses on creativity, innovation, the opportunity and the idea. Chapter 4 looks at creativity and innovation, providing a base for developing the idea. After a discussion of identifying an opportunity through the creation of an opportunity assessment plan (Chapter 5), this part concludes with Chapter 6 – creating and protecting the idea.

Part 3, The Business Plan, focuses on the aspects of the business plan. After a presentation of the overall business plan (Chapter 7), specific aspects of the business plan are discussed: the marketing plan (Chapter 8); the financial plan (Chapter 9); and the organizational plan (Chapter 10).

Part 4, The Venture, the final part of the book, deals with the venture and basically operationalizes the business plan. This part starts by discussing one of the four elements required: obtaining capital and other resources (Chapter 11). Following a discussion of launching (Chapter 12) and growing (Chapter 13) the venture, the book concludes with Chapter 14 – building a lasting company and ending the venture.

Many individuals – corporate executives, entrepreneurs, small business managers, professors from all over the world and the publishing staff – have made this book possible. Thanks go to my research assistants, Jonathan Beckley and Charise Foo, who provided significant research and editorial assistance. My utmost appreciation goes to my administrative assistant, Carol Pacelli, for her research and editing and without whom this book would have never been prepared in a timely manner.

I am deeply indebted to my wife, Tina; my daughters, Kary, Katy and Kelly; my son-in-law, Rich; and my grandchildren, Rachel, Andrew and Sarah, as well as Kaiya for their support and understanding of my time commitment in writing this book. It is to them and their generation that this book is particularly dedicated, as the world truly needs to understand entrepreneurs and the venture creation process.

PART I

Overview of the entrepreneur

1 Entrepreneurship: a historical perspective

Scenario: Tim and Karrie League – Alamo Drafthouse

A visit to the movie theater provokes a mix of emotions and anticipations. For some, it is a warm and nostalgic remembrance of your parents bringing you to watch a classic film that captivates you, influences you and stays in your memories into adulthood. For others, it is a chaotic and barely worth it race to throw yourself into a good seat, dodge any talkers (and their screaming children), balance your overpriced, oversized and overbuttered box of popcorn in your lap and sit through 20 minutes of excruciatingly dull advertisements. Alamo Drafthouse aims toward the first experience. Year-round, crowds of locals in Austin, Texas flock over to treat themselves to their favorite aspects of this unique joint that centers itself between a movie theater and a restaurant. Whether it is sipping a pint of local beer at the full bar in the lobby, or enjoying a nibble from the long menu of fresh and tasty entrees delivered right to your seat, or even simply coming for the mélange of indie, cult-classic and first-run films, Alamo Drafthouse offers a fusion of services truly unique to the cinema industry.

Founders Tim and Karrie League have been movie lovers from childhood into adulthood. Garnering that love of the cinema, the two leased out a small abandoned movie theater in the mid 1990s and remodeled it to run cult-classics and second-run films, sometimes incorporating unique add-ons like sing-along lyrics or live music. Taking advantage of Austin's creative and business-friendly culture, the Leagues turned their passion into a business that not only catered to the diverse tastes of their movie-obsessed audience but also incorporated their own values into their business model, taking out what they hated most about theaters and putting in more of what they loved. Alamo attendees can expect a fantastic experience even before the movie starts. Friendly, laid-back servers will quickly take your order and just as quickly deliver your food and beer to the skinny table in front of you. Instead of watching boring ads on the screen, attendees enjoy a smorgasbord of cartoons and vintage movie clips. And right before the movie starts, Alamo humorously but very seriously warns its viewers of its zero tolerance no talking/texting policy. Alamo is known to throw out movie disrupters and, no, you do not get your money back.

After 20 years, Alamo Drafthouse has established itself as a proud staple of the "Keep Austin Weird" culture, and has been recognized nationally as an innovator of the recently lacking-of-luster cinema industry. Alamo has also become the sole venue for film presentations during the city's famed South by Southwest annual film and music festival that attracts visitors and celebrities alike. With five theaters in Austin, three in San Antonio, several more spread throughout the rest of Texas and venues about to open in New York, Colorado and Virginia, Alamo Drafthouse is looking to bring its funky and addictive antics to fresh markets. And while expanding to different areas brings about the added risk of not generating as strong a following as in Austin, the Leagues and their team are confident that they will be able to work their quirky and slightly rebellious spirit into the hearts of movie lovers everywhere (see Online sources).

Introduction

As occurred in the case above, each day throughout the world thousands of new ventures are launched in spite of the odds of their existing five years later.

Who is an entrepreneur? What is entrepreneurship? What is new venture creation? These frequently asked questions reflect the increased national and international interest in entrepreneurs by individuals, university professors and students, and government officials. In spite of all this interest, a concise, universally accepted definition has not yet emerged. The development of the theory of entrepreneurship parallels to a great extent the development of the term itself. The word "entrepreneur" is French, and, literally translated, means "between-taker" or "go-between".

This chapter introduces entrepreneurship by looking at entrepreneurship and economic development and then entrepreneurship through the ages. Following the definition of entrepreneurship, profiles of some entrepreneurs over time are discussed. The chapter closes with a discussion of the nature of entrepreneurship.

Entrepreneurship and economic development[1]

Being an entrepreneur and creating value by establishing a new organization in both the profit and non-profit sectors in business as well as the arts impacts both economic and social conditions.[2] This creation process takes more time and effort than one can imagine and is by no means easy, with a high failure rate reaching over 70 percent in certain countries and environments.

For entrepreneurs to flourish and for new organizations to be created, four elements are required: an infrastructure that is supportive; an idea with unique value propositions; capital to get started and grow; and an entrepreneur to work toward making the venture a reality. This sounds very simple, but it is not. Laws and tax structures are not always encouraging, not all ideas are viable in a given market, capital is often not readily available for risky start-up opportunities and, of course, the right person has to be the driving force behind it all. Thinking of entrepreneurship in this way, it is no wonder strong business ventures do not emerge overnight.

Even entrepreneurship on a small scale can have great impact. "Gazelles" are businesses that may start out small but have swift, high growth potential. An infrastructure should be developed that supports both start-ups and these fast growth businesses. When times look bleak, people often look for one big, cataclysmic solution, which is impossible to find; yet, if they set their sights on a smaller scale – through resource allocation and the encouragement of innovation and risk taking – gazelles can be born and flourish from the many ventures started.

Entrepreneurship through the ages

Earliest period

An example of an early definition of an entrepreneur as a go-between is Marco Polo, who established trade routes to the Far East. As a go-between, Marco Polo would sign a contract with a money person (forerunner of today's venture capitalist) to sell the goods. A common contract during this time provided a loan to the merchant-adventurer at about a 22 percent rate including insurance. The capitalist was a passive risk bearer and the merchant-adventurer took the active role in trading, bearing all the physical and emotional risks. When the merchant-adventurer successfully sold the goods and completed the trip, the profits were divided with the capitalist taking most, up to 75 percent, while the merchant-adventurer settled for the remaining 25 percent.

Middle Ages

In the Middle Ages, the term "entrepreneur" was used to describe both an actor and a person who managed large production projects. In such large production projects, this individual did not take any risks, but merely managed the project using the resources provided, usually by the government of the country. A typical entrepreneur in the Middle Ages was the cleric – the person in charge of great architectural works, such as castles and fortifications, public buildings, abbeys and cathedrals.

Seventeenth century

The connection between risk and entrepreneurship developed in the seventeenth century. During this period, an entrepreneur entered into a contractual arrangement with the government to perform a service or to supply stipulated products. Since the contract price was fixed, any resulting profits or losses were the entrepreneur's. One entrepreneur in this period was John Law, a Frenchman, who was allowed to establish a royal bank. The bank eventually evolved into an exclusive franchise to form a trading company in the New World – the Mississippi Company. Unfortunately, Law's monopoly led to his downfall when he attempted to push the company's stock price higher than the value of its assets and the company collapsed.

Richard Cantillon, a noted economist and author in the 1700s, understood Law's mistake. Cantillon developed one of the early theories of the entrepreneur and is regarded by some as the founder of the term. He viewed the entrepreneur as a risk taker, observing that merchants, farmers, craftsmen and other sole proprietors "buy at a certain price and sell at an uncertain price, therefore operating at a risk".[3]

Eighteenth century

In the eighteenth century, the person providing capital (money provider) was differentiated from the one who needed capital (entrepreneur). This reflected the industrialization occurring throughout the world. Many of the inventions developed during this time were reactions to the changing world, such as the inventions of Eli Whitney and Thomas Edison. Both Whitney and Edison were developing new technologies and were unable to finance their inventions themselves. Whereas Whitney financed his cotton gin with expropriated British crown property, Edison raised capital from private sources to develop and experiment in the fields of electricity and chemistry. Both Edison and Whitney were capital users (entrepreneurs), not providers (venture capitalists).

Nineteenth and twentieth centuries

In the late nineteenth and early twentieth centuries, entrepreneurs were frequently not distinguished from managers and were viewed mostly from an economic perspective:

> Briefly stated, the entrepreneur organizes and operates an enterprise for personal gain. He pays current prices for the materials consumed in the business, for the use of the land, for the personal services he employs and for the capital he requires. He contributes his own initiative, skill and ingenuity in planning, organizing and administering the enterprise. He also assumes the chance of loss and gain consequent to unforeseen and uncontrollable circumstances. The net residue of the annual receipts of the enterprise after all costs have been paid, he retains for himself.[4]

Andrew Carnegie is a good example using this definition. Carnegie adapted and developed new technology in the creation of products for economic vitality. From a poor Scottish family, Carnegie made the American steel industry one of the wonders of the industrial world, primarily through his unremitting competitiveness rather than his inventiveness or creativity.

In the middle of the twentieth century, the notion of an "entrepreneur as an innovator" was established.

> The function of the entrepreneur is to reform or revolutionize the pattern of production by exploiting an invention or, more generally, an untried technological method of producing a new commodity or producing an old one in a new way, opening a new source of supply of materials or a new outlet for products, by organizing a new industry.[5]

The concept of innovation and newness is an integral part of entrepreneurship and the act of introducing something new is one of the most difficult tasks for the entrepreneur. It takes the ability not only to create and conceptualize but also to understand all the forces at work in the environment. Edward Harriman, who reorganized the Ontario and Southern railroad through the Northern Pacific Trust, and John Pierpont Morgan, who developed a large banking house by reorganizing and financing the nation's industries, are examples of entrepreneurs fitting this definition. These organizational innovations are frequently as difficult to develop successfully as the more traditional technological innovations (transistors, computers, lasers) that are usually associated with being an entrepreneur.

Definitions of the entrepreneur

The concept of an entrepreneur varies depending on whether from a business, managerial or personal perspective. The concept from these different perspectives is reflected in the following definitions:

- To an economist, an entrepreneur is one who brings resources, labor, materials and other assets into combinations that make their value greater than before, and also one who introduces changes, innovations and a new order. To a psychologist, such a person is typically driven by certain forces – the need to obtain or attain something, to experiment, to accomplish or perhaps to escape the authority of others. To one businessman, an entrepreneur appears as a threat, an aggressive competitor, whereas to another business- man, the same entrepreneur may be an ally, a source of supply, a customer or someone who creates wealth for others, as well as finds better ways to utilize resources, reduce waste and produce jobs others are glad to get.[6]
- Entrepreneurship is the dynamic process of creating incremental wealth. Wealth is created by individuals who assume the major risks in terms of equity, time and/or career commitment or pro- vide value for some product or service. The product or service may or may not be new or unique, but value must somehow be infused by the entrepreneur by receiving and locating the necessary skills and resources.[7]

Although each of these definitions views entrepreneurs from a differ- ent perspective, they both contain such similar notions as newness, organizing, creating, wealth and risk taking. Yet each definition is somewhat restrictive, since entrepreneurs are found in all professions – education, medicine, research, law, architecture, engineering, social work and distribution. To include all types of entrepreneurial behavior, the following definition of entrepreneurship is a better fit: Entrepreneurship is the process of creating something new with value by devoting the necessary time and effort, assuming the accompanying financial, psychic and social risks, and receiving the resulting rewards of monetary and personal satisfaction and independence.[8]

This definition stresses four basic aspects of entrepreneurship. First, entrepreneurship involves creating – creating something new of value. The creation has to have value to the entrepreneur and value to the customer. Second, entrepreneurship requires the devotion of the necessary time and effort. Only those going through the entrepreneurial process truly appreciate the significant amount of time and effort it takes to create something new and make it operational. Assuming the necessary risks is the third aspect of entrepreneurship. These risks take a variety of specific forms but are in financial, psychological and social areas.[9] The final part of the definition involves the rewards of being an entrepreneur. The most important of these rewards is independence, followed by personal satisfaction and profit in for-profit organizations.

Examples of entrepreneurial leadership

There are numerous examples of entrepreneurial leaders in each century in various areas. These individuals and their stories provide understanding of the concept of entrepreneurship in a variety of areas.

Saint Peter

After the death of Jesus, his closest follower, Peter, was left with a decision. He could either distance himself from a convicted criminal or he could follow his passion and continue the teachings of his leader. Peter chose to accept the entrepreneurial approach – accepting risk and creating something new – the Roman Catholic Church.

Starting in Jerusalem and neighboring areas of Palestine, Peter and his followers began to expand their teachings to surrounding areas of the Roman world. Like many entrepreneurs, Peter knew that a critical mass was necessary for his endeavor to succeed. He championed the benefits of what he proclaimed and how to achieve it. His dedication took him across great distances and often into hostile environments.

By the time of his death around 64 AD, the foundations of the now Roman Catholic Church were laid. Peter's work of creating a new church had been set into motion by his actions. His work to establish the Roman Catholic Church is reflected in many ways, but perhaps the most fitting is that his tomb lies beneath the grounds of the church that bears his name – St Peter's Basilica. Two thousand years later, the spirit of Peter's entrepreneurial activities still exists. The fact that he was able to offer something that people would be interested in is evidenced by the fact that there are currently over 2 billion Christians, a market size any entrepreneur would love to achieve.[10]

Edward Teach (Blackbeard the Pirate)

From 1716 to 1718, Blackbeard the Pirate ruled the seas from the Atlantic seaboard through the Caribbean. He was feared by the people living on the coast of North Carolina as well as the sailors in many seafaring vessels. Often portrayed as ruthless and brutal, Blackbeard was also a businessman and leader who flourished in his trade like few before or after him.

By 1716, he was no longer known as Edward Teach but by Blackbeard the Pirate, his menacing face and figure well known along the coast of the British colonies. Because people were scared to begin with, he often would not need to resort to violence to take their boats or property.

The life of a pirate on Blackbeard's boat, the *Queen Anne's Revenge*, was usually better than the life on the farms or plantations that made up most of society of early eighteenth-century America. All booty taken by the pirates would be divided evenly among the crew, one part each, save the captain's two. The pirates who joined Blackbeard's command usually came from the lowest classes of society and were joining because they often faced few prospects on shore. Some were former members of the British Navy who found the conditions and treatment they received so lacking that they took up Blackbeard's call for hands.[11]

During his two-year reign, Blackbeard is thought to have captured over 25 vessels as well as his most famous moment – the siege of Charleston, South Carolina in the spring of 1718. He controlled one of the wealthiest cities in the colonies for nearly two weeks. After negotiations described as quite business-like, the leaders of the city decided to deliver the medical supplies demanded, which ended his blockade.[12]

Blackbeard was finally captured and killed in 1718 off the coast of the Outer Banks of North Carolina by Lieutenant Robert Maynard. Blackbeard's entrepreneurial spirit was evident in the way he managed his crew, the tactics he took to build his reputation and the financial rewards he gained from his actions. Though they were illegal, Blackbeard's piracy reflected an independent man battling against the established order.

Louis Pasteur

Going against the established way of thinking is an entrepreneurial tendency. It is this desire for independence, both in thought and action, which allows someone to create something new. Such actions might bring with them consternation from peers and communities as the thinking is against the accepted norms; it is only by pushing these boundaries that discoveries can be made.

Louis Pasteur is an example of a scientist whose contributions to his field, and society as a whole, truly revolutionized not only the scientific community but also the lives and habits of people all around the world. Pasteur had achieved a moderate level of success in his field of academia, rising to become the Dean and Professor of Chemistry at the Faculty of Sciences in Lille, France.

It was during a visit to the countryside that Pasteur began to explore the field of alcoholic fermentation, as the wine and beer makers in the region were having problems fermenting their brews. Although some scientists believed that yeast was the cause of fermentation, they were often ridiculed by the scientific experts of the day. Pasteur began to investigate the area and, after several years of experimentation, was able to identify the critical factors of fermentation and the role of yeast in the process. In 1862, he identified what was his most famous discovery, the one that bears his name, the idea that by heating milk, wine or beer to a specific temperature for a short period of time, he was able to kill the microorganisms responsible for premature spoilage. Pasteurization revolutionized not only the safety of certain foods by killing the bacteria present in them but also the manner in which they were consumed by allowing for increased transportation, resulting in the transformation of the milk industry from a very local and farm-centric market to one of transporting dairy products across great distances without sacrificing safety or quality.

Like so many entrepreneurs and discoverers, Pasteur was not satisfied with the success he had achieved, so he continued in his search for new challenges. His combination of intellect, ego and brashness helped push him from one discovery to the next.[13]

Continuing his model of using experimentation and scientific analysis to develop a better understanding, Pasteur went on to what are his two most important discoveries – his theories on germs and how to control them and the creation of a vaccination against rabies. Through his studies of both germs themselves and the way that hospitals were being run, Pasteur brought to the attention of doctors the necessity of proper sterilization and sanitation in order to prevent the spread of disease from one patient to another through germ contamination. This was a radical change to the medical profession and one that would mark incalculable improvements on both the treatment and its success rate.

His work on viruses, and rabies in particular, was equally revolutionary. Pasteur was the first person to find that a weak form of a virus could be used as protection against a stronger, more deadly form of that virus. Pasteur's process of vaccination was later applied to other diseases affecting both humans and livestock such as cholera, anthrax and malaria.

Pasteur's contributions to science and humanity were deep and lasting. Although rewarded with accolades and commendations by his peers and society later in his life, money was not the result nor was it the motivator. Pasteur sought the independence to pursue what he wanted in a way that he saw best.

John Rockefeller

John Rockefeller was an extraordinary American entrepreneur and philanthropist. From a young age, Rockefeller believed the most important thing in life was to make as much money as possible.[14] Through hard work, determination and a strong competitive nature, he achieved his goal and more by becoming the world's first billionaire. He also supported multiple hospitals and schools, while establishing his own philanthropic organizations.

At the age of 18, his entrepreneurial spirit first appeared as he became a partner in a commission house. Realizing the importance of credit borrowing, he spent time building a strong reputation through which he took out loans and used this money to capitalize his business, making even more money for himself before paying the loan back when it became due.

In 1870, Rockefeller along with his brother and three other entrepreneurs established the Standard Oil Company in Cleveland, Ohio. Standard Oil soon became one of the most profitable refineries in Cleveland. Through controversial, but legal, deals with his local railroad cartels, he managed to secure rebates and discounts leaping far ahead of his competition. By 1872, Standard Oil had bought out all but 4 of its 26 local rivals.

Standard Oil's monopolistic business practices drew much criticism from politicians and journalists alike. In 1911, the Supreme Court of the United States ruled that Standard Oil was a monopoly that could no longer continue, declaring that it had to be broken into 34 different companies. Out of this fracture came many oil companies still well known today including Conoco, Amaco, Chevron, Exxon and Mobil; Rockefeller held substantial shares in each one.

Not dissuaded by the actions of the court, Rockefeller chose to change his entrepreneurial pursuits away from making money and toward giving it away. Holding a substantial position in Standard Oil's equities, he felt the need to disperse his wealth to those less fortunate in places where he thought the money could be put to good use; this started the rise of American social philanthropy. The Rockefeller Foundation was established in 1913 to "promote well-being" by expanding opportunities for poor and venerable individuals on an international scale. There were many institutions funded through Rockefeller, including medical, academic and research centers all over the world.

Rockefeller accomplished much in terms of personal and professional achievements. From a young age to his death in 1937, his strong discipline and willpower allowed him to first create value in ways that had not been done before, and then to distribute that value to the people he felt needed it most. His legacy and philanthropy will continue for many decades to come.

Madame CJ Walker

Entrepreneurs often find opportunities and success in spite of great odds and obstacles. Madame CJ Walker (born Sarah McWilliams) was an example of one such person.[15] Born to former slaves in Louisiana, a black woman in the recently desegregated south in 1867 would have faced just about every impediment imaginable in achieving success.

CJ Walker began losing her hair. While many who had lived through such a life might have decided this was just another complication to a life already filled with too many, CJ Walker saw this as an opportunity. After trying many lotions, potions and remedies, she finally found one that worked. If it had worked for her, maybe there were other people who might be interested in purchasing the product. She started as a sales agent for that product created by another black woman, Annie Malone, and moved to Denver.

In Denver, she met and married a St. Louis newspaper man who had a gift for marketing. It was here that she was able to transform into a businesswoman. She had identified an unserved market, hair care products for black women, and realized the many opportunities that were available in this market. She renamed the product "Madam Walker's Wonderful Hair Grower" and began to advertise in black newspapers throughout the country as a scalp conditioning and hair straightening formula. They set up a manufacturing facility to address the growing demand and she began to travel across the country, especially the south, to build awareness of the lotion.

After three years, demand was so high that CJ Walker was able to expand her company, building a beautician school in Pittsburgh to train other women to sell her products door-to-door. By 1914, only ten years after she had initially arrived in Denver with $2 in her pocket, CJ Walker was the first self-made female black millionaire in the United States. At one point, she employed over 3000 women and had a wide range of hair and skin care products.

Her success allowed her to do things that no black woman had done before in the United States. CJ Walker is an example of an entrepreneur who saw an opportunity and, even without the skills or background in the field, she did whatever it took, made sacrifices in her life, and overcame all of the odds to not only be a successful businesswoman by every measure but also an inspiration to countless women who followed her.

Muhammad Yunus

The Grameen Bank is a Bangladeshi micro-lending institution that lends to the poorest men and women in Bangladesh based on trust and accountability without demanding collateral. It is the only means of access to capital for the poor in Bangladesh enabling them to become micro entrepreneurs, catalysing the development of enhanced socio-economic conditions for millions who are otherwise denied opportunity to advance their conditions. The bank was started by Muhammad Yunus, who later won the Nobel Peace Prize for his work in microfinance. The project was started in 1976. By October 2011, the bank had 8.349 million borrowers, of whom 97 percent were women. Its 2565 branches provide services to over 97 percent of all the villages in Bangladesh.[16]

Muhammad Yunus is an example of a selfless entrepreneur. His entrepreneurial vision is to allow other people to become successful entrepreneurs.[17] He believes that not all entrepreneurs need a large capital infusion or enormous venture capital seed money; sometimes it only takes a few dollars in the right environment to get an idea up and running.

The idea of microfinance was not something new when Yunus returned to his home in Bangladesh in 1976 after teaching economics in the United States for several years. But it was something that many people, both institutional lenders and private agencies, were hesitant to do because of the perceived difficulty in recouping loans to poor and high risk people. The common belief was that this was not a sustainable business model; that such activities were better left to the aid agencies and non-governmental organizations (NGOs), not to for-profit enterprises.

In 1976, then Professor of Economics at Chittagong University, during a visit to the village of Jobra to study poverty in rural villages, Yunus made his first loan of $27 to a group of local craftsmen in order to see the impact. His intention was not to revolutionize the banking industry in developing countries or to lay the seeds for what would become more than a $5 billion industry. The first loan was merely to help those people who needed a small amount of money to do something valuable in their lives.

After seeing the impact of this first loan and the way in which he was repaid, Yunus began to envision a model that could work throughout impoverished villages. He found that the poor would often quickly repay their loans with few problems. Although the loans would often be for less than $20, these loans would have far-reaching impact that would be felt within the villages. People could be proud businesspeople. Yunus also focused on lending to women, realizing that their success would have a much stronger impact than would occur by lending to men.

Yunus continued to expand his loan practices throughout Bangladesh in the 1970s. By the early 1980s, he had expanded to other developing countries and in 1983, he formed the Grameen Bank, the institutional home of his micro-lending practices. Yunus's impact is best shown though the proliferation and movement of microfinance into the mainstream of the financial services industry. The Grameen Bank has grown to over 2500 branches, employing 22000 people and disbursing over $6 billion in loans to 7 million people. Although the goal of the Grameen Bank is to help the impoverished, it is still a for-profit institution that has turned a profit almost every year.

In 2006, Yunus and the Grameen Bank were recognized for their impact on society and the lives of so many people around the world and won the Nobel Peace Prize. This award reflects the belief that allowing entrepreneurial activities to flourish, at all levels, can bring peace to communities and offer hope to those who may not have had it before. Muhammad Yunus was not the first of the "social entrepreneurs", but his impact will arguably leave a significant mark. Yunus revolutionized an industry and taught millions how to be entrepreneurs.

James Dyson

In 1977, James Dyson was trying to clean up a recently purchased old farmhouse in the British countryside.[18] Frustrated by the lack of suction power in the vacuum cleaner he was using, he began to think of ways to solve this problem. Five years and 5126 prototypes later, he had built the Cyclone, a bagless vacuum that used centrifugal force to create intense suction power that would not degrade with use. At this point, Dyson was still an inventor, coming up with some designs for a product that he thought people might want. His entrepreneurial spirit came forward in the subsequent years in his efforts to bring his vacuum cleaner to market.

The vacuum cleaner industry at the time was dominated by a few large, well-established companies led by Hoover and Electrolux. It was not an industry that was viewed as having particularly sophisticated or technically advanced products. Without the financial resources to manufacture and market his new product, Dyson first attempted to just sell his vacuum cleaner to one of the large companies. No one was interested. Running low on capital and without a manufacturer in Europe, Dyson was finally able to convince a Japanese company called Apex to distribute the Cyclone in Japan. The licensing agreement with Apex offered him a small percentage royalty payment up to a fixed amount. Sales of the product exploded in Japan even though it was priced at about $2000 per vacuum.

Based on the experience in Japan, Dyson decided that he would need to establish his own company if he wanted to successfully launch in the British market. After several meetings with venture capitalists, he was finally able to secure the financing necessary to build the manufacturing facilities needed.

By 1995, only a year after its release, Dyson's vacuum cleaners were selling about 28 000 units each week to become the top selling upright vacuum in the country, even priced at about £300. His entrepreneurial spirit pervaded his corporate structure as he wanted to keep the focus on innovation and improvement rather than bureaucracy.

A few years later, Dyson entered the competitive US market and within a few years had earned 15 percent of the market. The resolution of his patent infringement lawsuit against Hoover netted him over $4 million, allowing him to expand production facilities in Asia and continue the research and development (R&D) work his company is dependent on.

The entrepreneurial spirit within James Dyson has allowed him to succeed after years of failure and disappointments, to battle much larger and established competition and keeps him looking for new ideas. It allowed him to turn one day's cleaning dissatisfaction into a large fortune, which now provides the independence that allows him the flexibility in his quest for innovation.

Debbi Fields

Entrepreneurship is often about surviving through difficult times while waiting for success to come. Most entrepreneurs find their first steps into a new endeavor to be extremely difficult and frustrating, and must learn from these experiences in order to earn their place in a crowded market. Debbi Fields was a housewife with no business experience when she opened her first cookie store in Palo Alto, California in 1977.[19]

Debbi Fields's passion for her cookies allowed her to look at that first day of scant sales not as a rejection but rather a learning lesson on what she should do the next day. The next day she set out with a tray of her cookies and walked the street, giving a free cookie to everyone she met. Some people walked past, others took a sample and a few returned to the store to purchase more. After doing this for several weeks, she had finally built a market for her cookies.

After building a strong local market for her cookies, Fields began to expand from Northern California. As she expanded, she continued to focus on the lessons she learned in her first days of business: to market to a customer who does not know you, you sometimes have to give some things away.

Debbi Fields was able to grow her single cookie store to over 1000 stores across the country before selling control to an investment group for nearly $300 million. Although not her intent in opening her first store, the financial gain was a great reward for taking the risk of trying to sell people a product that they could easily make in their own homes.

Debbi Fields also served as an example to other women. She proved that even in today's hypercompetitive environment you need to have a passion for your idea, perseverance to overcome the inevitable difficulties that will arise, and consistent focus on your customers' needs and how to make them happy.

Peter Jackson

By 2003, Peter Jackson had turned the New Zealand film industry from a regional center to a major player in Hollywood productions, built a state of the art production and digital effects facility and showed that an outsider to the Hollywood establishment could become one of the industry's most sought after and popular directors.[20] Achieving this level of success meant taking significant risks and strong persistence; Jackson sacrificed many years of his life in the pursuit of his dream to turn the well-known works of J.R.R. Tolkien into *The Lord of the Rings*

Trilogy. His success was in part because of his distancing himself from the Hollywood establishment, allowing him to make the films as he envisioned them. After ten years, Jackson can look back at the three movies, the 17 Academy Awards won, the more than $1 billion in box office receipts and the success that his vision and leadership brought.

Growing up on the North Island of New Zealand in the 1960s, Peter Jackson had an early affinity for movies, sometimes shooting scenes in his backyard with an 8 mm camera. By 1987, he had learned enough about filmmaking to attempt to make his own movie, *Bad Taste*, which he eventually took to the Cannes Film Festival where it received little acclaim. Jackson, though, was able to sell its rights for enough money to pay back the costs of production.

Jackson continued to expand his skills, making low-budget horror movies. During this time, he began to work with several people who would become partners in his future films; Jackson realized the importance of surrounding yourself with talented people. After the success of his film *Heavenly Creatures* in 1994, Jackson began to draw the attention of Hollywood. *The Frighteners*, released in 1996 starring Michael J. Fox, was a critical and commercial disappointment, but did give Jackson the recognition necessary to pursue his ultimate dream, *The Lord of the Rings*.

When he initially pitched his idea for *The Lord of the Rings* to movie studios, none were interested. Who would want to invest hundreds of millions of dollars on a no-name director from New Zealand who wanted to do his own visual effects, and complete most of the filming far away from Hollywood's prying eyes? While Jackson wanted to make three movies, the studios wanted him to condense them into two. Jackson held on to his vision, finally obtaining funding from a relatively small studio, New Line Productions, best known for the *Teenage Mutant Ninja Turtles* films. Jackson then retreated to New Zealand's capital city Wellington, where he began to build the team and infrastructure needed to create his films.

Over the course of the next two years, Jackson shot all three films simultaneously. He felt that if all three films were shot at once, the studio was less likely to prevent future releases if the first one performed poorly. He utilized computer generated images (CGIs) in a way no other film had. Fantastic locations were created on the computer, actors donned motion-capture suits so their movement could be transferred to a computer-designed character in a most unique way never before done. He hired local talent in order to build up the nascent New Zealand film industry.

With great anticipation the first film, *The Fellowship of the Ring*, released in 2001, met with strong reviews: "Against all odds in an era of machine-made spectaculars, Mr. Jackson and his collaborators have created a film epic that lives and breathes, that's swept by almost palpable weather".[21] The film grossed over $310 million. The two remaining films were released over the following two years, combining to an additional $800 million at the box office. Cumulatively, the three films combined over $4 billion in worldwide ticket revenue, DVD sales and merchandise. Jackson's contract with the studio netted him nearly 7.5 percent of this, making him one of the wealthiest men in New Zealand.

In many ways, Peter Jackson is the antithesis of the traditional Hollywood director. He took enormous risks to make his movies the way that he wanted, not how a studio executive did. He faced and overcame numerous challenges and obstacles, devising innovative and creative ways to do something many thought were not possible. And, in the end, his success occurred in the form of both critical acclaim and financial independence. He indeed dreamed and had a vision.

Steve Jobs

Reflection upon Steve Jobs, the man, conjures up a cacophony of conflicting ideas about his personality: perfectionist, brute, visionary, dictator, genius. Yet, no one can deny the impact made by Jobs's legacy, Apple Inc., which lives on not only having created a whole new market for consumer-friendly tech ware and gadgets, but also forever putting a dent in the world's ever changing notion of digital communication.

Having grown up in a flourishing Silicon Valley in the 1960s and 1970s, Steve Jobs emerged as a young success, taking interest in the surrounding technology industry, eventually dropping out of college while starting Apple with young technical mind, Steve Wozniak. While their success with selling computers, specifically the Apple II computer, had launched Apple into early achievement, competing for market share with established tycoons such as IBM proved to be a major roadblock. By the mid 1980s, Jobs had been pushed out of his own billion dollar company due to irreconcilable vision differences between him and Apple's board. That didn't stop or even slow Jobs's drive and passion, and Jobs immediately continued to build his new business, NeXT Inc., developing and selling computers for education and business purposes. While building the NeXT line, Jobs also invested in a newly spun-off graphics department from Lucasfilm, Pixar Animation Studios, ultimately becoming the company's Chief Executive Officer (CEO). With the help of Jobs and other Pixar leaders including Ed Catmull, Alvy Ray Smith and John Lasseter, Pixar Animation Studios eventually transformed into a renowned, leading computer-animation company.

Apple bought NeXT in 1996 and eventually reinstated Jobs as Apple's CEO. Jobs's NeXT operating system thus became the starting point for Apple's Macintosh operating system, and paved the way to success through progressive development and strengthening of Apple software and hardware. Jobs's unrelenting tenacity and perfectionism pushed the company into becoming a leading designer and distributor of consumer-friendly digital devices, providing not only a sleek and stylish product but also a powerful, fine-tuned and complex system software built on the premise of consumer-level functionality and productivity.

Steve Jobs's tenacity did not conclude with the success of Apple, but effectively revolutionized the world of entrepreneurship. Small, medium and large companies zealously committed themselves to finding the key to how Jobs was able to push his company to earth-shattering success. What did he do to become the legend that he is now? Was it his network with other smart icons like Steve Wozniak and Apple designer Jonathan Ive? Was it his visionary mindset? His genius? Was it simply a matter of efficient business planning and execution? Or perhaps it was his controversial disregard for social and business norms that routinely bordered on bullying and frequently left employees and suppliers affronted and bewildered. Jobs's style of leadership moved blatantly against any technique based on employee nurturing and encouragement.[22] However, his extreme method of command has caused a curious stir in the ideals of how successful companies should be led. Debates can now be seen between those managers arguing for a critical, direct management of employees and those managers who continue to uphold a more supportive business culture.

Like him or not, no one can ignore the impact Steve Jobs has had on the technology industry and in the ever changing realm of digital communication. The world will forever be impacted by Apple's products like the iPod, the Mac computer, the iPhone and the iPad, which was one of Jobs's last product reveals before his death in 2011 due to complications from pancreatic cancer. And whether critics portray him personally as a god or a devil, Steve Jobs will forever be known as the man who built Apple to become a cultural symbol embraced by the world for years to come.

The nature of entrepreneurship

As indicated in these profiles, entrepreneurship plays an important role in profit and non-profit organizations, in medicine, religion, science, the arts and in the growth and prosperity of regions and nations. Large-scale outcomes in each of these areas can have quite humble beginnings: the entrepreneurial opportunity begins at the nexus of an enterprising individual solving a need that is the basis for a lucrative opportunity. As indicated, there is no prescribed or predetermined path that has to be taken but there are some common traits and experiences.

These traits, which will be discussed in the next chapter, include risk taking, being a visionary, being able to fail, persistence, being a team player and commitment. For the entrepreneur today who starts their own enterprise, the experience is filled with enthusiasm, frustration, anxiety and hard work. There is a high failure rate due to such things as poor sales, too high costs, lack of capital, hypercompetition or lack of skills or managerial ability. Even though the financial, social and emotional risk can be high, so can the rewards.

Summary

This chapter has introduced the concept of entrepreneurship by looking at the term itself, entrepreneurship and economic development, the definition, and profiles of entrepreneurs in the arts, business, medicine, religion and science. The chapter closed with a discussion of the overall nature of entrepreneurship and its future.

NOTES

1 Material in this section is expanded on in an article by Stephanie Arthur and Robert D. Hisrich, "Entrepreneurship through the ages: lessons learned", *Journal of Enterprising Culture* (June 2011), **19** (1), 1–40.

2 Shane Greenstein, "Steve Jobs and the economics of one entrepreneur", *IEEE Micro* (2011), **31** (6), 64–5.

3 Robert F. Hebert and Albert H. Link, *The Entrepreneur – Mainstream Views and Radical Critiques* (New York: Praeger Publishers, 1982), p. 17.

4 Richard T. Ely and Ralph H. Hess, *Outlines of Economics*, 6th edn (New York: Macmillan, 1937), p. 488.

5 Joseph Schumpeter, *Can Capitalism Survive?* (New York: Harper & Row, 1952), p. 72.

6 Karl Vesper, *New Venture Strategies* (Englewood Cliffs, NJ: Prentice Hall, 1980), p. 2.

7 Robert C. Ronstadt, *Entrepreneurship* (Dover, MA: Lord Publishing, 1984), p. 28.

8 Adapted from Robert D. Hisrich, Michael P. Peters and Dean A. Shepherd, *Entrepreneurship*, 9th edn (Burr Hills: McGraw-Hill/Irwin, 2013), pp. 8–11.

9 Brooks Robinson, "Just say 'no' to the safe route", *Smart Business Atlanta* (2013), **10** (12), 6.

10 http://www.religioustolerance.org/worldrel.htm (accessed 18 February 2014).

11 C.R. Pennell (ed.), *Bandits at Sea: A Pirates Reader* (New York: New York University Press, 2001), p. 142, available at http://site.ebrary.com/lib/tbrd/Doc?id=10032500&ppg=155 (accessed 18 February 2014).

12 Joel K. Bourne Jr, "Blackbeard lives", *National Geographic* (August 2006), **210** (1), 146–61.

13 David Cohn, *The Life and Times of Louis Pasteur* (1996), available at http://www.labexplorer.com/louis_pasteur.htm (accessed 18 February 2014); John Waller, *Discovery of the Germ* (Cambridge, UK: Totem Books, 2002), p. 75.

14 N.S.B. Gras, "A new study of Rockefeller", *Bulletin of the Business Historical Society* (October 1941), **15** (4), 52; Rockefeller Foundation (5 April 2007), available at http://www.rockfound.org/about_us/about_us.shtml (accessed 18 February 2014).

15 http://www.africawithin.com/bios/cj_walker.htm (accessed 18 February 2014).

16 Dewan Mahboob Hossain, "Social capital and microfinance: the case of Grameen Bank, Bangladesh", *Middle East Journal of Business* (2013), **8** (4), 13–21.

17 http://www.grameen-info.org/bank/GBGlance.htm (accessed 18 February 2014).

18 D.V.R. Sheshadri and Jane Henry, "Dyson appliances: the 'never-say-die' spirit of entrepreneurship", *South Asian Journal of Management* (2006), **13** (1), 107–28; Joshua Levine, "Carpet diem", *Forbes* (14 October 2002), 206–10; Steve Hamm, "The vacuum man takes on wet hands: James Dyson moves beyond cyclonic vacuums to bring the world a better hand dryer", *BusinessWeek* (2 July 2007), 84–6.

19 Paulette Thomas, "Lessons from . . . the cookie queen", *Wall Street Journal* (New York), Eastern edition (30 March 1998), R6; http://www.ltbn.com/hall_of_fame/Fields.html (accessed 18 February 2014).

20 Brett Pulley, "Hollywood's new King Kong", *Forbes* (5 July 2004), 102–11.

21 Joe Morgenstern, "Review/film – it's Hobbit forming: 'Lord of the Rings' trilogy gets off to magical start – gamble on an offbeat director pays off in lush Tolkien epic", *Wall Street Journal* (New York), Eastern edition (21 December 2001), W1.

22 Richard Branson, "Steve was never satisfied", *Canadian Business* (2013), **86** (16), 32.

Online sources

http://drafthouse.com/about.

http://www.entrepreneur.com/article/224235.

2 The entrepreneur and entrepreneurial decision making

Scenario: Kathy Giusti – Multiple Myeloma Research Foundation

Kathy Giusti had the whole package. In her formative years, she had worked hard to attain her Bachelor's degree in Biological Sciences and completed her MBA from Harvard Business School. Through hard work and perseverance, she moved up through large companies such as Merck and Gillette, ultimately settling into an executive position at pharmaceutical giant, G.D. Searle & Co. She had a loving husband and a one-year-old daughter, whom she adored. Everything in her life seemed successfully aligned. And then, in 1996, Kathy received a call from her doctor about some routine blood work results – the tests showed evidence of cancer cells. The doctor diagnosed her with multiple myeloma, a rare and orphan form (meaning affecting less than 200 000 people) of blood cancer, and gave her three years to live. This news turned Kathy Giusti's life upside down.

Refusing to allow her new predicament to control her, Kathy instead took the disease head-on. As information through the internet was not as prevalent in the 1990s as it is now, Kathy researched scientific journals and articles at her library. She actively reached out to specialists and researchers in the field, and even attended conferences dedicated to related cancer research and treatment development. The more she uncovered, the more enraged she became – why was there so little research and funding for her type of cancer? Why so few treatments? Large pharmaceutical companies concentrated their efforts on more widespread cancers like breast, skin and colon cancer. Were these patients any more special than those with rarer forms? Kathy was beside herself, realizing the other truth behind those companies. Pharmaceutical firms, R&D companies and research institutions had traditionally kept their information under guarded lock and key, secretly stashing their own research for their own benefits rather than for the benefit of those patients waiting for a cure.

It was then that Kathy saw an opportunity. Applying her business education, her medical education as a pre-med undergraduate student and her working knowledge from her years in pharmaceutical firms, Kathy launched the Multiple Myeloma Research Foundation (MMRF). MMRF's business strategy centers on what she originally felt was missing in the cancer R&D industry – collaboration. Currently, 16 member institutions make up the foundation's "consortium". As members of the foundation, these centers receive monetary funding and other types of supportive resources, as well as access to MMRF's extensive tissue bank. However, in order to remain part of the group, all centers must disclose their research to each other. Collaborations on projects are highly encouraged in order to spread information and ideas in the hope of finding a treatment faster. Not only does the foundation go against the behaviors of medical research companies, who traditionally hide their research from their competitors, but it also remains highly and controversially involved in its members' operations. Projects must be approved by its Board of Directors (including Kathy), and consortia members are given annual grades on how quickly and effectively they turn around their projects. Although the demands are intense, members can rest assured that MMRF will support their needs and continue to remind them that the battle does not lie with each other but with the cancer, itself.

If building the MMRF was not trying enough, Kathy had been battling multiple myeloma the entire time. Fortunately, she had a diverse and encouraging support network that had stood by her side since the beginning. Old Harvard classmates helped to develop the foundation's first business plan. Several even sat on the original Board of Directors. Friends with legal backgrounds assisted with federal regulations. Family and friends helped to execute fundraising events. Last but not least, Kathy's twin sister, Karen, co-founded the organization and donated her stem cells in a transplant operation that pushed Kathy into remission. Now, with her cancer under control and her family and friends rallying behind her, Kathy can continue building her foundation, obliterating traditional industry norms and giving people with multiple myeloma hope for a cure (see Online sources).

Introduction

This chapter continues in providing a better understanding of entrepreneurship by focusing on the entrepreneur and particularly entrepreneurial decision making. First, aspects of the entrepreneur, his or her orientation and thinking are discussed. This is followed by a look at what it means to act like an entrepreneur. The entrepreneurial decision process, the possibility of new venture formation and the typical background and characteristics of an entrepreneur are then presented. The chapter concludes with a discussion of the entrepreneurial process, including role models and networks, and the various types of entrepreneurs.

Aspects of being an entrepreneur

A key aspect of being an entrepreneur is the ability to identify an opportunity and develop a solution to the problem this opportunity presents. This is so important that an entire chapter – Chapter 5 – is devoted to this topic. Here we shall address that doing this requires an entrepreneurial action. An entrepreneurial action means that the individual solves the problem by developing and then launching a new product/service, new process and/or an entirely new entity. Entrepreneurs act on what they believe is a worthwhile opportunity despite the high levels of risk and uncertainty involved. Doing this requires judgment about the level of risks and uncertainty involved in developing and launching a solution to the problem. One student who had a great new idea, had the needed $300 000 funding secured and had a partnership established with a large multinational company – American Express – broke down when asked when are you going to launch. She responded, "I just can't do it". This is the essence of being an entrepreneur – just doing it in spite of all the obstacles, lack of security and the high levels of risk and uncertainty involved. This judgment is aided by the individual's prior knowledge, which comes from their background and characteristics discussed later in this chapter. These of course also impact an individual's ability to recognize the opportunity in the first place. Generally, individuals with a background in technology and/or marketing can better identify an opportunity caused by a change in the environment or the level of technology.[1]

Once the opportunity is identified, then an individual has to decide whether this is an opportunity that he or she wants to address. The questions that need to be answered are: Is this an opportunity for me? Do I have the knowledge and skills to successfully do this? Do I have access to the resources to do this? Frequently, a negative response to one of these questions precludes a particular opportunity from being addressed. An opportunity to replace the cheap plastic bags currently used in grocery stores in the United States that end up in landfills with a cost-effective biodegradable alternative has not yet been successfully addressed. The knowledge is not there yet to do this at the needed cost/price point for the grocery store. Areas of the United States that have a significant number of sun days such as Phoenix, Arizona with over 320 should be solar powered. Yet, a solution to retrofit existing buildings, particularly in the residential market, takes significant resources.[2]

This decision to act on the opportunity deemed worth pursuing requires entrepreneurial thinking – deciding whether or not an opportunity is feasible to pursue based on the knowledge and skills needed and resources involved. Entrepreneurs not only think differently than other entrepreneurs, each entrepreneur thinks and acts differently to each opportunity.

Acting entrepreneurially

When an entrepreneur decides to pursue an opportunity by developing a new product/service/entity or enter a new market, he or she does this intentionally. Rarely is this an unintentional behavior. When engaging in this intentional behavior, the entrepreneur must perceive that the action to be taken is both feasible and desirable, which is discussed later in this chapter. The feasibility part has to do with an entrepreneur's self-efficacy – the connection that he or she can successfully execute all that is required to successfully solve the problem and act on the opportunity. This requires an individual to perceive himself or herself as having the personal capability to perform – to do the particular tasks needed to solve the problem. High self-efficacy leads to increased persistence and performance while low self-efficacy does not. Sometimes high self-efficacy can be mistaken for arrogance on the part of the entrepreneur. An entrepreneur needs to be careful not to allow his or her high self-efficacy and feeling competent to do the job lead to the perception of his or her being arrogant. A certain level of self-efficacy is needed as too low self-efficacy reduces both effort and performance.

A high degree of self-efficacy coupled with the perception that an entrepreneurial action is desirable leads to an entrepreneurial action. The higher the level of perceived desirability and feasibility, the stronger the intent to act entrepreneurially.

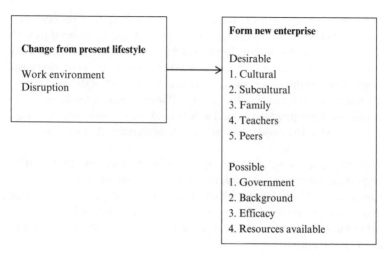

Figure 2.1   Decisions for a potential entrepreneur

Entrepreneurial decision process

An individual who recognizes an opportunity and comes up with a creative solution to solve the problem identified by the opportunity usually undertakes the entrepreneurial decision process at least to some degree. The process that entails a movement from something to something, from a present lifestyle to form a new enterprise is indicated in Figure 2.1. The process results in the formation of millions of new ventures despite economic uncertainty, high probability of failure, high levels of risk and uncertainty, high interest rates, inflation, lack of infrastructure and recession.

Change from present lifestyle

The decision to leave a career or lifestyle is not an easy one. It takes a great deal of energy and courage to change and do something new and different. Although individuals tend to start businesses in areas that are familiar, two work environments have been particularly productive in spawning new enterprises: R&D (technology) and marketing. While working in technology (R&D), individuals develop new product ideas or processes and often leave to form their own companies when these new ideas are not accepted by their present employers. Similarly, individuals in marketing have become familiar with the market and customers' unfulfilled wants and needs, and they frequently leave to start new enterprises to feed these needs.

Perhaps an even stronger incentive to overcome the inertia and leave a present lifestyle to create something new comes from a negative force – disruption. A significant number of companies are formed by people who have retired, who are relocated due to a move by the other member in a dual-career family or who have been laid off. There is probably no greater force than personal dislocation to galvanize a person's will to act. A study in one major city in the United States indicated that a number of new business listings in the Yellow Pages increased by 12 percent during a layoff period. Another cause of disruption that can result in company formation is someone's completion of an educational degree. For example, a student who is not promoted after receiving an MBA degree may become frustrated and decide to leave and start a new company. Another is when one partner in a dual-earning household takes a new position and the other moves as well and does not find a comparable position.

What causes this personal disruption to result in a new company being formed? The decision to start a new company occurs when an individual perceives that forming a new enterprise is both desirable and possible.

Desirability of new venture formation

The perception that starting a new company is desirable results from an individual's culture, subculture, family, teachers and peers. A culture that values an individual who successfully creates a new business will spawn more venture formations than one that does not. The American culture places a high value on being one's own boss, having individual opportunities, being a success and making money – all aspects of entrepreneurship. Therefore, it is not surprising to find a high rate of company formation in the United States. On the other hand, in some countries successfully establishing a new business and making money are not as highly valued and a failure becomes a disgrace. Countries with cultures that more closely emulate this attitude do not have as high a business formation rate. It will be interesting to watch which develops a strong pro-entrepreneur culture.

No culture is totally for or against entrepreneurship. Many subcultures that shape value systems operate within a cultural framework. There are pockets of entrepreneurial subcultures in the United States. Although the more widely recognized ones include Route 128 (Boston), Silicon Valley (California) and the North Carolina Triangle, some less-known but equally important entrepreneurial centers are Los Angeles, Denver, Seattle and Austin. These subcultures support and even promote entrepreneurship – the forming of a new company – as one of the best occupations. No wonder more individuals actively plan new enterprises in these supportive environments.

There are also variations within these subcultures caused by family traits. Studies of companies in a variety of industries throughout the world indicate that a very high percentage of the founders of companies had fathers and/or mothers who valued independence. The independence achieved by company owners, professionals, artists, professors or farmers permeates their entire family life, giving encouragement and value to their children's company-formation activities.

Encouragement to form a company is further stimulated by teachers, who can significantly influence individuals to regard entrepreneurship as a desirable and viable career path. Schools with exciting courses in entrepreneurship and innovation tend to develop entrepreneurs and can actually drive the entrepreneurial environment in an economic area. The number of entrepreneurship courses a person takes increases the probability of starting a venture. Both the Massachusetts Institute of Technology (MIT) and Harvard facilitate the entrepreneurial environment around Route 128; Stanford is in the Silicon Valley; the University of North Carolina, North Carolina State and Duke are the points of the North Carolina Triangle; and Case Western Reserve University facilitates entrepreneurship in the Cleveland area. A strong university education base is an important factor for entrepreneurial activity and company formation in an area.

Finally, peers are very important in the decision to form a company. An area with an entrepreneurial pool and a meeting place where entrepreneurs and potential entrepreneurs can discuss ideas, problems and solutions spawns more new companies than an area where these are not available.

Possibility of new venture formation

Although the desire derived from the individual's culture, subculture, family, teachers and peers needs to be present before forming a new venture is considered, the second feature necessary centers around this question: What makes it possible to form a new company? Several factors – government, background, efficacy and available resources contribute to the creation of a new venture[3] (see Figure 2.1). The government contributes by providing the infrastructure to help and support a new venture. It is no wonder that more companies are formed in the United States – given the roads, communication and transportation systems, utilities and economic stability – than in other countries. Even the US tax rate for companies and individuals is better than in countries such as Ireland, England or Germany. Countries that have a repressive tax rate on businesses or individuals can suppress company formation since companies will not have the money to start and grow and monetary gain cannot be achieved. Since the social, psychological and financial risks are still present, the entrepreneur must also have the necessary background. Formal education and previous business experience give a potential entrepreneur the skills needed to form and manage a new enterprise. Although educational systems are important in providing the needed business knowledge, individuals will tend to be more successful in forming businesses in fields in which they have worked. Entrepreneurs are not born: they develop – and emerge.[4] A discussion of backgrounds and characteristics follows in the next section of this chapter.

Efficacy, previously discussed, the conviction that you can succeed also impacts the possibility. The higher the level of self-efficacy, the higher the probability of forming a successful new venture.

Finally, resources, particularly financial ones, must be readily available. Although most of the start-up money for any new company comes from personal savings, credit, friends and relatives, there is often a need for additional risk capital. Risk capital availability plays an essential role in the development and growth of entrepreneurial activity. More new companies form when risk capital is readily available.

Background and characteristics

Why are some individuals more likely to go through the entrepreneurial decision process and be entrepreneurs? As indicated in the previous section and Figure 2.1, background and characteristics provide an indicator of whether an entrepreneur perceives the opportunity as possible. These include age, education and work history and experience.

Age

The relationship of entrepreneurs and the entrepreneurial career process and age has been carefully researched.[5] Most entrepreneurs initiate their entrepreneurial career and start a new venture between the ages of 22 and 45. Women tend to start their first significant venture a little later than men in their middle 30s compared to early 30s for men. Today, particularly in the United States, starting a new venture later in life is becoming more and more frequent when children have left the home and there are fewer financial concerns. Individuals, particularly those who are not satisfied with their current job, decide they want to do something they really like and have passion for and decide to start a new venture.

Education

Generally, entrepreneurs are better educated than the general population in almost every country researched. Education plays an important role in the upbringing of an entrepreneur and affects the level of education obtained as well as their ability to start a new venture and overcome the problems confronted. A formal education or degree is not necessary for starting a new venture and having a successful entrepreneurial career as indicated in the careers of such entrepreneurial luminaries as Andrew Carnegie, Henry Ford, J.B. Fuqua, Bill Gates and William Lear. Education does provide a good background particularly when it is related to the field of the venture or when financial resources need to be obtained. It is an indication of the persistence and accomplishment of an entrepreneur when raising capital. Such educational areas as engineering, finance, logistics, marketing, management and supply chain management can help an entrepreneur be successful. And of course any impact education has on the entrepreneur's ability to communicate effectively in both the spoken and written word is important in any entrepreneurial activity.

The general education of an entrepreneur provides knowledge, skills and problem-solving capabilities that can be used through the process of developing, launching, managing and growing a new venture. Even though this is the case, while education is a positive influence on the chance that an individual will recognize a new opportunity, it has not been shown to impact whether that individual will create a new business to solve the problem identified in the opportunity recognized.[6]

Work history and experience

Work history and experience are not only important in the decision to launch a new venture by making it seem possible; they also have been shown to impact its growth and success. As indicated, job dissatisfaction, frustration and boredom often motivate an individual to launch a new venture; previous industrial experience affects the actual launch and growth of the venture, particularly when it is in such areas as financing, marketing, distribution channels, manufacturing or product/service planning and development.

As the venture launches and grows, managerial experience, particularly if it is in the same industry, becomes very important in solving the problems and overcoming the obstacles to success. This is even more important when more and more employees are added and the venture reaches significant amounts of capital or goes public. Previous experience in the industry is one of the few demographic variables that has been attributed to the success of a new venture.

Previous experience as an entrepreneur is also beneficial as serial (repeat) entrepreneurs tend to have a better chance of success than nascent entrepreneurs. This previous start-up experience provides the know-how and expertise in starting and running an independent venture. It helps in deciding which information is relevant, making timely decisions and setting up benchmarks for appropriate control and management of the enterprise.[7]

The entrepreneurial process

The overall process of starting a new venture is indicated in the entrepreneurial process. An entrepreneur needs to first find, evaluate and develop an opportunity and then overcome the forces that resist the creation of something new. The process has four distinct phases: (1) identification and evaluation of the opportunity; (2) development of the business plan; (3) determination of the required resources; and (4) management of the resulting enterprise (Table 2.1). Although these phases proceed progressively, no one stage is dealt with in isolation or is totally completed before the work on other phases occurs. For example, to successfully identify and evaluate an opportunity (phase 1), an entrepreneur must have in mind the resources, particularly financial resources, needed.

Table 2.1 Aspects of the entrepreneurial process

Identify and evaluate the opportunity	Develop the business plan	Resources required	Launch and manage the enterprise
• Opportunity assessment • Creation and length of opportunity • Real and perceived value of opportunity • Risk and returns of opportunity • Opportunity versus personal skills and goals • Competitive environment • Creating opportunity assessment plan	Section 1 1. Title Page 2. Table of Contents 3. Executive Summary Section 2 1. Description of Business 2. Description of Industry 3. Technology Plan 4. Marketing Plan 5. Financial Plan 6. Production Plan 7. Organizational Plan 8. Operational Plan 9. Summary Section 3 • Appendices (Exhibits) Creating a business plan	• Determine resources needed • Determine existing resources • Identify resource gaps and available suppliers • Develop access to needed resource suppliers	• Develop launch plan • Establish culture • Understand key variables for success • Identify problems and potential problems • Implement control systems • Develop management style • Develop growth strategy

Identify and evaluate the opportunity

Opportunity identification and evaluation is probably the most frustrating task. Most good business opportunities do not just suddenly appear, but rather result from an entrepreneur's alertness to possibilities, or in some cases, the establishment of mechanisms that identify potential opportunities. For example, one entrepreneur asks at every cocktail party whether anyone is using a product that does not adequately fulfill its intended purpose. This person is constantly looking for a need and an opportunity to create a better product. Another entrepreneur always monitors the play habits and toys of her nieces and nephews. This is her way of looking for any unique toy product niche for a new venture.

Since this important topic is the focus of Chapters 4 and 5, it will only be examined in an overview fashion here. Although most entrepreneurs do not have formal mechanisms for identifying business opportunities, some sources are often fruitful: consumers and business associates; members of the distribution system; and technical people. Often consumers are the best source of ideas for a new venture. How many times have you heard someone comment, "If only there was a product that would . . ." This comment can result in the creation of a new business. One entrepreneur's evaluation of why so many business executives were complaining about the lack of good technical writing and word-processing services resulted in the creation of her own business venture to fill this need. Her technical writing service grew to ten employees in two years.

Due to their close contact with the end user, channel members in the distribution system also see product needs. One entrepreneur started a college bookstore after hearing all the students complain about the high cost of books and the lack of service provided by the only bookstore on campus. Many other entrepreneurs have identified business opportunities through a discussion with a retailer, wholesaler or manufacturer's representative.

Finally, technically oriented individuals often conceptualize business opportunities when working on other projects. One entrepreneur's business resulted from seeing the application of a plastic resin compound in developing and manufacturing a new type of pallet while developing the resin application in another totally unrelated area – casket moldings.

Whether the opportunity is identified by using input from consumers, business associates, channel members or technical people, each opportunity must be carefully screened and evaluated. This evaluation of the opportunity is perhaps the most critical element of the entrepreneurial process, as it allows the entrepreneur to assess whether the specific product or service has the returns needed compared to the resources required. As indicated in Table 2.1, this evaluation process involves looking at the length of the opportunity, its real and perceived value, its risks and returns, its fit with the personal skills and goals of the entrepreneur and its uniqueness or differential advantage in its competitive environment.

The market size and the length of the window of opportunity are the primary basis for determining the risks and rewards. The risks reflect the market, competition, technology and amount of capital involved. The amount of capital needed provides the basis for the return and rewards.

Finally, the opportunity must fit the personal skills and goals of the entrepreneur.[8] It is particularly important that the entrepreneur be able to put forth the necessary time and effort required to make the venture succeed. Although many entrepreneurs feel that the desire can be developed along with the venture, typically it does not materialize. An entrepreneur must believe in the opportunity so much that he or she will make the necessary sacrifices to develop the opportunity and manage the resulting organization. This is his or her passion. The opportunity can be best evaluated using an opportunity assessment plan, which is discussed in Chapter 5.

Develop a business plan

A good business plan must be developed in order to exploit the defined opportunity. This is a very time-consuming phase of the entrepreneurial process. An entrepreneur usually has not prepared a business plan before and does not have the resources available to do a good job. Although the preparation of the business plan is the focus of Chapter 7, it is important to understand the basic issues involved as well as the three major sections of the plan (see Table 2.1). The three sections each have a specific purpose. Section 1 contains the most important document when raising capital – the two-page executive summary. Section 2 is the main body of the business plan and needs to contain each of the essential elements (description of business, description of industry and market, technology plan, marketing plan, financial plan, production plan, organizational plan, operational plan and summary). In some businesses, such as a non-technical service like a restaurant or online service provider, there usually is not a need for a technology plan or a production plan. Often the production plan becomes an outsourcing plan since it is usually more cost-effective and requires a lower capital raise to outsource any production for at least the first three years. One coaster manufacturing company started by outsourcing and has continued the practice today with revenues of about $800 000. The final section – Section 3 – contains the backup support material for Section 2. These include such things as résumés of the entrepreneur and management team, brief biographies of the board of advisors, market and industry statistics, list of suppliers, any signed contracts and important articles on the industry, market and their growth rates. No new material should be introduced in Section 3. A good business plan is essential in developing the opportunity and determining the resources required, obtaining those resources and successfully managing the resulting venture.

Determine the resources required

The resources needed for addressing the opportunity must also be determined. This process starts with an appraisal of the entrepreneur's present resources. Any resources that are critical need to be delineated from those that are just helpful. Care must be taken not to underestimate the amount and variety of resources needed. The downside risks associated with insufficient or inappropriate resources should also be assessed.

Acquiring the needed resources in a timely manner while giving up as little equity and control as possible is the next step in the entrepreneurial process. An entrepreneur should strive to maintain as large an ownership position as possible, particularly in the start-up stage. As the business develops, more funds will probably be needed to finance the growth of the venture, requiring more ownership to be relinquished. Alternative suppliers of financial resources, the focus of Chapter 11, along with their needs and desires need to be identified. By understanding resource supplier needs, the entrepreneur can structure a deal that enables the resources to be acquired at the lowest possible cost and the least loss of control.

Launch and manage the enterprise

After resources are acquired, the entrepreneur must use them to implement the business plan. The launch strategy and plan need to be developed and implemented. Focus, focus, focus is the key phrase in doing this. The operational problems of the enterprise must also be examined. This involves implementing a management style and structure, as well as determining the key variables for success. A control system must be established, so that any problem areas can be quickly identified and resolved. Some entrepreneurs have difficulty managing and growing the venture they created.

Role models and support systems

Role models are very important in a person not only initially becoming an entrepreneur but also in their career path following the initial venture launch.[9] Successful entrepreneurs are frequently catalysts for a potential entrepreneur both from a positive or negative lens. Some entrepreneurs are viewed as great success stories that others want to emulate and others as indicators that if they can do it, so can I. In either case, these role models encourage others to "just do it".

An even more important role that these role models can perform is being a mentor during and after the launch of a venture. While entrepreneurs usually perceive the advice from other entrepreneurs who have already been through the process as best, many different types of individuals can serve as a mentor. The most important thing is that each entrepreneur should have at least one mentor who can serve as the sounding board for ideas and help solve any problems. This advisory support system is critical for new venture success providing information, advice and guidance on a wide variety of issues such as valuation, how much equity is fair for a certain level of investment, organizational structure, channel member selection, outsourcing and partnership agreements. The mentor can help the entrepreneur establish the needed networks that will help in the success of the new venture.

The network of contacts and connections established will continue to expand and will have two aspects: centrality (the distance of the entrepreneur to all other individuals and the total number of individuals in the network) and density (the extensiveness of the tie between the entrepreneur and each individual in the network). The density (strength of the tie) reflects the frequency, level and reciprocity of the relationship between the entrepreneur and the individual in the network. The more frequent, in-depth and mutually beneficial this relationship between the entrepreneur and the individual, the stronger and more durable the tie and the network between the two.[10] Some networks are more informal than others but nonetheless important.

Two types of networks are important for the entrepreneur: a personal network and a business network.

Personal Support Network

It is very important for the entrepreneur to establish a personal support network to provide the support needed during the more difficult times of starting and growing a venture. This cheering squad, usually consisting of family and friends, helps the entrepreneur overcome the many difficulties and obstacles involved in the entrepreneurial process. Being an entrepreneur can be a very lonely experience as the final responsibility for the success or failure of the venture lies with them. Usually the biggest supporter is the entrepreneur's spouse or partner. They are viewed as so important in the success of the venture that many financial providers will not invest or lend to the venture until they have been introduced to them.

Of course, when there is no partner or spouse in the picture, then a friend(s) usually takes this role. These friends cannot only provide encouragement and personal support but also in many cases business advice as well. Other family members – grandparents, uncles, brothers, sisters – can also serve in this personal support capacity.

Business Support Network

In addition to the personal support, an entrepreneur needs to establish a business support network. This access to needed business advice from the mentor/advisor helps the entrepreneur make the best decision possible when confronted with the problem occurring in the venture. Usually this person is looked on as a mentor as he or she is an advisor, coach and sounding board. To perform these roles, a mentor needs to be an expert in the field and as such is usually another entrepreneur.

Sometimes an entrepreneur can be a part of a group or network of business associates besides the mentor(s). This group is usually other entrepreneurs or self-employed individuals or they work in the industry of the entrepreneurial venture and often meet on a regular (usually monthly) basis. The group can consist of suppliers as well as buyers and can be the potential source of supply as well as potential customers.[11]

A trade association can offer a good business support network. By having information and knowledge in an industry, trade associations can be very helpful in the launch and growth of a new venture in the industry.

Even personal groups that an entrepreneur participates in can become a business support network. Affiliations developed through participation in sporting events, hobbies, clubs, civic activities and school groups can be excellent sources of advice, information and even referrals. These social networks have become increasingly important due to the many specific social platforms as well as the more generic ones such as Facebook and LinkedIn. Regardless of the type, both personal and business support networks are important for the entrepreneur throughout their entrepreneurial career and the various types of enterprises started.

Mary Kay Ash developed five makeup products from her home in Dallas, Texas. She started with a small store and a big vision. The vision was to empower women to employ themselves selling her products and further help empower other women to do the same. Today more than 3 million women, working as independent beauty consultants, sell over 200 Mary Kay products in over 35 countries. Over the last 50 years, Mary Kay has not only offered women popular beauty products but also the opportunity to transform their lives and empower other women in the process. Mary Kay Cosmetics has grown from her humble home-based beginnings to a multinational company bringing in over $3 billion in annual revenue.

Types of enterprises

Entrepreneurs and the kinds of business they start are different. While there are many paths to being an entrepreneur, there are four broad categories that can be used to classify the new venture: home-based entrepreneur; cyber entrepreneur; traditional entrepreneur; and serial entrepreneur.

A significant number of ventures are home-based businesses.[12] Some of these are hobby, consulting or freelance businesses that can essentially be operated from the home of the entrepreneur. Technology has made it possible to do business successfully from anywhere so a traditional office space is not essential to start or operate a business. A home-based business provides more opportunity to be a part of the family and avoid the travel time to an office location. One family doctor loved having his office connected to his house as it was easier to see emergency patients quickly. In some cases, a business will start as a home-based business and then expand to a traditional entrepreneurial business when the revenue and number of customers are too large to be adequately taken care of from the home.

The second classification, the cyber (internet) entrepreneur, transacts all their business with customers, suppliers and strategic partners on the internet. This can be providing goods as well as services. One student who met a group of talented yet impoverished women in a small village in Peru started an internet business selling Alpaca accessories made by these women, donating 20 percent of the profits back to the village. The internet itself has made it much easier for all entrepreneurs to communicate and sell their products and services.

A traditional entrepreneur, if there is such a person, generally starts a brick and mortar business outside the home and grows it to be a success, employing numerous individuals and increasing the facilities. These individuals build sustainable companies that can have accelerated growth to become the next large companies in a country.

Finally, the serial entrepreneur is one who loves starting, growing and exiting businesses. These individuals start a new venture soon after the one they are presently involved in is over, hopefully through a successful exit. It is the thrill of starting, growing and successfully exiting a venture that drives the serial entrepreneur. They prefer to leave the actual management issues of the venture to someone else.

Another useful classification system divides start-ups into three categories: lifestyle firms; foundation companies; and high-potential ventures. A lifestyle firm is privately held and usually achieves only modest growth due to the nature of the business, the objectives of the entrepreneur and the limited money devoted to R&D. This type of firm may grow after several years to 30 or 40 employees and have annual revenues of about $2 million. A lifestyle firm exists primarily to support the owners and usually has little opportunity for significant growth and expansion.

The second type of start-up – the foundation company – is created from R&D and lays the foundation for a new business area. This firm can grow in five to ten years from 40 to 400 employees and from $10 million to $20 million in yearly revenues. Since this type of start-up rarely goes public, it usually draws the interest of private investors only, not the venture capital community.

The final type of start-up – the high-potential venture – is the one that receives the greatest investment interest and publicity. While the company may start out like a foundation company, its growth is far more rapid. After five to ten years, the company could employ around 500 employees, with $20 million to $30 million in revenue. These firms are also called "gazelles" and are integral to the economic development of an area.

Given that the results of the decision making process need to be perceived as desirable and possible for an individual to change from a present lifestyle to a radically new one, it is not surprising that the type and number of new business formations vary greatly throughout the world.

Summary

In focusing on the entrepreneur and entrepreneurial decision making, this chapter has provided an understanding of the aspects of an entrepreneur and his or her orientation as well as what it means to act entrepreneurially. The typical background and characteristics of an entrepreneur – age, education, work history and experience – were discussed. After describing the entrepreneurial decision process, the entrepreneurial process and role models and networks, the chapter concluded by discussing the types of enterprises created using two broad classification systems.

NOTES

1 Elizabeth J. Rozell, Kenneth E. Meyer, Wesley A. Scroggins and Aimin Guo, "Perceptions of the characteristics of successful entrepreneurs: an empirical study in China", *International Journal of Management* (2011), **28** (4), 60–71.

2 This is fully developed in a model of entrepreneurial action; see Jeffery S. McMullen and Dean A. Shepherd, "Entrepreneurial action and the rule of uncertainty in the theory of the entrepreneur", *Academy of Management Review* (2006), **31**, 132–42.

3 Hedia Fourati and Habib Affes, "Financial constraints, human and social capital and risk-taking attitude in the foundation of new firms", *Strategic Change* (2011), **20** (5/6), 219–32.

4 Jason Daley, "Born or made?", *Entrepreneur* (2013), **41** (10), 64–72.

5 See Robert C. Ronstadt, "Initial venture goals, age, and the decision to start an entrepreneurial career", in *Proceedings*, 43rd Annual Meeting of the Academy of Management (August 1983), p. 472; Robert C. Ronstadt, "The decision not to become an entrepreneur", in *Proceedings*, 1983 Conference on Entrepreneurship (April 1983), pp. 192–212; Moren Lévesque, Dean A. Shepherd and Evan J. Douglas, "Employment or self-employment: a dynamic utility-maximizing model", *Journal of Business Venturing* (2002), 189–210; Robert D. Hisrich and Candida G. Brush, *The Woman Entrepreneur: Starting, Financing and Managing a Successful New Business* (Lexington, MA: Lexington Books, 1986); Robert D. Hisrich and Candida G. Brush, "The woman entrepreneur: management skills and business problems", *Journal of Small Business Management* (January

1984), 30–7; Robert D. Hisrich, "Women entrepreneurs: problems and prescriptions for success in the future", in *Women-owned Businesses* (New York: Praeger Press, 1989), pp. 3–32.

6 See Javier Gimeno, Timothy B. Folta, Arnold C. Cooper and Carolyn Y. Woo, "Survival of the fittest? Entrepreneurial human capital and the persistence of underperforming firms", *Administrative Science Quarterly* (1997), **42**, 750–83; Per Davidsson and Benson Honig, "The role of social and human capital among nascent entrepreneurs", *Journal of Business Venturing* (2003), **18**, 301–31; Dawn R. DeTienne, Dean A. Shepherd and Julio O. De Castro, "The fallacy of 'only the strong survive': the effects of extrinsic motivation on the persistence decisions for underperforming firms", *Journal of Business Venturing* (2008), **23**, 528–46.

7 Arnold C. Cooper, Timothy B. Folta and Carolyn Y. Woo, "Entrepreneurial information search", *Journal of Business Venturing* (1995), **10**, 107–20; Mike Wright, Ken Robbie and Christine Ennew, "Venture capitalists and serial entrepreneurs", *Journal of Business Venturing* (1997), **12** (3), 227–49; Per Davidsson and Benson Honig, "The role of social and human capital among nascent entrepreneurs", *Journal of Business Venturing* (2003), **18**, 301–31.

8 Jason Arentz, Frederic Sautet and Virgil Storr, "Prior-knowledge and opportunity identification", *Small Business Economics* (2013), **41** (2), 461–78.

9 Shirley S. Almquist and Elizabeth M. Angrist, "Role model influences on college women's career aspirations", *Merrill-Palmer Quarterly* (July 1971), **17**, 263–97; Jayne E. Strake and Charles R. Granger, "Same-sex and opposite-sex teacher model influences on science career commitment among high school students", *Journal of Educational Psychology* (April 1978), **70**, 180–86; Howard Aldrich, Ben Rosen and William Woodward, "The impact of social networks on business foundings and profit: a longitudinal study", in *Proceedings*, 1987 Conference on Entrepreneurship (April 1987), pp. 154–68.

10 See, for example, Howard Aldrich and Catherine Zimmer, "Entrepreneurship through social networks", in *The Art and Science of Entrepreneurship* (Cambridge, MA: Ballinger, 1986), pp. 3–24; Ha Hoang and Bostjan Antoncic, "Network-based research in entrepreneurship: a critical review", *Journal of Business Venturing* (2003), **18**, 165–88; Sue Birley, "The role of networks in the entrepreneurial process", *Journal of Business Venturing* (1985), **1**, 107–17; Arnold C. Cooper and William C. Dunkelberg, "Entrepreneurship and paths to business ownership", *Strategic Management Journal* (1986), **7**, 53–68; B. Johannisson, "Networking and entrepreneurial growth", in D. Sexton and H. Landström (eds), *The Blackwell Handbook of Entrepreneurship* (Oxford: Blackwell, 2000), pp. 26–44.

11 Ibid.

12 T.S., "Humble beginnings", *Entrepreneur* (2011), **39** (6), 108.

Online sources

http://www.fastcompany.com/3007768/creative-conversations/using-data-treat-cancer-and-drive-innovation.

http://www.parade.com/37077/francarpentier/25-kathy-giusti-mission-to-cure-multiple-myeloma/.

http://www.themmrf.org/.

3   Corporate, government and social entrepreneurship

Scenario: Ken Kutaragi – Sony Corporation/Sony PlayStation

Ken Kutaragi sat in his Tokyo living room watching his daughter immersed in the new Nintendo game console he had just brought home. Listening along to its music and sound effects, Ken noted that the game's audio was subpar. If only there was a way to improve this. Fortunately, Ken Kutaragi had the skills to do so. He had a Bachelor's degree in electrical engineering and had been, since graduation, working in the sound lab at Sony Corporation. Kutaragi mulled over this issue and finally came up with a possible solution – Nintendo could develop an advanced chip dedicated only to the console's sound, effectively improving its quality. Receiving permission from his managers at Sony, Kutaragi began working on a side project with Nintendo, aiding in the creation of the SPC7000 chip that enhanced Nintendo's consoles and increased their product's value.

At the time, Sony's senior executive management had not known of Kutaragi's collaboration with Nintendo. And once word had got around about the success of Nintendo's new sound chip, they opposed Kutaragi's involvement and attempted to fire him. Norio Ohga, Sony's CEO at that time, stopped the senior management. Witnessing Kutaragi's innovative spirit and entrepreneurial drive, Ohga could not simply allow the release of an employee of such caliber, even if it meant another company was benefiting from it. After all, any technological innovation, even if not from his own company, would benefit the future of electronics. Ohga kept Kutaragi in Sony Corporation and encouraged him to continue his consulting projects for Nintendo.

Kutaragi resumed his positions at both Sony and Nintendo. Contemplating the future of the gaming industry, Kutaragi realized that the next step would be to continue advancing the consoles themselves. This meant pushing out the use of large, blocky game cartridges and ushering in thinner CD-ROMs. Kutaragi worked incessantly on his new idea and finally developed for Nintendo a system using the newly developed CD-ROM technology. Soon after, Nintendo unexpectedly cancelled the project. Why cancel a project that could yield the turning point for gaming? Kutaragi refused to let his project fall by the wayside, and instead brought his project back to his own company and urged Sony to bring gaming consoles into their product line.

At that time, Sony was not interested in moving into the gaming industry, their primary focus being on other types of consumer electronics. Head management unsurprisingly bucked the idea and brushed Kutaragi's project off as a mere child's toy. CEO Norio Ohga once again saw the potential of the new gaming console and, convinced of the console's inherent capabilities, accepted Kutaragi's project and effectively entered Sony into Japan's gaming industry. The console was named the Sony PlayStation and was released to the public in 1994. Sales of the PlayStation quickly overtook Nintendo's system, as well as the system sold by established gaming company, Sega. While Sony had invested $2.5 billion into Kutaragi's project, Sony's sales and reputation has far exceeded that investment. Sony's gaming segment, Sony Computer Entertainment, is now one of the largest, most popular and more revered gaming companies in the world. Thanks to the support of Sony CEO Norio Ohga, Kutaragi stayed on with Sony, continuing to contribute to the development of the PlayStation line, being forever immortalized in history as "The father of the PlayStation" (see Online sources).

Introduction

As indicated in Chapter 1, entrepreneurship is not a modern concept; rather, examples can be traced back to 550 BC in the case of Confucius. Not only do entrepreneurs contribute by themselves to the economic and social well-being of society, thinking and acting entrepreneurially can impact any organization. Aspects of entrepreneurship (opportunity, recognition, idea generation and development, resource determination and acquisition, and launching, growing and harvesting the venture) can be and should be found in all types of organizations. This chapter focuses on managerial versus entrepreneurial decision making, corporate entrepreneurship, government entrepreneurship and social entrepreneurship.

Managerial versus entrepreneurial decision making

The difference between entrepreneurial and managerial styles can be viewed from five key business dimensions: strategic orientation; commitment to opportunity; commitment of resources; control of resources; and management structure.[1] Managerial styles are called the administrative domain.

Strategic orientation

The entrepreneur's strategic orientation depends on his or her perception of the opportunity. This orientation is most important when other opportunities have diminishing returns accompanied by rapid changes in technology, consumer economies, social values or political rules. When the use of planning systems as well as measuring performance to control current resources is the strategic orientation, the administrative (managerial) domain is operant, as is the case with many large multinational organizations.

Commitment to opportunity

In terms of the commitment to opportunity, the second key business dimension, the two domains vary greatly with respect to the length of this commitment. The entrepreneurial domain is pressured by the need for action, short decision windows, a willingness to assume risk and few decision constituencies and has a short time span in terms of opportunity commitment. The administrative (managerial) domain is not only slow to act on an opportunity but once action is taken, the commitment is usually for a long time span, too long in some instances. There are often no mechanisms set up in companies to stop and re-evaluate an initial resource commitment once it is made – a major problem in the administrative (managerial) domain.

Commitment of resources

An entrepreneur is used to having resources committed at periodic intervals that are often based on certain tasks or objectives being reached. These resources, often acquired from others, are usually difficult to obtain, forcing the entrepreneur to maximize any resources used. This multistage commitment allows the resource providers (such as venture capitalists or private investors) to have as small an exposure as possible at each stage of business development and to constantly monitor the track record being established. Even though the funding may also be implemented in stages in the administrative domain, the commitment of the resources is for the total amount needed. Administratively oriented individuals respond to the source of the rewards offered and receive personal rewards by effectively administering the resources under their control.

Control of resources

Control of resources follows a similar pattern. Since the administrator (manager) is rewarded by effective resource administration, there is often a drive to own or accumulate as many resources as possible. The pressures of power, status and financial rewards cause the administrator (manager) to avoid rental or other periodic use of the resource. The opposite is true for the entrepreneur who – under the pressures of limited resources, the risk of obsolescence, a need for flexibility and the risks involved – strives to rent, or otherwise achieve periodic use of, the resources on an as-needed basis.

Management structure

The final business dimension, management structure, also differs significantly between the two domains. In the administrative domain, the organizational structure is formalized and hierarchical in nature, reflecting the need for clearly defined lines of authority and responsibility. The entrepreneur, true to his or her desire for independence, employs a flat organizational structure with informal networks throughout.

Corporate entrepreneurship

The area of corporate entrepreneurship is addressed in terms of: definition and interest; managerial versus entrepreneurial culture; climate for corporate venturing; leadership characteristics; aspects of corporate entrepreneurship; implementing and evaluating a corporate entrepreneurship program; and benefits of corporate entrepreneurship to the company and to its employees.

Definition and interest

Given the differences in managerial versus entrepreneurial thinking, what actually is corporate entrepreneurship and why the increased interest in the topic?

Corporate entrepreneurship, which is often referred to as intrapreneurship or corporate venturing, is the process by which an individual inside an organization pursues opportunities independent of the resources they currently control; this involves doing new things and departing from the usual ways and creating something new of value. This results in the development, renewal and innovation within that organization. Corporate entrepreneurship requires encouraging and facilitating entrepreneurial behaviors within an established organization. It can be viewed as a system that enables individuals to be creative and invent technologies and new ways of doing things.

Companies such as IBM recognized the value of corporate entrepreneurship in increasing corporate growth. Hewlett-Packard (HP), 3M, Thermo Electron Corporation and Xerox have experienced significant success in corporate entrepreneurship. Entrepreneurship can also be indirectly encouraged as in the case of Starlight Telecommunications. William O'Brien and Pete Nielsen resigned from GTE to start this new firm due to lack of support.

A broad definition of corporate entrepreneurship was proposed by Guth and Ginsberg, who stressed that corporate entrepreneurship encompasses two major phenomena: new venture creation within existing organizations and the transformation of organizations through strategic renewal.[2] This renewal usually involves formal or informal activities aimed at creating new businesses or processes in established companies at the corporate, division (business), functional or project levels. The ultimate aim of the renewal is to improve a company's competitive position and financial performance.

There has been an increased interest in corporate entrepreneurship due to a variety of events occurring on social, cultural and business levels. On a social level, there is an increasing interest in "doing your own thing" and doing it on one's own terms. Individuals who believe strongly in their own talents frequently desire to create something of their own. They want responsibility and have a strong need for individual expression and freedom in their work environment. When this freedom is not there, frustration can cause that individual to become less productive or even leave the organization to achieve self-actualization elsewhere. This new search for meaning, and the impatience involved, has recently caused more discontent in structured organizations than ever before. When meaning is not provided within the organization, individuals often search for an institution that will provide it. Corporate entrepreneurship stimulates and then capitalizes on individuals in an organization who think that something can be done differently and better.

Most people think of Xerox as a large bureaucratic Fortune 100 company. Although, in part, this may be true of the giant company, Xerox has done something unique in trying to ensure that its creative employees do not leave, like Steve Jobs did to form Apple Computer, Inc. In 1989, Xerox set up Xerox Technology Ventures (XTV) for the purpose of generating profits by investing in the promising technologies of the company, many of which would have otherwise been overlooked. Xerox wanted to avoid mistakes of the past by having "a system to prevent technology from leaking out of the company", according to Robert V. Adams, President of XTV.

The fund has supported numerous start-ups thus far, similar to Quad Mark, the brainchild of Dennis Stemmle, a Xerox employee of 25 years. Stemmle's idea was to make a battery-operated, plain paper copier that would fit in a briefcase along with a laptop computer. While for ten years the idea was not approved by Xerox's operating committee, the idea was finally funded by XTV and Taiwan's Advanced Scientific Corporation. As is the case with all the companies funded by XTV, 20 percent of each company is owned by the founder and key employees. This provides an incentive for employees like Dennis Stemmle to take the risk, leave Xerox and form a technology-based venture.

XTV provides both financial and non-financial benefits to its parent, Xerox. The funded companies provide profits to the parent as well as the founders and employees, and now Xerox managers pay closer attention to employees' ideas as well as internal technologies. Is XTV a success? Apparently so, if replication is any indication. The XTV concept contains an element of risk in that Xerox employees forming new ventures are not guaranteed a management position if the new venture fails. This makes XTV different from most intrapreneurship ventures in companies. This aspect of risk and no guaranteed employment is the basis for AT&T Ventures, a fund modeled on XTV.

External factors have also caused an increase in this interest in corporate venturing. These include such things as hypercompetition, rapidly changing technology in an industry and shorter product life cycles, which have forced companies to be more innovative, to continuously develop new products/services or product/service improvements, which in turn has led to implementing one way to do this – corporate venturing.

Managerial versus entrepreneurial culture

Smaller, aggressive, entrepreneurially driven firms are developing more new products and becoming major factors in most markets. Recognizing the results that occur when employees in other large corporations catch this "entrepreneurial fever", many companies are now attempting to create the same spirit and culture in their organizations. What are the differences among managers, entrepreneurs and corporate entrepreneurs?

The typical corporate culture has a climate and a reward system that favors conservative decision making. Emphasis is on gathering large amounts of data as the basis for a rational decision and then using the data to support the decision should the proposed results not occur. Risky decisions are often postponed until enough facts can be gathered or a consultant hired to "illuminate the unknown". Caution is valued higher than new opportunities as a wrong turn has the potential to negatively affect the entire corporation and usually more importantly, at least to the decision maker, the individual's career. Frequently, there are so many sign-offs and approvals required for a large-scale project so that no individual feels personally responsible. Some corporate cultures emphasize decision making initiatives funneling from a top-down, hierarchical structure. Few have the power and responsibility to create any entrepreneurial changes.

The traditional corporate culture differs significantly from a corporate entrepreneurship culture. Guiding principles in a traditional corporate culture include: adhere to the instructions given from top management; do not make any mistakes; do not fail; do not take the initiative but wait for instructions; stay within your turf; and protect your backside. This restrictive environment is, of course, not conducive to creativity, flexibility, independence, ownership or risk taking – the guiding principles of corporate entrepreneurship. Rather, it is an environment directed at promoting efficiency of current resources.

There are also differences in the shared values and norms of the two cultures. The traditional corporation is hierarchical in nature, with established procedures, reporting systems, lines of authority and responsibility, instructions and control mechanisms. These support the present corporate culture and do not encourage creativity and new product, service or venture creation. The culture of a corporate entrepreneurial firm is in stark contrast to this model. Instead of a hierarchical structure, a corporate entrepreneurial climate has a flat, fluid organizational structure encouraging networking, teamwork, sponsors and mentors.[3] Close working relationships help establish an atmosphere of trust that facilitates the accomplishment of visions and objectives. Tasks are viewed as fun, personalized events, not chores, with participants gladly putting in the hours necessary to get the job done. Instead of building barriers to protect turfs, individuals make suggestions within and across functional areas, resulting in a cross-fertilization of ideas. This approach can also produce an internally competitive environment where barriers still exist as certain projects or functions compete to create the next best idea, as in the case of Microsoft's culture.

These two cultures produce and hire different types of individuals and have different management styles. A comparison of traditional managers, entrepreneurs and corporate entrepreneurs reveals several differences (Table 3.1). While traditional managers are motivated primarily by promotion and typical corporate rewards, entrepreneurs and corporate entrepreneurs thrive on independence and the ability to create.

There is a different time orientation in the three groups with managers emphasizing the short run, entrepreneurs the long run and corporate entrepreneurs somewhere in between. Similarly, the primary mode of activity of corporate entrepreneurs falls between the delegation activity of managers and the direct involvement of entrepreneurs. Whereas corporate entrepreneurs and entrepreneurs are moderate risk takers, managers are much more cautious about taking any risks. Protecting one's corporate career and turf is a way of life for many traditional managers, and risky activities are avoided.

Whereas traditional managers tend to be most concerned about those at a higher level in the organization, entrepreneurs serve themselves and their customers, and corporate entrepreneurs add sponsors to these entrepreneurial categories. This reflects the respective

Table 3.1   Comparison of traditional managers, entrepreneurs and corporate entrepreneurs

	Traditional managers	Entrepreneurs	Corporate entrepreneurs
Primary motives	Promotion and other traditional corporate rewards, such as office, staff and power	Independence, opportunity to create and money	Independence and ability to advance in the corporate rewards
Time orientation	Short-term, meeting quotas and budgets, weekly, monthly, quarterly and annual planning horizons	Survival and achieving 5–10-year growth of business	Between entrepreneurial and traditional managers, depending on urgency to meet self-imposed and corporate timetable
Activity	Delegates and supervises more than direct involvement	Direct involvement	Direct involvement more than delegation
Risk	Careful	Moderate risk taker	Moderate risk taker
Status	Concerned about status symbols	Not concerned about status symbols	Not concerned about traditional corporate status symbols; desires independence
Failure and mistakes	Tries to avoid mistakes and surprises	Deals with mistakes and failures	Attempts to hide risky projects from view until ready
Decisions	Usually agrees with those in upper management positions	Follows dream with decisions	Able to get others to agree to help achieve dream
Who serves	Others	Self and customers	Self, customers and sponsors
Family history	Family members worked for large organization	Entrepreneurial small business, professional or farm background	Entrepreneurial, small business, professional or farm background
Relationship with others	Hierarchy as basic relationship	Transactions and deal making as basic relationship	Transactions within hierarchy

Source: Adapted from Robert D. Hisrich and Claudine Kearney, *Corporate Entrepreneurship* (New York: McGraw-Hill, 2012), p. 72.

background of the three types of individuals. Instead of building strong relationships with those around them the way entrepreneurs and corporate entrepreneurs do, managers tend to follow the relationship explicitly outlined in the organizational chart.

Climate for corporate venturing

How can the climate for corporate entrepreneurship be established in an organization? In establishing an intrapreneurial environment, certain factors and leadership characteristics need to be operant.[4] The overall characteristics of a good intrapreneurial environment are summarized below.

- organization operates on frontiers of technology
- new ideas encouraged
- trial and error encouraged
- failures allowed
- no opportunity parameters
- resources available and accessible
- multidisciplinary teamwork approach
- long time horizon
- volunteer program
- appropriate reward system
- support of top management.

The first of these is that the organization operates on the frontiers of technology. Since research and development are key sources for successful new product ideas, the firm must operate on the cutting edge of the industry's technology, encouraging and supporting new ideas instead of discouraging them, as frequently occurs in firms that require a rapid return on investment and a high sales volume.

Experimentation – trial and error – is encouraged. Successful new products or services usually do not appear fully developed; instead, they evolve. It took time and some product failures before the first marketable computer appeared. A company wanting to establish an intrapreneurial spirit has to establish an environment that allows mistakes and failures in developing new innovative products. This is in direct opposition to the established career and promotion system of the traditional organization. Yet without the opportunity to fail in an organization, few, if any, corporate intrapreneurial ventures will be developed. Almost every entrepreneur has experienced at least one failure in establishing a successful venture.

An organization should make sure that there are no initial opportunity parameters inhibiting creativity in new product development.

Frequently in an organization, various "turfs" are protected, frustrating attempts by potential intrapreneurs to establish new ventures. In one Fortune 500 company, an attempt to establish an intrapreneurial environment ran into problems and eventually failed when the potential intrapreneurs were informed that a proposed new product and venture was not possible because it was in the domain of another division.

The resources of the firm need to be available and easily accessible. As one intrapreneur stated, "If my company really wants me to take the time, effort and career risks to establish a new venture, then it needs to put money and people resources on the line". Often, insufficient funds are allocated not to creating something new but instead to solving problems that have an immediate effect on the bottom line. Some companies – like Xerox, 3M and AT&T – have recognized this problem and established separate venture capital areas for funding new internal as well as external ventures. Even when resources are available, all too often the reporting requirements become obstacles to obtaining them.

A multidisciplinary team approach needs to be encouraged.[5] This open approach, with participation by needed individuals regardless of area, is the antithesis of the typical corporate organizational structure. Examining successful cases of corporate venturing shows that one key to success was the existence of "skunkworks" involving relevant people. Developing the needed teamwork for a new venture is further complicated by the fact that a team member's promotion and overall career within the corporation are based on his or her job performance in the current position, not on his or her contribution to the new venture being created.

Besides encouraging teamwork, the corporate environment must establish a long time horizon for evaluating the success of the overall program as well as the success of each individual venture. If a company is not willing to invest money without a guarantee of return for five to ten years, it should not attempt to create a corporate entrepreneurship environment. This patient attitude toward money in the corporate setting is no different from the investment/return time horizon used by venture capitalists and others when they invest in an entrepreneurial effort.

The spirit of corporate entrepreneurship cannot be forced upon individuals; it must be on a volunteer basis. There is a difference between corporate thinking and intrapreneurial thinking, with certain individuals performing much better on one side of the continuum or the other.

Most managers in a corporation are not capable of being successful intrapreneurs. Those who do emerge from this self-selection process must be allowed the latitude to carry a project through to completion. This is not consistent with most corporate procedures for new product development, where different departments and individuals are involved in each stage of the development process. An individual willing to spend the excess hours and effort to create a new venture needs the opportunity and the accompanying reward of completing the project. An intrapreneur falls in love with the newly created internal venture and will do almost anything to help ensure its success.

Another characteristic is a reward system. An individual needs to be appropriately rewarded for all the energy, effort and risk taking expended in the creation of the new venture. Rewards should be based on the attainment of established performance goals. An equity position in the new venture is one of the best rewards for motivating and eliciting the amount of activity and effort needed for success.

Finally, and perhaps most importantly, the corporate venturing activity must be wholeheartedly supported and embraced by top management, both by their physical presence and by making sure that the personnel and financial resources are available. Without top management support, a successful intrapreneurial environment cannot be created.

Leadership characteristics

Within this overall corporate environment, certain individual characteristics have been identified that constitute a successful intrapreneur:

- understands the environment
- visionary
- flexible and creates management options
- encourages teamwork
- encourages open discussion
- builds a coalition of supporters
- persists.

An entrepreneur needs to understand all aspects of the environment. Part of this ability is reflected in the individual's level of creativity, which generally decreases with age and education in most individuals. To establish a successful corporate venture, the individual must be creative and have a broad understanding of the internal and external environments of the corporation.

The person who is going to establish a successful new corporate venture must also be a visionary leader – a person who dreams great dreams. Although there are many definitions of leadership, the one that best describes what is needed for intrapreneurship is: "A leader is like a gardener. When you want a tomato, you take a seed, put it in fertile soil and carefully water under tender care. You don't manufacture tomatoes; you grow them". Another good definition is that "leadership is the ability to dream great things and communicate these in such a way that people say yes to being a part of the dream". Martin Luther King Jr said, "I have a dream" and articulated that dream in such a way that thousands followed him in his efforts, in spite of overwhelming obstacles. To establish a successful new venture, the corporate entrepreneurial leader must have a dream and overcome obstacles in achieving it by selling the dream to others.

The third necessary characteristic is that the leader must be flexible and create management options. A corporate entrepreneur does not "mind the store", but rather is open to and even encourages change. By challenging the beliefs and assumptions of the corporation, a corporate entrepreneur has the opportunity to create something new in the organizational structure.

The corporate entrepreneur needs a fourth characteristic: the ability to encourage teamwork and use a multidisciplinary approach. This also violates the organizational practices and structures taught in most business schools that are apparent in established organizational structures. In forming a new venture, putting together a variety of skills requires crossing established departmental structure and reporting systems. To minimize disruption, the corporate entrepreneur must be a good diplomat.

Open discussion must be encouraged in order to develop a good team for creating something new. Many corporate managers have forgotten the frank, open discussions and disagreements that were a part of their educational process. Instead, they spend time building protective barriers and insulating themselves in their corporate empires. A successful new corporate venture can be formed only when the team involved feels the freedom to disagree and to critique an idea to reach the best solution. The degree of openness among the team depends on the degree of openness of the intrapreneur.

Openness leads also to the establishment of a strong coalition of supporters and encouragers. The corporate entrepreneur must encourage and affirm each team member, particularly during difficult times. This encouragement is very important, as the usual motivators of career paths and job security are not operational in establishing a new corporate venture. A good corporate entrepreneur makes everyone a hero.

The final characteristic is persistence. Throughout the establishment of any new intrapreneurial venture, frustration and obstacles will occur. Only through the corporate entrepreneur's persistence will a new venture be created and successful commercialization result.

Aspects of corporate entrepreneurship

While the aspects of corporate entrepreneurship can vary from organization to organization, the four fundamental ones that affect the level of corporate entrepreneurship occurring are indicated below:

$$L = I + O + 2C$$

Where:

L = Level of Corporate Entrepreneurship
I = Innovation
O = Ownership
C = Creativity
C = Change

Each of these four aspects – innovation, ownership, creativity and change – are discussed in turn.

Innovation

While innovation is highly valued and a central aspect of most organizations as indicated in the speeches of their top administrators and the aggressive expenditures on it, few organizations are satisfied with the return on their spending. According to surveys on corporation innovation, which drew responses from about 3000 global executives, innovation is at or near the top of the company's agenda with 43 percent of the respondents considering it one of their three most important strategic priorities and 23 percent considering it their top priority.

Yet, in spite of its priority, satisfaction with the return on innovation spending has decreased over the last three years. The satisfaction level decreased from 52 percent in 2006 to 46 percent in 2007 to 43 percent in 2008. This dissatisfaction with the return on the spending has also caused a decrease in the amount of spending on innovation from 72 percent (2006) to 67 percent (2007) to 63 percent (2008).

Dissatisfaction with the return on spending on innovation occurs at all levels of many organizations regardless of the industry. Many factors affect this poor return, such as: a non-corporate entrepreneurial culture; an aversion to risk; the inability to select the right ideas to commercialize; a lack of internal coordination; a long development time from idea to market launch; an inability to institute "best practices" to capitalize on idea; and the desire to always hit a home run. This last concern reflects a wrong assumption. Venture capitalists' track records show that out of ten investments, generally there are: one very big success; two successes; four walking wounded or living dead (not good, not bad), in which exit would be desired if the money invested would be recouped; and three failures.

One way to gain a perspective on this aspect is to understand the types of innovations. As indicated in Figure 3.1, the majority of innovative events are ordinary innovations – innovations that represent a small change in the way things are generally done; how the product looks, tastes or performs; or even in the packaging itself. The next

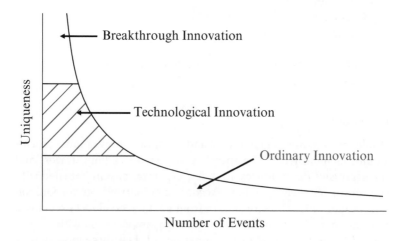

Figure 3.1 Innovation chart

most frequent in occurrence are the technological innovations. These are innovations that have some more advanced technological aspect than what is presently occurring in the market. Frequently these are protected by a patent or copyright. Big successes come from breakthrough innovations, the smallest number of innovative events where a radical transformation occurs from what is then taking place in the market. The personal computer, cell phone, social networks and the internet are indeed breakthrough innovations. Organizational managers need to manage their expectations and realize that although a breakthrough innovation and a resulting home run can occur, most innovative events in their organizations will be technological or ordinary ones.

Ownership

Ownership is also essential to corporate entrepreneurship in an organization and reflects the overall organizational environment or culture. In this sense, ownership means owning and feeling responsible for one's job, having the desire to perform the job in the most efficient and effective manner and in essence loving to go to work.

Creativity

The third aspect of successful corporate entrepreneurship is creativity. Creativity – the ability to bring into being from one's imagination something unique and original – is very important and yet often lacking in many organizations. Eight of the most frequently used creative-solving techniques are discussed in the following pages. This is the focus of the next chapter – Chapter 4.

Change

In order for corporate entrepreneurship to thrive in an organization, the final "C" of the formula – change – must continuously be allowed and encouraged. Organizational change should ideally be the result of an accumulation of smaller steps (changes) taken over time. Adam Smith in his *Theory of Moral Sentiments* referred to this as "gradual greatness". People tend to be more accepting of change if they can see and experience the steps slowly. New technologies, strategies, structures and/or rapid business expansion originate from smaller experimental steps and reflect the transference of knowledge and continual practice in the organization.

The idea that change in an organization should occur incrementally and collectively rather than suddenly suggests that an entrepreneurial organization should be continually experimenting and modifying around the edges of the core business. Change, discovery and renewal are fundamental aspects of this type of organization. As this becomes more apparent, managers are encouraged to develop creative, individualistic approaches and unexpected solutions to problems. This leads to charismatic individual leadership and inventive, creative decision making. Yet it might be necessary, in order to begin this process, to let go some of the existing managers who neither possess the skills nor desire to develop these softer skills.

Implementing a corporate entrepreneurship program

There are many ways to implement and operationalize a corporate entrepreneurship program. A general approach, which can be tailored to the specific objectives of an organization, is indicated below.

- Develop the vision and objectives of the program with key members of the management team.
- Develop example(s) of the proposal to be submitted; establish the evaluation criteria; and determine the amount of money available.
- Select members of the evaluation committee.
- Announce the start of the program with proposal submissions due in four to six weeks.
- Select winning proposals.
- Form venture teams.
- Communicate results and provide information on the program internally throughout the company on a regular basis.
- Implement and structure the corporate entrepreneurial activity and climate.

Vision statement

The first step in the process is for the CEO and key members of the management team to develop the vision (mission) of the program. This is extremely important to avoid the syndrome "without a detailed map, many roads will get you there". Some common elements in a mission statement are customer focus, quality product or service, employees are important, innovative activity, consistent quality delivery of product or service and ethics and social responsibility.

Elements of the program

Once the vision for the corporate entrepreneurship program has been established, several examples of a submission for support of a corporate entrepreneurial idea should be written. Ideally, these would be examples of the submission itself but at least should contain the elements needed. Having these examples has significantly increased the number of corporate entrepreneurship proposals received in companies being assisted by the author. Also, the proposal evaluation criteria and the amount of money available should be determined.

Evaluation committee

A committee that will be evaluating the proposals needs to then be established. This committee needs to include an individual from each important functional area and should reflect some diversity in terms of position in the company. The CEO or head of the division should not be a member of the selection committee. Being a member of the committee compromises the ability of the CEO or division head to champion the entire program.

Program announcement

The next step is to announce the program throughout the company about four to six weeks before the proposal submission deadline. The announcement should include examples or elements of the submission required, the amount of money available, the evaluation criteria and the members of the evaluation committee. The proposal announcement should come from the highest-level position in the group involved such as the CEO or division head and should include an enthusiastic message encouraging every employee to participate. This support will significantly increase the degree of participation and the number of proposals submitted.

Proposal selection

At the same time that the winning proposals are selected and announced, carefully crafted letters indicating why other proposals were not accepted, along with encouragement to submit a proposal in the next round of proposals, should be sent to the individuals submitting proposals that were not funded. Complete transparency is needed in the selection process in order to establish an environment that is very positive for the corporate entrepreneurship activities.

Venture team formation

Where needed, the individuals with the winning proposals should be helped in their selection of a venture team. While assistance should be available, the corporate entrepreneur should make the final decision and ask whomever he or she feels would be a good team member. Alternative individuals should be identified, as usually some of the individuals asked will not want to participate. It is extremely important that no employee be forced to participate as companies have experienced problems when this occurs.

Communicate results

In order for the corporate entrepreneurship process to become an integral part of the corporate culture, information on the activities of the funded venture proposals should be distributed regularly throughout the company. An internal company newsletter or at least e-mail blasts are two means to accomplish this. Periodically, the CEO or division head should show support through the same medium. Successes should be celebrated.

Implement the program

The second date for proposals should be announced at least four weeks before the due date; ideally, it would be announced along with the selection of the winning proposals of the first round. This enhances the acceptance of the program and makes it a regular activity of the company and part of the corporate culture. The author has had good success in implementing corporate entrepreneurship programs in both large and medium-sized companies using this approach. The actual corporate entrepreneurship program differed significantly by company, reflecting its vision and objectives.

Benefits of a corporate entrepreneurship program

The benefits of establishing and implementing a corporate entrepreneurship program are now discussed in terms of benefits to the company and benefits to the employees.

Benefits to the company

The principal benefits of corporate entrepreneurship to the company are indicated below. One of the most important benefits is the increase in morale through the establishment of a new corporate culture. Employees will "own their jobs" and want to make their positions operate in the best possible, most efficient ways. The new culture will make it fun for employees to come to work.

Employees liking what they do results in a reduction in employee turnover. Given the high cost of recruiting, hiring and training a new employee, higher retention rates result in substantial savings as well as retaining trained, experienced employees.

Employees are motivated to make sure the company does as well as possible. Can you imagine the quality of output and performance that result from an experienced, motivated team? These highly motivated employees will contribute to increase in revenues, reduction of costs and increase in profits.

Corporate entrepreneurship provides new business concepts. These can include new products or services, better systems and new ways of doing things. These new ways of doing things will be the norm as employees are encouraged to try new things for the best performance of their positions. Failure will be allowed and experimentation encouraged.

This will result in the company evolving into a more flexible organizational structure. There will be little or no turf protection, and teams can be easily formed to carry a project from start to finish. New products or services and new customers will occur and present customers will be more satisfied.

With flexibility and newness constantly occurring, organizational learning will be an integral part of the company's operation. Learning results in employees being able to do multiple jobs, grow in their own competencies and increase the productivity of the company.

All these benefits will result in increased revenues and profits. New products or services, new customers and more efficient operations will reduce operational costs, increase revenues and increase profits.

Benefits to the employees

The major benefits of corporate entrepreneurship to the employees are shown below. With a flexible organizational structure and corporate entrepreneurial culture, employees will feel self-actualized. Experiencing self-achievement will in turn enhance loyalty, efficiency and performance.

Increased job satisfaction is a common result of corporate entrepreneurship. With a culture of trial and error and try and experiment, employees actively make sure their jobs are done in the best possible way to the extent of being excited to come to work. This is perhaps the greatest benefit of corporate entrepreneurship for employees. Employees who are happy with their jobs and the company will make sure everything possible is done for the company to grow and prosper.

With a learning organization operating, employees will increase their skills. And of course employees with increased skills feel better about themselves and their ability to perform better and more efficiently.

Financial and non-financial rewards will be given to employees involved. Performance-based pay rewards will regularly occur, as will non-financial rewards. Successful activities will be heralded, rewarded and made known throughout the organization. The trial-and-error culture will allow employees to be more creative and open to change the way their jobs are done, to invent new processes and to develop new products and services.

Governpreneurship: entrepreneurship in government

If small and medium-sized enterprises and, as previously discussed, large organizations can be entrepreneurial, what about organizations not in the private sector? Can entrepreneurship occur in public sector organizations? Can it occur in government and/or governmental agencies?

Public sector entrepreneurship, which is called governpreneurship, becomes more and more important when public revenues are reduced, catastrophes occur and more services are requested.[6] While there are no proven models for achieving public sector entrepreneurship, whether it can occur and the degree it does depends to a great extent on its internal and external environments. Since entrepreneurship is a universal concept, it can be a part of non-profit organizations as well as government and other public sector organizations. Governpreneurship is discussed in terms of: a framework; aspects and transforming; government entrepreneurs; managing internal and external politics; and building a coalition.

Framework

Public sector organizations are usually large and hierarchical with somewhat guaranteed sources of funding and being more removed from their stakeholders (voters, politicians and other political institutions). The more the government is bureaucratic, the lower the entrepreneurial activity and spirit.

The emergence of entrepreneurship in the public sector has raised some concerns and questions regarding the responsibility of public managers and politicians. The political authority needs to be taken into account when designing and implementing new policies and/ or programs. Particularly, public interest must be kept in mind as government employees need to be civic-minded. Singapore, a city known for governpreneurship, has a top-down, strategic approach to entrepreneurship that includes: policies that reduce barriers and encourage foreign direct investment; subsidies for researchers or firms in targeted industries; emphasis on creativity and innovation at public universities; and recruiting professionals to develop policies and mentor the next generation and entrepreneurial growth.

The pillars of governpreneurship provide the framework for looking at this phenomenon. The external and internal environments provide the two major pillars. External pillars include funding, dynamism, stakeholders and time. The internal pillars are internal politics, funding/budgets, managing policy, control systems, behavior and reward/ motivation.

These pillars determine the differences between public and private sector entrepreneurship indicated in Table 3.2. There are fundamental key differences with respect to the level of diversity in objectives, diversity in decision making, authority risk/rewards, motivation, availability

Table 3.2   Differences between public and private sector entrepreneurship

	Public sector entrepreneurship	Private sector entrepreneurship
Objectives	Greater diversity and multiplicity of objectives; greater conflict among objectives	More clearly defined goals and objectives; greater consistency among objectives
Decision making	Less decision making autonomy and flexibility; more constraint on procedures and operations; subject to public scrutiny; major decisions have to be transparent	Greater degree of flexibility and autonomy in the decision making process; more participative and independent in their decision making
Authority	More authoritarian; more centralized or centrally controlled	More democratic; more decentralized
Risks/rewards	Risk and reward trade-offs favor avoiding mistakes; lower financial incentives; does not share enterprise's profits	Identifies risk factors and aims to minimize them; calculated risk taker; invest personal capital in the business; higher financial incentives; profitability is fundamental to generate income
Motivation	Lower commitment and job satisfaction	Greater level of commitment and job satisfaction
Funding and profit	Not constrained by narrow profit; easier to obtain funding for risky projects; easier to raise capital; does not have a profit motive, instead are guided by political and social objectives	Can be constrained by narrow profit; more difficult to access and obtain funding for risky projects; difficult to raise capital; profit-oriented
Restrictions	Restrictions on growth and power that face the private sector are not applicable to the public sector	Can be restrictions on the growth and power of the enterprise
Independence	Obtains independence by overcoming dependencies	Obtains independence by avoiding or minimizing dependencies

Source: Adapted from Claudine Kearney, Robert Hisrich and Frank Roche, "Facilitating public sector corporate entrepreneurship process: a conceptual model", *Journal of Enterprising Culture* (2007), **15** (3), 275–9.

of funds, restrictions and levels of independence. Generally, entrepreneurship in the public sector relies less on particular individual
attributes and more on group motivation and interest. For governpreneurship to occur, individuals need to be able to operate at the institutional level. Personal qualities and motivation become less important.

Aspects and transformation

When looking at the cases of governpreneurship such as the Celtic
Tiger or the Saudi Arabia Government Investment Authority (SAGIA),
several ways emerge that a government or any public sector organization can use to transform itself into a more entrepreneurial organization. One easy way is to reduce the bureaucracy and formal structure
by installing a decentralized structure and decision making process.
This, coupled with encouraging and rewarding creative behavior, goes
a long way to stimulating innovative behavior.

Establishing clearly defined goals and objectives is also important.
Identifying the desired outcomes and then measuring any deviations
that occur impacts the government employee's perception of what is
the behavior sought.

Third, developing a competitive strategy that establishes incentives to
increase efficiency and effectiveness, best use of available resources
and a long-term orientation encourages governpreneurship. And at
the same time, this increases the morale and culture for the government employee.

Fourth, establishing partnerships with the private sector aides this process.[7] These public-private partnership agreements usually result in the
development of creative solutions to problems and good utilization of
resources.

Finally, it is important to have a focus on customer satisfaction.
This focus and the alignment of budgets and spending to obtain this
leads to a more creative and innovative organization that supports
governpreneurship.

Government entrepreneurs

Who is this government employee who will be a government entrepreneur? Little research has been done on the topic. One way to answer

this question is to look at the differences between public sector and private sector entrepreneurship. As indicated in Table 3.2, the differences become more easily identifiable on the basis of several dimensions: objectives; decision making; authority; risks/rewards; motivation; funding and profit; restrictions; and independence. The nature of the constituency and external environments of the two significantly influences these differences. Turbulence and crisis create a need for action that can be served by individuals with creative solutions. To accomplish this often requires redesigning or restructuring the system and a longer time orientation, perhaps as long as 10 to 15 years with short-term goals established during this period of time.

Government entrepreneurs have persistence (fortitude) and good interpersonal skills allowing them to build coalitions. They are able to seek out constituencies needed for the creation and approval of the initiative and continue on in the face of adversity and numerous obstacles inherent in the extra constraints of the government.

The government entrepreneur needs to ignore the limitations and obstacles present and install a creative solution to the problem. One challenging problem confronting the government entrepreneur may be corruption. Corruption and unethical behavior comes in many forms. The government entrepreneur needs to be familiar with the country's anti-corruption laws and policies and any businesses that have a reputation for both ethical/unethical behavior. This and a knowledge of the global and national resources available to report and combat corruptive unethical practices help reduce the risks and improve the circumstances for the government entrepreneur.

Finally, government entrepreneurs need to develop several competencies to be successful. These include: energy; desire to achieve; being change-oriented; challenging the ways things are being done; focusing on the opportunity; being innovative and creative; taking moderate risks; and desiring that the constituency affected will be satisfied.

Managing internal and external politics

One of the biggest problems for government entrepreneurs is managing and navigating the internal and external politics. The impact and source of each of these need to be identified and a plan developed for coping with each. For example, Sir Colin Campbell when becoming

Vice Chancellor of Nottingham University established a formalized university management group to confront the internal dissent and the political nature of higher education in the United Kingdom.

To successfully manage the internal politics, a government entrepreneur needs to understand the overall culture of the government. Usually this culture is devoid of competition, creativity and risk taking. The culture is further impacted by the government system of motivation and reward. Since the government has to serve multiple, diverse constituencies, the decision making process tends to be one of slowly giving concessions and finding the most appropriate consensus.

This internal culture requires the government entrepreneur to diagnose the roadblocks and understand the hierarchy and individuals that need to be influenced. Also, it is important for him or her to align themselves with the right type of government employee.

Similarly, there are many external forces that need to be dealt with. These include: the lobbyist; court of public opinion; executive branch; the court system; the elected officials; and the labor unions. Lobbyists can be individuals, collections of individuals and/or corporations who exert influence and shape the terms and results of the debate. The court of public opinion includes full-time journalists at credentialed news outlets, bloggers, social media and pollsters. This force is best handled by employing or seeking counsel of a trusted communications manager or press secretary.

The third external force, the executive branch, enforces the legislative acts voted on by elected officials. This, coupled with the fourth, the court system, requires careful attention by the government entrepreneur. Particularly important is to understand the ability of the executive branch to unilaterally make decisions and the rulings by the court system usually in response to a grieved external party.

The last two external forces – the elected officials and labor unions – must also be dealt with. Elected officials can encourage or prevent governpreneurship by inserting an amendment, calling for hearings and using parliamentary procedures. Labor unions can be critical to the process as well as they have the ability to act in the form of their collective bargaining power.

Building a coalition

A coalition, a diverse group of individuals or organizations that come together to work for a common goal, is an excellent way for a government to break through bureaucratic red tape and foster governpreneurship. The key to establishing a highly effective and sustainable coalition is to make sure it is designed, developed and managed in a systematic way. A strong coalition can lead to significant changes in systems and policy. A coalition bridges the gap that exists in the meaning attached to an event by one person or organization and the meaning attached by another.

David Bishop, a law professor at Hong Kong University, wanted to create opportunities for his students who struggled to find meaningful work. He offered a group of students the opportunity to run a social venture if he contributed the time and capital to start it. After brainstorming on various possible social ventures, the students selected Soap Cycling. Soap Cycling collects and processes the leftover soap bars from hotels and distributes the soap through NGOs to families in low-income communities in Asia. This not only reduces chemical waste in landfills but helps the poor avoid easily preventable disease, as diarrhea kills over 800 000 children under five each year. In its first year, it produced and distributed over 300 000 bars of soap to some of the poorest communities in Asia.

Social entrepreneurship

Social entrepreneurship has made significant contributions to communities and society in general by adopting business models to offer innovative and creative solutions to complex social issues. Despite increased interest in social entrepreneurship and the credence of the growing impact of social entrepreneurship, there has been somewhat limited research in the area.

One challenge is that the definition of social entrepreneurship has been developed in a number of different domains such as not-for-profits, for-profits, public sector organizations and a combination of the three. Social entrepreneurship can be broadly defined as innovative activity with a social objective in the for-profit sector, such as social commercial ventures; non-profit sector; public sector; or even across sectors in terms of hybrid organizations that combine for-profit and non-profit approaches.

Social entrepreneurship can be more narrowly defined as the application of business expertise and market skills in the for-profit, non-profit or public sector when these organizations develop more innovative approaches in business activities. Common across all definitions of social entrepreneurship is that its core objective is to create social value rather than personal and stakeholder wealth.

Even though all of the above definitions of entrepreneurship, corporate entrepreneurship and social entrepreneurship have slightly different perspectives, they contain similar concepts since entrepreneurship involves creative activity. The core components of entrepreneurship involve the discovery and exploitation of opportunities. In fact, an entrepreneurial event cannot occur without identifying and addressing an opportunity.

Table 3.3 depicts a typology that identifies the similarities and differences between the three types of entrepreneurship and entrepreneurs: private sector, corporate and social. This table indicates that entrepreneurship and entrepreneurs are characterized as having a preference for creating activity, manifested by some degree of proactiveness and innovativeness. The core components of entrepreneurship include the discovery and exploitation of opportunities.

Since social entrepreneurship has similar aspects of entrepreneurship, corporate entrepreneurship and governpreneurship, it is addressed in terms of: developing the social concept; measuring social value; earned income; and securing donations through fundraising.

Developing the social concept

Developing a social enterprise involves establishing the mission, describing the opportunity and venture and developing a viable business model. Each of these aspects needs to be expressed clearly and succinctly so that the importance and aspects of the social enterprise are clearly understood.

Once the social problem and opportunity are identified, the social entrepreneur needs to create a mission statement for the social enterprise. This mission statement needs to discuss what the social enterprise will do; the uniqueness (unique selling propositions) of the idea; the value it creates and how this value will be measured; and the metrics of success and their measurement.

Table 3.3 Similarities and differences between private, corporate and social entrepreneurs and entrepreneurship

	Private entrepreneurs/ entrepreneurship	Corporate entrepreneurs/ entrepreneurship	Social entrepreneurs/ entrepreneurship
Objectives	Freedom to discover and exploit profitable opportunities; independent and goal-orientated; high need for achievement	Require freedom and flexibility to pursue projects without being bogged down in bureaucracy; goal-orientated; motivated but are influenced by the corporate characteristics	Require the freedom and resources to serve their constituencies; add value to existing services; address social problems and enrich communities and societies; driven by the desire for social justice
Opportunity	Pursue an opportunity, regardless of the resources they control; relatively unconstrained by situational forces	Pursue an opportunity independent of the resources they currently control; doing new things and departing from the customary to pursue opportunities	Show a capacity to recognize and take advantage of opportunities to create social value by stimulating social change; develop a social value proposition to challenge equilibrium
Focus	Strong focus on the external environment; competitive environment and technological advancement; primary focus is on financial returns and profit maximization	Focus on innovative activities and orientations such as development of new products, services, technologies, administrative techniques, strategies and competitive postures; primary focus is economic returns generated through innovation	Aim to create value for citizens by focusing on serving long-standing needs more effectively through innovation and creativity; aim to exploit social opportunities and enhance social returns, social wealth and social justice

Innovation	Create value through innovation and seizing that opportunity without regard to either resources (human and capital); produce resources or endows existing resources with enhanced potential for creating wealth	A system that enables and encourages individuals to use creative processes that enable them to apply and invent technologies that can be planned, deliberate and purposeful in terms of the level of innovative activity desired; instigation of renewal and innovation within the organization	Create practical, innovative and sustainable approaches to social problems for the benefit of society in general; mobilize ideas and resources required for social transformation
Risk taking	Risk taking is a primary factor in the entrepreneurial character and function; assume significant personal and financial risk but attempt to minimize them	Calculated risk taker; recognize that risks are career related	Recognize the social value-creating opportunities and key decision making characteristics of innovation, proactivity and risk taking; accept an above average degree of risk
Character and skills	Self-confident; strong business knowledge	Self-confident; strong self-belief that they can manipulate the system; strong technical or product knowledge; good managerial skills	Self-confident; high tolerance for ambiguity; strong political skills

Source: Robert D. Hisrich and Claudine Kearney, *Corporate Entrepreneurship* (New York: McGraw-Hill, 2012). pp. 16–17.

A valuable business model needs to be formulated to accomplish this mission and to indicate the financial feasibility of the social enterprise. The business model, a blueprint for how the social enterprise will create value, actually provides an outline of how the mission statement will be actualized. The business model has four aspects:

1. Mission statement (brief summary of the opportunity, activities, values, goals and metrics for success of the social enterprise).
2. Network (discussion of the network of the social enterprise, which includes donors, volunteers, supplies and collaborators).
3. Interface (detailed description of how the social enterprise will connect and deliver the services described to its beneficiaries who primarily are the targeted clientele but also donors, staff, volunteers and community).
4. Resources (discussion of the fundraising and earned income of the social enterprise).

Measuring social value

Measuring the impact of a social enterprise can be difficult in part because it has a double bottom line. A social enterprise must maximize its social impact of the mission while meeting financial budgets. It is important for the success of the social enterprise to be as precise as possible in measuring its social value, organizational efficiency and health, overall effectiveness and financial stewardship.

One thing that is important for every social enterprise is accountability. To show its accountability, a social enterprise must measure on at least a yearly basis the outcomes or impacts of its efforts. The measurements provide information to clients, donors and the general public about the performance and effectiveness of the social enterprise.

Several additional measurements provide valuable information to these three groups. These include: (1) benchmarking the performance of the social enterprise with a leading social enterprise working in the same area; (2) benchmarking the present performance of the social enterprise against its performance in previous years; and (3) indicating the extent to which the social enterprise achieved its stated objectives and milestones in its business plan.

Another important measure is social purpose value – the value that the social enterprise creates in society.[8] It can be measured in terms of the costs saved to society or the revenues generated by positively impacting a person's life. When an employed person becomes a part of the workforce, there is a social cost saving in the reduction in welfare payment and a social revenue generated in terms of the taxes the employed person will pay.

The following measurements should also be taken:

$$\text{equity balance} = \frac{\text{total assets} - \text{liabilities}}{\text{total revenues}}$$

$$\text{administrative costs} = \frac{\text{total administrative costs}}{\text{total costs}}$$

$$\text{operating margin} = \frac{\text{total revenue} - \text{total costs}}{\text{total revenue}}$$

$$\text{return on investment} = \frac{\text{total revenue} - \text{total costs}}{\text{total revenue}}$$

$$\text{enterprise index of return} = \frac{\text{enterprise value}}{\text{philanthropic money raised}}$$

$$\text{social purpose index of return} = \frac{\text{social purpose value}}{\text{philanthropic money raised}}$$

Each of these measurements provides information on the effectiveness, efficiency, impact and social return on investment of the social enterprise.

Earned income

Income for a social enterprise comes from three primary sources: donations, government organizations and fee income. Most social enterprises in the United States receive two-tenths of their income from donations, three-tenths from government organizations and five-tenths from fee income and other earned income sources.

Fee income can be obtained in a number of ways by a social enterprise. It can come from the sale of a commercial product and through endeavors operated directly or indirectly through separately incorporated entities.

Another source of income for a social enterprise is from membership fees. This is basically done through two types of membership organizations. One type of membership organization charges a membership fee and provides benefits primarily to its members. The second one is a public-serving organization, which serves both paying members and the public at large.

Donations and fundraising

Most social enterprises, particularly in the United States, rely on donations from bequests, corporations, foundations and individuals. Most of the charitable donations come from individuals.

Donations are obtained through employment by the social enterprise of a variety of fundraising efforts. These can be grouped into six broad categories: direct mail; fundraising events; personal relationships; telefunding; traditional media; and virtual means of publicity (e-philanthropy). Usually, social enterprises use a blended approach of several of these techniques to raise the needed donation amount. For most social enterprises, more could be spent in this area as the return per dollar spent is quite high. The size of the budget to attract donors of a social enterprise should reflect the type of donor being asked. There are basically five types of donors: potential donors; new donors; core donors; lapsed but reactivated donors; and lapsed donors. Each type requires a fundraising effort that will be appealing to them.

Summary

This chapter has focused on three different types of entrepreneurs: corporate, government and social entrepreneurs. After a discussion of managerial and entrepreneurial decision making, corporate entrepreneurs were discussed in terms of definition and interest, corporate culture, aspects, implementing and evaluating a corporate venturing program and the benefits of corporate entrepreneurship to the company and to its employees.

Government entrepreneurship (governpreneurship) was then presented. This public sector entrepreneurship was looked at in terms of a framework, aspects and transforming, government entrepreneurs, managing the internal and external politics and building a coalition. The chapter concluded with a discussion of the aspects of social entrepreneurship: developing the social concept, measuring social values, earned income and securing donations and fundraising.

NOTES

1 These differences are discussed in Howard H. Stevenson and William A. Sahlman, "Importance of entrepreneurship in economic development", in Robert D. Hisrich (ed.), *Entrepreneurship, Intrapreneurship, and Venture Capital* (Lexington, MA: Lexington Books, 1986), pp. 1–6.

2 William D. Guth and Ari Ginsberg, "Corporate entrepreneurship", *Strategic Management Journal* (1990), **11** (4), 5–15.

3 Donald F. Kuratko, Jeffrey S. Hornsby and Jeffrey G. Covin, "Diagnosing a firm's internal environment for corporate entrepreneurship", *Business Horizons* (2014), **57** (1), 37–47.

4 Ellen Enkel and Sanjay Goel, "Smoothing the corporate venturing path: rules still count", *Journal of Business Strategy* (2012), **33** (3), 30–39.

5 Peerasit Patanakul, Jiyao Chen and Gary S. Lynn, "Autonomous teams and new product development", *Journal of Product Innovation Management* (2012), **29** (5), 734–50.

6 The concept is introduced and discussed in Robert D. Hisrich and Amr Al-Dabbagh, *Governpreneurship: Establishing a Thriving Entrepreneurial Spirit in Government* (Cheltenham, UK and Northampton, MA, USA: Edward Elgar, 2013).

7 Joseph Mann, "Public-private partnerships toward a better future", *Latin Trade (English)* (2013), **21** (3), 66.

8 Cheryl Clark and Linda Brennan, "Entrepreneurship with social value: a conceptual model for performance measurement", *Academy of Entrepreneurship Journal* (2012), **18** (2), 17–39.

Online sources

http://www.intrapreneurshipconference.com/the-sony-playstation-an-intrapreneurship-story/.

http://www.intrapreneurshipinstitute.com/resources/intrapreneurship-case-study-of-the-sony-corporation%E2%80%99s-playstation/.

http://www.playstationlifestyle.net/2013/08/02/daily-reaction-happy-birthday-to-ken-kutaragi-the-history-of-playstations-father/.

PART II

Innovation and the idea

4 Creativity and innovation

Scenario: Gabor and Andras Forgacs – Modern Meadow

Americans cannot live without their hamburgers. The French love their fois gras. The Japanese's love for sushi has survived the tests of time. But what time will also tell you is that, eventually, the world will run out of meat. Countries trudge along with their traditional animal farming methods, breeding and raising animals, slaughtering them and processing their meat, then finally shipping those products to companies and families for consumption. And while we are currently freely eating as much meat as we like, there is no denying that the earth's population will one day outgrow our steadily declining resources.

Modern Meadow could solve this. Co-founded by a team of four innovators skilled in the fields of biotechnology, bioengineering and entrepreneurship, Modern Meadow is a 2011 start-up leading the revolution in biomolecular food reproduction. The company is led by a father-son team, Gabor and Andras Forgacs, who had together previously founded Organovo Inc., a company using their innovative 3D printer to develop human tissue. After Organovo's success had made human tissue printing a reality, people began to ask Gabor if the next reality would be to print animal tissue in the form of meat. He thought they were out of their minds. But after recognizing the similarities of his human product with a potential animal product and the list of possibilities stemming from this idea, Gabor eventually came around.

Now, Modern Meadow is using Organovo's innovative printer and pushing its limits even further, focusing primarily on the printing of three-dimensional leather and raw animal meat. The process starts with the acquisition of the types of molecular cells needed for the product. Those biopsied cells are then induced to multiply and form collagen, and the resulting product is placed into special printing cartridges and printed into a thin sheet. Those sheets are what are layered together millions of times over to produce the three-dimensional product. Of course, the process becomes much more complex, since creating raw meat requires making every component, from the fat to the vessels to the muscles. Other companies have already succeeded in printing other types of food, such as whipped cream and chocolate. But what Modern Meadow's innovation does differently is print using live material in the form of real cells.

The company is still working on this project, not yet having brought it up to the level they would need for it to be commercially viable. However, Modern Meadow's perseverance to start this lab-created meat revolution is already leading other companies to involve themselves in this idea. Many see this innovation as a breakthrough that will provide humans with an alternative to our current resource-intensive farming practices. Raising and processing meat requires a slew of energy and natural resources, from fossil fuels to water and land. There is also the concern with the impact to the environment related to greenhouse gases and other ozone-depleting emissions. It is hoped that not only will this 3D meat printer create a slowing of our global resource usage but it will also help in the fight against hunger in underdeveloped nations.

Even so, controversies will still be there throughout the beginning phase of this new innovation. Will these products really look and taste like meat? Will bringing food home from a lab instead of from a grocery store be too difficult for some people to accept? Why would anyone want to try what sounds a bit more like a crazy science experiment? Well, if Modern Meadow succeeds with their 3D meat printer, then maybe the question to ask is "Why not?" (see Online sources).

Introduction

As is the case with Modern Meadow, creativity and innovation are essential aspects for any entrepreneur. Creativity and innovation are frequently used interchangeably. However, there are some fundamental distinctions between the two concepts. This chapter explores these two concepts by first looking at creativity, its aspects, the creative process and creative problem-solving techniques. Following a discussion of the link between creativity and innovation, the chapter concludes by focusing on the many aspects of innovation.

Creativity

Creativity is the core of innovation and necessary to develop innovative business concepts. It is fundamental for identifying the patterns and trends that define an opportunity.[1] While there are numerous perspectives including psychological, social, individual and organizational, creativity is the application of an individual's ability to identify and develop new ideas, processes or concepts in novel ways. It is the act of relating previously unrelated things in novel and useful ways – a deviation from conventional perspectives. Both novelty and usefulness are necessary conditions for an idea to be considered creative.

There is no one idea of creativity that is appropriate for all fields of endeavor. Creativity calls on both cognitive and non-cognitive skills, curiosity, intuition and determination. Creativity is not just a revolutionary changing product that comes from world-renowned innovators like Alexander Graham Bell, Thomas Edison, Sigmund Freud or more recently James Dyson or the late Steve Jobs. Creativity is the ability to consistently produce different and valuable results. A key aspect in producing valuable outcomes is commitment and focus to channel creativity and achieve desirable results in light of potential limitations.[2]

Creativity is a process that can lead to incremental improvements or breakthrough innovations (see Figure 3.1). While breakthrough innovations such as penicillin, the computer and the automobile are great, most innovations make incremental improvements to existing product lines rather than risk bringing something radically new to market. Technological innovations such as voice and text messaging and the jet airplane occur more frequently than breakthrough innovations and are, in general, at a lower level of scientific discovery and advancement. Incremental innovation is the form of innovation that occurs most frequently. It usually extends a technological innovation into a better product or service with a different and usually greater market appeal. American Express is always looking to extend, modify and enhance its services. Organizations like Apple, General Electric, 3M, Microsoft and Nokia have been able to continuously innovate and transform themselves to serve new and growing markets by developing innovative products and delivering them effectively. Creativity and innovation does not just happen; it requires both general knowledge and field-specific knowledge, because creative individuals cannot know what is novel without a comprehension of what is already known in any specific area.

The final and most frequent type of innovations are ordinary innovations. In Italian and Spanish *mio* means mine. For Kraft Foods Group it has translated into money for a new ordinary innovation. The beverage brand was created and launched as the first nationally marketed "liquid water enhancer"; it has rocketed out of the gate. Sales were on pace to at least double those of 2012 to more than $200 million and now it is spawning imitations from companies such as Coca-Cola.

Mio had already reached a 12.28 percent share in the fruit-drink mix category, with sales of $14.4 million in the 52 weeks ending 7 October 2012 trailing only private label and Kool-Aid (also a Kraft brand), according to SymphonyIRI.

The liquid is basically Tang for a new age. Mio comes in a squeezable container that is small enough to fit into a purse or pocket. Kraft markets the brand to millennials, whom the company says crave the type of customization that Mio affords. Users either squeeze a bunch or a little into a glass of water.

But Kraft did not have the market cornered for much longer. Coca-Cola launched a similar product in Fall 2012, Dasani Drops, billed as a "zero-calorie liquid beverage enhancer" that the company says "offers a new twist on the water-drinking routine".

"Dasani Drops is the perfect solution for those who want to mix things up with a refreshing splash of flavor in their day", said John Roddey, Vice President – Water, Tea and Coffee for Coca-Cola North America. Like Mio, Dasani Drops come in a small, squeezable bottle and is meant to be an on-the-go option. An integrated marketing campaign and sampling efforts supported the launch.

Creativity can range from low levels to relatively high levels. Lower-level creativity frequently involves incremental modifications and adjustments of an existing idea or a combination of two or more previously unrelated ideas in a novel and useful way. Higher-level creativity involves more radical or breakthrough contributions. There are different forms of creativity:

- Creativity that develops new ideas, processes or concepts.
- Creativity that modifies existing ideas, processes or concepts, for example:
  - a new, improved version that is more efficient and effective

- • additional features and functions added
- • performs in a different setting
- • targets a new audience.
- Creativity that combines things that were previously unrelated.

Whether creativity is entirely new, modified or a combination of previously unrelated things, it is a process of developing novel and useful ideas, processes or concepts. Creativity and innovation without people does not happen. It needs people who are willing and eager to utilize their core competencies in the most creative and innovative ways. Being creative involves the following:

- being open-minded and objective
- perseverance and dedication to continuously seek and produce ideas
- an ability to put existing or new ideas together in different ways
- drive and ability to overcome obstacles or find alternative solutions
- moderate risk taker
- intrinsic motivation
- internal locus of control
- desire to achieve and grow
- driven by growth and development.

The creative process

Creativity is originality that is realistic, viable and marketable. Three key aspects of organizational creativity are knowledge, drive and ability. Knowledge of the course of action is required for opportunity identification, problem solving and decision making. Drive refers to the passion, desire and motivation to do something new and novel with the confidence to proceed as a first mover. This individual has an internal locus of control and is driven by a sense of achievement and self-fulfillment. Ability refers to the ways in which an individual seeks to identify a solution to a problem by adopting diverse and creative techniques in order to accurately assess and evaluate the situation and identify the best and most viable course of action. The following five components are the essential aspects of the creative process:

- preparation
- incubation

- illumination
- validation
- implementation.

Preparation is the background, experience and knowledge that an individual brings to the opportunity recognition process. It is through the preparation stage that the individual attempts to find answers to the question, problem or challenge. At this stage, it is important to fully understand the issue in order to have the required knowledge to find the best possible solution.

Incubation is the stage where an individual considers an idea or thinks about a problem. Time and space is necessary to reflect on the solution or considerations that may not be immediately forthcoming. The incubation stage frequently occurs when individuals are involved in activities totally unrelated to the question, problem or challenge. This stage is valuable as it is important to identify where extra help may be needed in order to progress forward.

The illumination stage involves the individual coming up with an outline of an answer to the question, problem or challenge. Frequently this answer needs to be further refined and modified.

In the validation stage, the individual tries to select the choice with a calculated level of risk and uncertainty. The ultimate success of the chosen alternative depends on whether it can be translated into action. This stage often requires further modification and adjustments to fit the organizational culture. At this stage, the idea is subject to scrutiny and analyzed for its viability. This is a particularly challenging stage of the creative process because it requires the individual to objectively reflect on the viability of the idea.

Implementation involves the use of managerial, administrative and persuasive abilities to ensure that the selected alternative is carried out effectively. This is the transformation of the creative idea into reality.

Innovation occurs through cycles of divergent creative thinking, which brings about many potential alternatives, followed by convergence to a selected solution. Divergence is breaking from the normal and familiar ways of doing things. It is focused on coming up with new ideas and solutions. It expands the number of potential solutions through the process of creativity. It is the most dynamic and social phase and underpins the creative process. Convergence is the achievement of some agreement regarding the benefits of a given idea and the value in pursuing that idea. It removes any non-viable options. It is an assessment in terms of the implementation issues. Unless the convergence stage is well managed, the most viable and innovative ideas may be lost. Creativity depends on a repeated cycle of divergence and convergence to first create a diversity of options and then determine the best ideas to implement. This process takes time and depends on the question, problem or challenge that the organization is facing.

The creative process involves both logical and analytical thinking in the preparation, validation and implementation stages. In addition, it calls for imagining, using intuition, conceptualizing and synthesizing in the incubation and illumination stages.

21st Amendment Brewery created and launched Lower De Boom barleywine-style ale in cans provided by Ball Corp. It is believed to be the first craft beer launched in an 8.4-oz can. "Traditionally, due to their higher alcohol content, barleywines were served in small bottles", explained Shaun O'Sullivan, co-founder of 21st Amendment Brewery in San Francisco. "Lower De Boom is a powerfully balanced, American-style barleywine packed with citrusy Pacific Northwest hops, making the 8.4-oz 'nip' can the perfect size to pay homage to the past".

"By being the first craft brewery to put their beer in our 8.4-oz can, 21st Amendment has found a unique way to differentiate their brand in a manner that pays tribute to the past", said Robert M. Miles, Senior Vice President of Sales, for Ball's metal beverage packaging division, Americas. "Distinctive can size and graphics are two great ways that brewers can elevate their brands in the marketplace. And because cans are impenetrable to oxygen and light, the result is better tasting beer which is crucial to every successful brewer".

Creative problem-solving techniques

While creativity is an important characteristic of a successful entrepreneur, unfortunately it declines with age, education and lack of use, as well as in a bureaucratic environment. Creativity generally declines in stages beginning when a person starts school.[3] It continues to deteriorate through the teens and continues to progressively decrease through ages 30, 40 and 50. Also, the latent creative potential of an individual can be stifled by perceptual, cultural, emotional and organizational factors. Creativity can be unlocked and creative ideas and innovations generated by using any of the creative problem-solving techniques indicated below:

- brainstorming
- reverse brainstorming
- checklist method
- free association
- collective notebook method
- attribute listing
- big-dream approach
- parameter analysis.

Brainstorming

The first technique, brainstorming, is probably the most well-known and widely used for both creative problem solving and idea generation. In creative problem solving, brainstorming can generate ideas about a problem within a limited time frame through the spontaneous contributions of participants. A good brainstorming session starts with a problem statement that is neither too broad (which would diversify ideas too greatly so that nothing specific would emerge) nor too narrow (which would tend to confine responses). Once the problem statement is prepared, 6–12 individuals are selected to participate. Finding individuals who are diverse from one another can also add extra value and insight to a brainstorming session. To avoid inhibiting responses, no group member should be a recognized expert in the field of the problem. All ideas, no matter how illogical, must be recorded, with participants prohibited from criticizing or evaluating during the brainstorming session. With this in mind, excluding certain upper-level management in the initial brainstorming session may be an effective way to reduce pressure and concern about possible repercussions.

Reverse brainstorming

Reverse brainstorming is similar to brainstorming except that criticism is allowed. In fact, the technique is based on finding fault by asking the question, "In how many ways can this idea fail?" Since the focus is on the negative aspects of a product, service or idea, care must be taken to maintain the group's morale. Reverse brainstorming can be effectively used before other creative techniques to stimulate innovative thinking.[4] The process usually involves the identification of everything wrong with an idea, followed by a discussion of ways to overcome these problems. Reverse brainstorming usually produces some worthwhile results, as it is easier for an individual to be critical about an idea than to come up with a new idea.

Checklist method

In the checklist method, a new idea is developed through a list of related issues or suggestions. The entrepreneur can use the list of questions or statements to guide the direction of developing entirely new ideas or concentrating on specific "idea" areas. The checklist may take any form and be of any length. One general checklist is as follows:

- Put to other uses? New ways to use as-is? Other uses if modified?
- Adapt? What else is like this? What other ideas does this suggest? Does the past offer parallel opportunities? What could I copy? Whom could I emulate?
- Modify? New twist? Change meaning, color, motion, odor, form, shape? Other changes?
- Magnify? What to add? More time? Greater frequency? Stronger? Larger? Thicker? Extra value? Plus ingredient? Duplicate? Multiply? Exaggerate?
- Minify? What substitute? Smaller? Condensed? Miniature? Lower? Shorter? Lighter? Omit? Streamline? Split up? Understated?
- Substitute? Who else instead? What else instead? Other ingredient? Other material? Other process? Other power? Other place? Other approach? Other tone of voice?
- Rearrange? Interchange components? Other pattern? Other layout? Other sequence? Transpose cause and effect? Change track? Change schedule?
- Reverse? Transpose positive and negative? How about opposites? Turn it backward? Turn it upside down? Reverse roles? Change shoes? Turn tables? Turn other cheek?
- Combine? How about a blend, an alloy, an assortment, an ensemble? Combine units? Combine purposes? Combine appeals? Combine ideas?

Free association

One of the simplest yet most effective methods that entrepreneurs can use to generate new ideas is free association. This technique is helpful in developing an entirely new slant on a problem. First, a word or phrase related to the problem is written down, then another and another, with each new word attempting to add something new to the ongoing thought processes, thereby creating a chain of ideas ending with a new product idea emerging. It may be beneficial to do the first round of free association as individuals so that ideas from the group do not constantly sidetrack from completing the ideas of each individual. Then, bring the participants together for a group free association.

Collective notebook method

In the collective notebook method, a small notebook that easily fits in a pocket – containing a statement of the problem, blank pages and any pertinent background data – is distributed. Participants consider the problem and its possible solutions, recording ideas at least once, but preferably three times, a day. At the end of a week, a list of the best ideas is developed along with any suggestions. This technique can also be used with a group of individuals who record their ideas, giving their notebooks to a central coordinator who summarizes all the material and lists the ideas in order of frequency of mention. In addition, ranking the ideas by importance might be more helpful than ranking by frequency as most people initially think of generic solutions at first and then begin to develop more creative, valuable ideas later. The summary becomes the topic of a final creative focus group discussion by the group participants.

Attribute listing

Attribute listing is an idea-finding technique that requires the entrepreneur to list the attributes of an item or problem and then look at each from a variety of viewpoints. Through this process, originally unrelated objects can be brought together to form a new combination and possible new uses that better satisfy a need.

Big-dream approach

The big-dream approach to coming up with a new idea requires that the entrepreneur dream about the problem and its solution – in other words, think big. Every possibility should be recorded and investigated without regard to all the negatives involved or the resources required. Ideas should be conceptualized without any constraints until an idea is developed into a workable form.

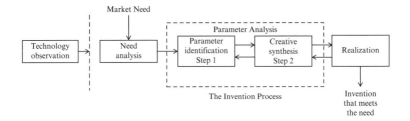

Figure 4.1 Illustration of parameter analysis

Parameter analysis

A final method for developing a new idea – parameter analysis – involves two aspects: parameter identification and creative synthesis. Step one (parameter identification) involves analyzing variables in the situation to determine their relative importance. These variables become the focus of the investigation, with other variables being set aside. After the primary issues have been identified, the relationships between parameters that describe the underlying issues are examined. Through an evaluation of the parameters and relationships, one or more solutions are developed; this solution development is called creative synthesis. This method is outlined in Figure 4.1.

Creativity and innovation

The link between innovation and creativity can be divided into three stages. The first stage comprises creativity through idea, activity, ability and skill; the second stage comprises invention through working model and prototype; and the final stage comprises innovation through successful commercial introduction of the invention.

Creativity is a process of generating ideas and innovation is the refinement and implementation of those ideas.[5] Creativity alone is not sufficient. Innovation is necessary to take the new or existing creative ideas and put them into action. It is the generation, acceptance and implementation of new ideas, products, services or processes. Within the context of the organization, the focus is on taking a creative idea and bringing it to fruition. From an organizational perspective, many great ideas never manifest beyond just that "great idea". To bring an idea from concept to market, it must be recognized for its potential; it must receive funding in an environment of limited and competing resources; and it must overcome potential obstacles, for example, technological challenges, competitive pressures, economic climate. The process by which this occurs is referred to as innovation and it is a fundamental process when talking about creativity within the organization.

Creativity without innovation has no real value. Similarly, without creative ideas to feed the innovation so it can develop and grow, innovation cannot accelerate. "Thus, no innovation is possible without the creative processes that mark the front end of the process: identifying important problems and opportunities, gathering information, generating new ideas, and exploring the validity of those ideas".[6]

Creativity is initiated and exhibited at the individual level. Creativity at the individual level is related to factors such as personality, motivation, competency and expertise. At the organizational level, certainly, environmental factors such as culture and climate influence creativity and therefore influence individuals' behavior. Innovation, on the other hand, operates much more at the organizational level. The focus is more on interrelationships, interactions and dynamism among components of the organization and its environment.

The lack or insufficiency in creativity and innovation is one of the biggest threats to organizations today. Organizations such as Bell Laboratories, 3M, Hallmark and Xerox practice creativity by looking more broadly for ideas within their industries rather than where everyone else is looking. Future opportunities are typically about being able to differentiate from what everyone else is doing and linking creative ideas into innovations that are commercially viable and generate value.

Neostem is a firm in the emerging industry of cellular therapy. Cellular therapy is a new therapeutic technology that uses stem cells for tissue regeneration and disease prevention and treatment. Neostem develops proprietary cellular therapy products and provides contractual services to other firms in the regenerative medicine industry. By combining these revenue-generating services with their own R&D for new products, the firm is able to generate cash flow and develop products in a more cost-effective manner.

Innovation

Innovation is a process that starts with an idea, proceeds with the development of an invention and results in the development or enhancement of products, services, processes or technological advancement as part of organizational innovativeness. Innovativeness reflects a tendency to engage in and support new ideas and create new processes, thereby moving away from established practices, processes and technologies. Innovative organizations place a strong emphasis on R&D. Innovation is not only the opening of new markets but also new ways of serving established and mature markets.

Elevation Brands, LLC and Ian's unveiled new innovative products and packaging at the Natural Products Expo West held 7–10 March 2013 by signaling a strong declaration for the allergy-friendly food company's product and marketing strategy under the new tagline "Friendly Foods for Life!" Best known for its 34 stock keeping units (SKUs) of allergy-friendly convenience foods, the new look supports a more powerful brand promise to deliver allergy-friendly foods you can trust to anyone with food intolerances/sensitivities. "Friendly Foods for Life!" is a multifaceted combination of product truths; allergy-friendly, family-oriented, convenience-friendly, taste-bud-friendly and health-friendly.

The addition of a leaf as the apostrophe in Ian's logo reinforces the all-natural aspect of Ian's product line while also helping to maintain its friendly, approachable personality. The new packaging puts trust front and center – literally – by featuring quick-read panels with icons and "No –" descriptions (No Gluten, No Wheat, No Eggs, No Dairy) that make it instantly easy to understand what the products do not contain. This saves the shopper from having to turn the packaging over and search small-type ingredient lists.

The move to broaden its product offering cross-category is supported by national trends including an increase in adult-onset food allergies as well as consumers' growing determination to make healthier food choices they can trust. Consumer demand for convenience, portability and varied usage occasions also drives Ian's product strategy.

Innovative organizations support new ideas, are experimental and creative in search of new improved practices and technologies.[7] The newness can consist of anything from a new product to a new distribution system to a method for developing a new organizational structure. Examples of these entrepreneurs include Edward Harriman, who reorganized the Ontario and Southern railroad through the Northern Pacific Trust, and John Pierpont Morgan, who developed his large banking house by reorganizing and financing the nation's industries. The most successful entrepreneurial organizations are those that link knowledge gained from their previous innovations into future innovation strategies.

Innovation, as an act of introducing something new, novel or advanced with the intention of benefiting the unit, some part of it or the wider society, is one of the most difficult tasks for an organization. It takes not only the ability to create, conceptualize and develop but also the ability to fully understand all the forces at work in the internal and external environment. The internal and external forces vary between different sectors and industries and every organization needs to have comprehensive knowledge and awareness of each aspect of the internal and external environment and the direct and indirect impact that the environment places on their innovation. Successful innovation under complexity, uncertainty and change can only be achieved through collaborative approaches that integrate knowledge inside and outside the organization. This has influenced organizations to start recognizing that they need to find new ways of accessing the knowledge needed to adapt to a continuously changing, increasingly complex and uncertain environment. Organizations need new ways of recognizing what they need to know by exploring, experimenting and networking with people and entities inside and outside the organization. This has led to the rise in what is termed "open innovation", which is intimately linked to the concept of core capability and how that affects an organization's innovation process. Moving from internal R&D to external connect and develop opens the door for small and medium-sized enterprises (SMEs) and large corporations to reach beyond their core competencies to remain competitive in an increasingly complex, uncertain and dynamic environment.

Traditionally, innovation has been more a private sector phenomenon where the impetus to successfully innovate or the application of new innovations in a given industry is fundamental to future growth and development. Innovation is equally important to the private sector organizations, public sector organizations and social enterprises. Private sector innovativeness is concerned with the creation or development of any product, service or process for the business that will lead to competitive success. Innovativeness in the public sector is more concerned with process improvements, new services and new organizational forms that will enhance the efficiency and effectiveness in the delivery of new and existing services. Innovativeness in social enterprises creates practical, innovative and sustainable approaches to social problems for the benefit of society in general, mobilizing ideas and resources required for social transformation.

Innovation is central to organizational competitiveness around the globe. Increased competition arising from globalization and technological advancement has heightened companies' needs to leverage and utilize resources to develop innovation within their organization. In today's society, individuals are constantly searching for higher standards of living and the newest, most sophisticated innovations that are introduced such as the iPhone, iPad, iTunes, eBay, Skype and Toyota Hybrid Prius. Increasingly, more sophisticated individual needs necessitate more rapid innovation, which in turn intensifies competition. Organizations that fail to innovate will fail to compete and very quickly will fail to exist. Innovation is a critical factor in the success and growth of organizations and societies.

Characterizations of innovation

A common factor in innovation is that it represents something new, whether a new product, service, process or technology. Innovation whether incremental (improvement to existing product lines) or breakthrough (unique and rare) will result in new ways of doing things, and changes the thought process to develop new ways of thinking about things. Innovation in organizations needs to be involved in:

- developing new products, services, processes or technologies
- developing new, more efficient methods of production
- identifying new markets both nationally and globally
- extending distribution beyond existing channels.

Innovation also needs to deliver customer value by creating a product or providing a service that not just meets but exceeds customers' needs, wants and expectations. Innovations are not always planned or deliberate; some of the most successful innovations were discovered by accident such as cell phones, cornflakes, nylon, penicillin, Post-its and

Teflon. Therefore, organizations need to be open to potential innovations beyond and in contrast to what they are aiming to achieve.

Phases of innovation

An innovation must progress through a number of phases before it is commercially viable. This applies to all innovations whether incremental or breakthrough in terms of product, service, process and technological advancement. These phases are:

* idea generation
* selection of most viable idea
* coalition building to transform the selected idea into reality
* implementation and commercialization of the developed or new product, service, process or technology.

Summary

This chapter has looked at two important aspects of entrepreneurship – creativity and innovation. After looking at creativity, its aspects and creative problem-solving techniques, the relationship and the differences between creativity and innovation were discussed. The chapter concluded with looking at innovation, its characteristics and phases.

NOTES
1   Some of this material is discussed in more depth in Robert D. Hisrich and Claudine Kearney, *Managing Innovation and Entrepreneurship* (Los Angeles, CA: Sage, 2014).
2   Todd A. Finkle, "Creativity, innovation and entrepreneurship: the case of H. Wayne Huizenga", *Journal of the International Academy for Case Studies* (2013), **19** (3), 71–85.
3   Costas Markides, "Do schools kill creativity?", *Business Strategy Review* (2013), **24** (4), 6.
4   "Better brainstorms", *Communication Briefings* (2012), **31** (10), 2.
5   "How to come up with a great idea", *Wall Street Journal* (New York), Eastern edition (29 April 2013), R1–R2.
6   Teresa M. Amabile, "Innovation and creativity quotes" (2004), available at http://www.inno-varsity.com/coach/quotes_innovation_process.html (accessed 20 February 2014).
7   Jay Rao and Joseph Weintraub, "How innovative is your company's culture?", *MIT Sloan Management Review* (2013), **54** (3), 29–37.

Online sources

http://modernmeadow.com/.

http://www.bbc.co.uk/news/technology-20972018.

http://www.inc.com/john-mcdermott/big-ideas/modern-meadow-in-vitro-meat.html.

5 Identifying opportunity

Scenario: Kevin Knight – Knight Solutions

Kevin Knight found his calling in the army at a very young age. In 1987, right after graduating from high school, he enlisted. However, fate took a different turn when, during a training activity, Knight sustained injuries to his face. The doctor told him he had lost sight in one of his eyes and effectively determined him unfit for duty. Knight was discharged before being deployed. Fortunately, this did not halt his ambitions and Knight continued on taking a different route with his life by successfully attending college, earning degrees from Norfolk and Cincinnati and gaining managerial experience through his time working for large corporations such as GM. Although his corporate experience had made him a success, Knight felt an entrepreneurial drive within him and after a while decided to start his own business.

During this time, Knight attended the funeral of a fallen soldier at a national cemetery. He observed that the grounds were not kept up as they should have been. A light bulb switched on. Here it was in front of him – an opportunity to not only start his own business but also find a way to serve his country. With renewed determination, Knight founded Knight Solutions, a construction company headquartered in Leesburg, Virginia. Knight Solutions was started using a $50 000 disabled veteran federal loan and focused initially on small contract jobs, such as restoring parking lots. Now Knight Solutions offers a range of services for private and public sector businesses and has surpassed $16 million in revenue.

One of Knight Solutions' most notable traits can be seen in its employees who are mainly military veterans. Since founding his company, Kevin Knight set off with a goal of hiring discharged military veterans, providing them with a stepping stone to begin their assimilation back into civilian life. Having had personal experience with the difficulties only experienced by vets, Knight knew that many men and women coming off the battlefield were not able to easily merge back into society. He knew of the challenges created by moving from a strict and hierarchical structured lifestyle to an unorderly one. Thus, Knight structures the operations of his company to mimic that of the military life. Order is highly regarded. Employees are managed with a hierarchical method of communication and instruction. Knight's specialized operational tactics are utilized as a comfort for those coming from a highly structured style of work, allowing his employees a smoother transition back into civilian society.

Knight Solutions does not just help out discharged veterans but also helps those veterans who have fallen during battle. The US federal government continues to grant the company contracts to restore national cemeteries, bringing them from once forgotten graveyards to honorable resting spots. Due to the lack of businesses that specialize in this type of restoration, Knight Solutions has been responsible for much of the jobs since its start in 2005. These national cemeteries, reserved for those who have served the country through the military, are handled distinctively as their physical appearances are to be managed according to strict guidelines known as shrine standards. Under these standards, many fine details are managed. Gravestones that are sinking into the ground are once again raised to stand tall and in line with one another as though they were soldiers themselves. Other parts of the grounds, such as the grass, are also returned to their original state. Kevin Knight did not serve his country in the way he had imagined since his childhood. And yet, Knight turned his story into another form of service. In creating Knight Solutions, Knight continues to not only serve his country but also the men and women who have survived our wars and their brothers and sisters who did not (see Online sources).

Introduction

As was the case for Kevin Knight, identifying the opportunity such as Knight Solutions is an important part of being an entrepreneur and particularly a successful one. Identifying the right opportunity either in the domestic or global market is an important ingredient for success. With so many potential market opportunities and prospective countries available, a critical issue for the entrepreneur is opportunity identification and market selection. This chapter focuses on this important topic by first looking at opportunity recognition. The three general opportunity assessment methods are discussed: trend analysis, demographic analysis and gap analysis. The chapter concludes with a discussion of sources of new ideas, methods of generating ideas and some good growing industries for starting a business and creating an opportunity plan.

Opportunity recognition

Some entrepreneurs need the ability to recognize a business opportunity; this is fundamental to the entrepreneurial process as well as growing a business. A business opportunity represents a possibility for the entrepreneur to successfully fill a large enough unsatisfied need that enough sales and profits result. There has been significant research done on the opportunity recognition process and several models developed.[1] One model that clearly identifies the aspects of this opportunity recognition process is indicated in Figure 5.1.

As indicated, recognizing an opportunity often results from the knowledge and experience of the individual entrepreneur and, where appropriate, the entrepreneurial business. This prior knowledge is a result of a combination of education and experience, and the relevant experience could be work related or could result from a variety of personal experiences or events. The entrepreneur needs to be aware of this knowledge and experience and have the desire to understand and make use of it. The other important factors in this process are entrepre-

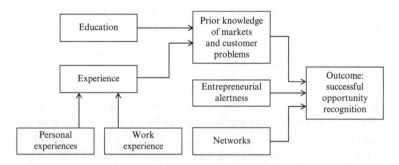

Source: From Alexander Ardichvili and Richard N. Cardozo, "A model of the entrepreneurial opportunity recognition process", *Journal of Enterprising Culture* (June 2000), **8** (2), 103–19. Reprinted with permission of World Scientific Publishing Co. Inc.

Figure 5.1   A model of the opportunity recognition process

neurial alertness and entrepreneurial networks. There is an interaction effect between entrepreneurial alertness and the entrepreneur's prior knowledge of markets and customer problems. Those entrepreneurs who have the ability to recognize meaningful business opportunities are in a strategic position to successfully complete the product planning and development process and successfully launch new ventures.

In March 2013, Whole Foods Market announced that all genetically modified organism (GMO) food products in their stores in the United States and Canada would require a GMO label by 2018. It is the first grocery store in the United States to take advantage of this new trend in health food. With increasing skepticism among consumers about GMO foods, particularly among health food consumers, it has created a valuable differentiated niche in the grocery store industry and perhaps has spearheaded a full movement toward GMO labeling. They currently sell more non-GMO project-verified products than any other retailer in North America making their labeling strategy hard to replicate for grocery stores that may wish to follow their lead.

Trend analysis

A trend, particularly a new one, often provides one of the greatest opportunities for starting a new venture, particularly when the entrepreneur is at the very start of a trend that will last for a period of time. This allows a new venture to be created and the idea serving the trend created, developed and marketed.

Energy trend

One significant concern for both consumers and industries revolves around energy – saving energy and having its source clean. Solar, wind and geothermal are viewed as the clean energy sources of the future but the amount of total energy consumed in the world supplied by these three sources is quite small. Some smaller businesses and single-family homes have installed solar energy as have many large corporations. While the number is increasing, it will take some time before this becomes a major source of energy.

Much more progress has been made in terms of energy savings such as solar hot water heaters, more energy-efficient appliances, electric cars and delivery vans, fuel-efficient engines in cars, planes and trains and energy-efficient lighting (light-emitting diode (LED) bulbs and lamps that cut out overhead lighting). Other energy-saving devices include: smart energy strips that automatically shut down at the time designated such as in the evening when offices are not being used; key cards needed to be able to turn on the lights in hotels and offices; and numerous new solar-powered devices.

Organic certification trend

There is an increasing consumption of organically certified food.[2] The sales growth in all organic food products including meat, dairy, fruit, vegetables, bread and snacks averages over 30 percent of total food consumption per year. Gluten-free product sales have also increased substantially over the last five years since first introduced. A similar increase has occurred in organic non-food items such as baby clothing, sheets and pillow cases.

Green trend

Overlapping to some extent the trends in energy and organically certified is the green trend. Water is one area of concern where more focus is on less water usage; reclamation programs for irrigation and desalination; and other water use efficiencies. Making recyclable products and having consumers and companies being more conscious of their recyclability is becoming more and more a habit. One entrepreneur is testing using worms to recycle food waste into fertilizer on a commercial basis and another uses a similar process to create energy.

Social and web trend

The social trend is accelerating throughout the world with more networking events and social media sights, and social platforms continue to increase in number and use. These include Facebook, Myspace, Twitter, LinkedIn, Vine, Instagram and Snapshot. Consumers who have engaged with a brand through social media have increased their spending on these brands by an average of 30 percent versus other customers. For example, Taco Bell has used Twitter to create a hip, fun presence turning some customers into strong spokespeople and supporters. This allowed Taco Bell, a brand of Yum! Brands, to successfully introduce and market Doritos Locos Tacos, achieving sales of around $100 million in the first ten weeks. In addition, due to cloud computing and nifty inventions like scanners, apps, digital books and media, the world is going digital. The web has aided this by creating many new forms of communication and purchasing, resulting in massive opportunities for entrepreneurs all over the world.

Health trend

With the average age increasing each year, significant changes are needed in health care devices and delivery platforms. As the world ages, many new opportunities occur in cosmetic products, niche expansion products and programs, personal health portals, point-of-care testing, fitness and relaxing centers and spas. New products such as Vibrant Brains, Fit Flops and Wit Fit are designed to capture this trend.

Demographic analysis

Another useful area to evaluate in looking for business opportunities is the demographics occurring and, most importantly, notable changes.[3] Several changing demographics include: dual household incomes; women entrepreneurs; aging population; increasing mobility; changing markets; different types of jobs; and an increasing number of partners. More and more families are having dual family incomes that put a premium on labor-saving devices or systems particularly in the service sector. Cleaning services, pool services, dog walking services, children pick up services and after-school day care are just a few services designed to save time for this segment. Gourmet to Go offered a food delivery service featuring all the necessary food materials and spices and an easy to use menu allowing even someone without any culinary talent to prepare a tasty, nutritious meal of choice in under 20 minutes. The aging of the world's population results in opportunities in a wide variety of areas for this segment, such as transportation, travel, education, health care and assisted living to mention just a few. It is no wonder some universities are encouraging retirement communities to be built near their campuses and offering education, arts and entertainment programming to this community, particularly when fewer resident students are present. Similarly, the increase in mobility and partnerships as well as changing and new markets have resulted in an increase in the number of women entrepreneurs throughout the world as well as different types of employment, particularly in the service sector.

Gap analysis

Gap analysis is another opportunity assessment method that is based on discovery gaps or opportunities presently in the market. These gaps or opportunities can be in the form of product line gaps, distribution gaps, usage gaps and competitive gaps.

1. Product line gaps:

- size related
- options related
- style-color, flavor, fragrance related
- form related
  - method or principle of operation
  - range of operation
  - product format
  - product composition
  - form of container
- quality (price) related
- distributor brand related.

2. Distribution gaps:

- coverage gap
- intensity gap
- exposure gap.

3. Usage gaps:

- non-user gap
- light user gap.

4. Competitive gaps.

Of these, the one most frequently used is finding product line gaps. This involves accessing products or services presently in the market on a wide variety of dimensions such as related to: size; options available; style-color, flavor, fragrance; form; quality (price); and distribution brand. By examining these dimensions of existing products, often an opportunity for a new or improved product/service can be identified. Gaps in distribution, usage or competition can also yield opportunities to develop a new product/service to meet this gap.

Sources of new ideas

Some of the more fruitful sources of ideas for entrepreneurs include consumers, existing products and services, distribution channels, the federal government and R&D.

Consumers

Potential entrepreneurs should always pay close attention to potential customers.[4] This attention can take the form of informally monitoring potential ideas and needs or formally arranging for consumers to have an opportunity to express their opinions. Care needs to be taken to ensure that the idea or need represents a large enough market to support a new venture.

Existing products and services

Potential entrepreneurs should also establish a formal method for monitoring and evaluating competitive products and services on the market. Frequently, this analysis uncovers ways to improve on these offerings that may result in a new product or service that has more market appeal and better sales and profit potential. Even existing companies need to do this. Sam Walton, founder of Walmart, would frequently visit competitive stores focusing not on what the competitive store did badly but rather on what it was doing very well, so he could implement the idea at Walmart. Jameson Inns established a policy whereby the manager of each of its inns (hotels) reports weekly on competitive hotels and their prices in their market areas.

Distribution channels

Members of the distribution channels are also excellent sources for new ideas because of their familiarity with the needs of the market. Not only do channel members frequently have suggestions for completely new products but they can also help in marketing the entrepreneur's newly developed products. One entrepreneur found out from a salesclerk in a large department store that the reason his hosiery was not selling well was its color. By heeding the suggestion and making the appropriate color changes, his company became one of the leading suppliers of non-brand hosiery in that region of the United States.

Federal government

The federal government can be a source of new product ideas in two ways. First, the files of the Patent Office contain numerous new product possibilities. Although the patents themselves may not be feasible, they can frequently suggest other more marketable product ideas. Several government agencies and publications are helpful in monitoring patent applications. The *Official Gazette*, published weekly by the US Patent Office, summarizes each patent granted and lists all patents available for license or sale. Also, the Government Patents Board publishes lists of abstracts of thousands of government-owned patents; a good resource for such information is the *Government-owned Inventories Available for License*. Other government agencies, such as the Office of Technical Services, assist entrepreneurs in obtaining specific product information.

Second, new product ideas can evolve in response to government regulations. The Occupational Safety and Health Act (OSHA) mandated that first-aid kits be available in business establishments employing more than three people. The kits had to contain specific items that varied according to the company and the industry. For example, the weather-proof first-aid kit needed for a construction company had to be different than the one needed by a company manufacturing facial cream or a company in retail trade. In response to OSHA, both established and newly formed ventures marketed a wide variety of first-aid kits. One new company, R&H Safety Sales Company, was successful in developing and selling first-aid kits that allowed companies to comply with the standards of the Act with minimum time and effort.

R&D

The largest source of new ideas is the entrepreneur's own "research and development" efforts, which may be a formal endeavor connected with one's current employment or an informal lab in a basement or garage. One research scientist in a Fortune 500 company developed a new plastic resin that became the basis of a new product, a plastic-molded modular cup pallet, as well as a new venture – the Arnolite Pallet Company, Inc. – when the Fortune 500 company was not interested in developing the idea and released it to the entrepreneur.

Methods of generating ideas

Even with such a wide variety of sources available, coming up with an idea to serve as the basis for a new venture can still pose a problem, particularly since the idea is the basis for the business. The entrepreneur can use several methods to help generate and test new ideas, such as focus groups, brainstorming, brainwriting and problem inventory analysis.

Focus groups

Focus groups have been used for a variety of purposes since the 1950s. In a focus group, a moderator leads a group of people through an open, in-depth discussion rather than simply asking questions to solicit participant response. For a new product area, the moderator focuses the discussion of the group in either a directive or a non-directive manner. The group of frequently 8–14 participants is stimulated by comments from each other in creatively conceptualizing and developing a new product idea to fill a market need. One company interested in the women's slipper market received its new product concept for a "warm and comfortable slipper that fits like an old shoe" from a focus group of 12 women from various socio-economic backgrounds. The concept was developed into a new women's slipper that was a market success. Even the theme of the advertising message came from comments of the focus group members.

In addition to generating new ideas, the focus group is an excellent method for initially screening ideas and concepts. With the use of one of several procedures available, the results can be analyzed more quantitatively, making the focus group a useful method for generating new product ideas.[5]

Brainstorming

The brainstorming method stimulates people to be creative by meeting with others and participating in an organized group experience. Although most of the ideas generated by the group have no basis for further development, sometimes a good idea emerges. This has a greater frequency of occurrence when the brainstorming effort focuses on a specific product or market area. When using brainstorming, four rules need to be followed:

1. No criticism is allowed by anyone in the group – no negative comments.

2. Freewheeling is encouraged – the wilder the idea, the better.
3. Quantity of ideas is desired – the greater the number of ideas, the greater the likelihood of the emergence of useful ideas.
4. Combinations and improvements of ideas are encouraged; ideas of others can be used to produce still another new idea.

The brainstorming session should be fun with no one dominating or inhibiting the discussion.

A large commercial bank successfully used brainstorming to develop a journal that would provide quality information to its industrial clients. The brainstorming among financial executives focused on the characteristics of the market, the information content, the frequency of issue and the promotional value of the journal for the bank. Once a general format and issue frequency were determined, focus groups of vice presidents of finance of Fortune 1000 companies were held in three cities – Boston, Chicago and Dallas – to discuss the new journal format and its relevancy and value to them. The results of these focus groups served as the basis for a new financial journal that was well received by the market.

Brainwriting

Brainwriting is a form of written brainstorming. It was created by Bernd Rohrbach at the end of the 1960s under the name Method 635 and differs from classical brainstorming by giving participants more time to think than in brainstorming sessions where the ideas are expressed spontaneously. Brainwriting is a silent, written generation of ideas by a group of people. The participants write their ideas on special forms or cards that circulate within the group, which usually consists of six members. Each group member generates and writes down three ideas during a five-minute period. The form is passed on to the adjacent person, who writes down three new ideas and so on until each form has passed all participants. A leader monitors the time intervals and can reduce or lengthen the time given to participants according to the needs of the group. Participants can also be spread geographically with the sheets rotated electronically.

Problem inventory analysis

Problem inventory analysis uses individuals in a manner analogous to focus groups to generate new product ideas. However, instead of generating new ideas themselves, consumers are provided with a list of problems in a general product category. They are then asked to identify and discuss products in this category that have the particular problem. This method is often effective since it is easier to relate known products to suggested problems and arrive at a new product idea than to generate an entirely new product idea by itself. Problem inventory analysis can also be used to test a new product idea.

An example of this approach in the food industry is illustrated in Table 5.1. One of the most difficult problems in this example was in developing an exhaustive list of problems, such as weight, taste, appearance and cost. Once a complete list of problems is developed, individuals can usually associate products with the problem.

Results from problem inventory analysis must be carefully evaluated as they may not actually reflect a new business opportunity. For example, General Foods' introduction of a compact cereal box in response to the problem that the available boxes did not fit well on the shelf was not successful, as the problem of package size had little effect on actual purchasing behavior. To ensure the best results, problem inventory analysis should be used primarily to identify product ideas for further evaluation.

New emerging industries

While every industry has some opportunities for an entrepreneur to develop a new product or service, there are certain industries that offer significant opportunities for doing this. These include: boutique beer, wine and spirits; consumer health technology; online education; specialty online retailing; and wearable computing.

Boutique beer, wine and spirits

There is a thirst for boutique alcohol in the form of beer, wine and spirits that started several years ago with microbreweries. According to Anything Research, microbrewery revenue grew 29 percent in 2012 and microdistillery revenue grew 32 percent in the same year. Look at the success of Boston Beer Company, Dog fish Head, Sierra Nevada and Six point in the beer sector. Skinnygirl Cocktails was so successful that it was purchased by Beam Global in 2011 for an undisclosed price.

Table 5.1 Problem inventory analysis

Psychological	Sensory	Activities	Buying Usage	Psychological/Social
A. Weight • fattening • empty calories	A. Taste • bitter • bland • salty	A. Meal planning • forget • get tired of it	A. Portability • eat away from home • take lunch	A. Serve to company • would not serve to guests
B. Hunger • filling • still hungry after eating	B. Appearance • color • unappetizing • shape	B. Storage • run out • package would not fit	B. Portions • not enough in package • creates leftovers	• too much last-minute preparation
C. Thirst • does not quench • makes one thirsty	C. Consistency/ Texture • tough • dry • greasy	C. Preparation • too much trouble • too many pots and pans • never turns out	C. Availability • out of season • not in supermarket	B. Eating alone • too much effort to cook for oneself • depressing when prepared for just one
D. Health • indigestion • bad for teeth • keeps one awake • acidity		D. Cooking • burns • sticks	D. Spoilage • gets moldy • goes sour	C. Self-image • made by a lazy cook • not served by a good mother
		E. Cleaning • makes a mess in oven • smells in refrigerator	E. Cost • expensive • takes expensive ingredients	

Consumer health technology

With the increasing cost of health, the aging population and the impact of the Affordable Care Act, new products and services are being developed in the consumer health technology industry.[6] This is a particularly exciting industry as it has a broad appeal to investors. Digital health care companies were able to raise $1.4 billion from venture capitalists in 2012, an increase of 66 percent from 2011.

New apps are emerging to help consumers monitor their glucose as well as start and maintain fitness programs. Noteworthy Medical Systems developed a patient record-keeping system that would allow consumers to carry all their health care records on a flash drive and was acquired by a German company in 2011.

Data mining provides significant opportunities, particularly if a trend is discovered for hospitals and large pharmaceutical companies. Acquisitions are common. Healthagen, maker of a health reference app (iTriage), was acquired in 2011 by Aetna and Massive Health, maker of Eatery (a meal tracking app), was bought by Jawbone in 2012.

Online education

As the cost of college keeps increasing and the job market is not expanding, more and more individuals are turning to increasing their capabilities and knowledge. According to an Education News Report, the content segment only of this online education will reach $72.9 billion by 2017.[7] Universities such as Harvard, MIT and Thunderbird School of Global Management are continuing to develop more online courses and certificate and degree programs, and corporations like the Apollo Group (University of Phoenix), 2U, the Minerva Project, Coursera and Kaplan in the profit sector do the same.

Specialty online retailers

Ecommerce is growing significantly worldwide and one segment of it is growing even faster, particularly in terms of new entrants into the market. These new specialty online retailers offer everything from Apache accessories and elk antlers for dogs, to personalized greeting cards, to vintage furniture and hardware, to vintage silver and glassware, to custom-made shirts and blouses and to photo printing. Acquisitions of some of these successful start-ups are also occurring.

JackThreads.com, a trendy men's fashion site, was bought by Thrillist and TinyPrints.com was acquired by Shutterfly.

Wearable computing

Probably the most rapidly changing are computing and telecommunications as technology continues to advance at such a rapid pace that products become obsolete in increasingly shorter periods of time. One aspect of this technological phenomenon is wearable computing. This is presently an $800 million industry and should be $1.6 billion in 2014 according to Juniper Research.[8] The biggest problems are the short battery life and convincing consumers that the new product/service needs to be purchased. Apple is working on watches and Microsoft is researching computer-enhanced glasses. And investment money for entrepreneurs does not seem to be a problem. Pebble, a start-up company, raised $10 million in 30 days on Kickstarter to develop a watch that downloads data from your phone and it appears that venture capitalists are interested in investing.[9]

Opportunity assessment plan

Once an opportunity has been identified, it should be evaluated through an opportunity assessment plan. This plan is not a business plan and focuses mainly on the idea and the market not on the business itself. It does not describe the organizational structure, the marketing plan, the financial plan and other aspects of the business plan discussed in Chapter 7. The opportunity assessment plan addresses four areas: a description of the idea for the product/service, the industry and the competition; the market – its size, trends and growth rate; an entrepreneurial self and team assessment; and the steps needed to translate the opportunity into a viable venture. The aspects of each of these four sections are outlined below.

Section 1: Description of idea, industry and competition

- A description of the product or service.
- The market need for the product or service.
- The specific aspects of the product or service.
- The competitive products available filling this need and their features.
- The companies in this product market space.
- The unique selling propositions of this product or service.

Section 2: Description of the market

- The market need filled.
- The social condition underlining this market need.
- Any market research data available to describe this market need.
- The size, trends and characteristics of the domestic and/or international market.
- The growth rate of the market.

Section 3: Team and self-assessment

- Why does this opportunity excite you?
- How does the product/service idea fit into your background and experience?
- What business skills do you have?
- What business skills are needed?
- Do you know someone who has these skills?

Section 4: Steps to create a viable venture

- Identifying each step.
- Determining the sequence of activities and putting these critical steps into some sequential order.
- Identifying what will be accomplished in each step.
- Determining the time and money required at each step.
- Determining the total amount of time and money needed.
- Identifying the source of this needed money.

Summary

This chapter has looked at identifying opportunities for a new venture. Following a discussion of opportunity recognition, three opportunity analysis techniques were discussed: trend analysis; demographic analysis; and gap analysis. After presenting some sources for new ideas and methods for generating new ideas, the chapter discussed industries that have significant opportunities available: boutique beer, wine and spirits; consumer health technology; online education; specialty online retailing; and wearable computers. The chapter concluded with a presentation of the opportunity assessment plan and its four aspects.

NOTES

1 For examples of this research and models, see Lenny Herron and Harry J. Sapienza, "The entrepre-
   neur and the initiation of new venture launch activities", *Entrepreneurship: Theory and Practice*
   (Fall 1992), 49–55; C.M. Gaglio and R.P. Taub, "Entrepreneurs and opportunity recognition",
   Proceedings, Babson Research Conference (May 1992), pp. 136–47; Lowell Busenitz, "Research
   on entrepreneurial alertness", *Journal of Small Business Management* (1996), **34** (4), 35–44; Scott
   Shane, "Prior knowledge and discovery of entrepreneurial opportunities", *Organizational Science*
   (2000), **11** (4), 448–69; Hean Tat Keh, Maw DerFoo and Boon Chong Lim, "Opportunity evaluation under risky conditions: the cognitive process of entrepreneurs", *Entrepreneurship: Theory and
   Practice* (Winter 2002), 125–48; Noel J. Lindsay and Justin Craig, "A framework for understanding
   opportunity recognition", *Journal of Private Equity* (Winter 2002), 13–25.
2 William A. Roberts Jr, "Natural and organic in the marketplace", *Prepared Foods* (2011), **180** (6),
   51–8.
3 Martha Mattare, Michael Monahan and Amit Shah, "A profile of micro-entrepreneurship in western Maryland: how demographic variables affect these nascent engines of opportunity", *Journal of
   Marketing Development and Competitiveness* (2011), **5** (3), 127–38.
4 Prabhat Vira, "Customers as best source of ideas", *MWorld* (2012), **11** (1), 35–7.
5 For an in-depth presentation on focus group interviews in general and quantitative applications,
   see "Conference focuses on focus groups: guidelines, reports and 'the Magic Plaque'", *Marketing
   News* (21 May 1976), 8; Keith K. Cox, James B. Higginbotham and John Burton, "Application of
   focus group interviews in marketing", *Journal of Marketing* (January 1976), **40** (1), 77–80; Robert
   D. Hisrich and Michael P. Peters, "Focus groups: an innovative marketing research technique",
   Hospital and Health Service Administration (July–August 1982), **27** (4), 8–21.
6 Precivil Carrera, "Do-it-yourself health care", *Health Affairs* (2013), **32** (6), 1173.
7 *Global "Smart Ed" Market to Reach $220 Billion by 2017*, available at http://www.educationnews.
   org/online-schools/report-global-smart-ed-market-to-reach-220-billion-by-2017/#sthash.oUuH-
   WAo7.dpuf (accessed 9 May 2014).
8 Greg Slabodkin, "Wearable device market to reach $1.5B by 2014" (6 November 2012),
   FierceMobileHealthcare, available at http://www.fiercemobilehealthcare.com/story/wearable-
   device-market-reach-15b-2014/2012-11-05#ixzz31FByS8kI (accessed 9 May 2014).
9 J.P. Mangalindan, "Meet Pebble Steel: a smartwatch for day and night", *Fortune* (2014), 1.

Online sources

http://investing.businessweek.com/research/stocks/people/person.
asp?personId=334746&ticker=KNX.

http://www.inc.com/laura-entis/inc-5000-applicant-of-the-week-knig
ht-solutions.html.

http://www.inc.com/magazine/201309/darren-dahl/knight-solutions-
improves-military-cemeteries.html.

http://www.knightsolutionsfirst.com/Company.

6 Creating and protecting the business idea

Scenario: Phanindra Sama – redBus

Phanindra Sama did not intend on becoming an entrepreneur. He had finished his degree in engineering and had already found his dream job as a Texas Instruments electrical engineer in Bangalore, India. The cushy offices, the good pay, an expected list of daily tasks to complete – all the comforts of a stable corporate job had completely spoiled him. Perhaps one constant drawback was the commute back and forth to work. Bangalore's population was booming in 2005, easily surpassing 6 million people with no indications of slowing. The city had grown to become one of the most densely populated in all of India, bringing with it a reputation for inconceivable traffic. It was now, thanks to this traffic, that Phanindra's life plan would be flipped upside down.

The Hindu festival of Diwali was just around the corner, and Phanindra was battling after-work traffic in an attempt to find a ticket booth for his bus ride back home to Hyderabad. He would be lucky if he got to the booth in time. He would also be lucky if they had any tickets left. He was not lucky that day. Frustrated with missing his bus back home to Hyderabad, Phanindra realized he was not the only one suffering through the madness. Many Indians had the same travel issues. At the time, the only way to buy bus tickets was to purchase one in person at a brick-and-mortar booth. Once you got there, ticket agents could only sell seats from buses they directly communicated with, leaving customers with few choices and no information about schedules and availability at other booths. There were also no postings of ticket fares, and thus no fixed pricing. Early preparation and a good amount of luck were needed if you planned on booking a ticket during a holiday, not forgetting the impending stress of repeating the process for your return ticket (roundtrip tickets were non-existent). Phanindra knew the use of bus travel in India was expanding with the growing population. Over 60 000 Indians traveled by bus each day. And while the bus business was booming, there seemed to be little interest in trying to organize the chaos into a smoother means of transportation.

The next year, Phanindra brought together a team of college classmates and started redBus.in, an online ticketing business that provided customers with an easier way of booking bus tickets around India. Using the team's own savings and an influx of third party investors, Phanindra molded redBus in a way that eliminated those previously accepted annoyances of booking tickets. Customers could book their tickets at home, at a transparent price and with the option of booking their return trips at the same time. The website, which currently links the schedules of over 1000 bus operators with over 10000 routes into one central hub, also allows customers a vastly larger pool of options to choose from. You can even see a layout of the bus seats. Phanindra's team eventually added software developed in-house, which were sold to existing travel agents and ticket booths that allowed them to tie into the hub.

redBus.in's sales grew ten-fold in its second year, six-fold in its third and doubled in its fourth. And in mid 2013, the company was successfully acquired by the Ibibo Group for $138 million, one of the largest overseas deals seen so far. Yet, what eventually follows a trail of success is a trail of eager followers, intent on taking advantage of the growing need for Indian ticketing sites. Other online start-ups have cropped up, bringing with them more choices in booking sites and more software options for travel agents and ticket booths. redBus, as the first entrant into the Indian market, will from now on need to battle these new sites for market share. However, in a population exceeding 1.2 billion people, less than 10 percent of total bus passengers actually use online ticketing. By continuing to fine-tune their website, software and other services, redBus can leverage their early entry and support systems to maintain the lead in India's evolving transportation industry (see Online sources).

Introduction

As occurred in the case of redBus, the basis for any business is the idea. Yet, this is often the most difficult aspect of entrepreneurship – coming up with an idea for the business and then developing it as well as the overall business concept. This chapter focuses on this by looking first at the overall concept of creativity and design thinking. Then, the different ways to classify new products are discussed along with the product planning and development process. After a presentation of aspects of developing the overall business concept, the chapter concludes with the various ways of protecting the idea and the concept.

Creativity

Creativity is the core of innovation and is necessary to develop innovative products and services and business concepts. While there are numerous perspectives including psychological, social, individual and organizational, creativity is the application of an individual's ability to identify and develop new ideas, processes or concepts in novel ways. It is the act of relating previously unrelated things in useful ways. These ideas, processes or concepts need to be useful and have value or meaning. Netflix is a highly creative company that recognized an opportunity and capitalized on the success of the DVD and the booming internet-streaming service. It was established in 1997 and since then has become a $9 billion powerhouse (crushing Blockbuster). Netflix has been one of the most successful dot-com ventures. Despite a series of hurdles that Netflix faced since July 2011, it was launched in the United Kingdom and Ireland on 9 January 2012. Creativity requires perseverance, passion and commitment – all of which is demonstrated by such companies as 3M, Apple, Amazon, Facebook, Google, Salesforce.com, Samsung, Twitter and Virgin Atlantic Airways.

There is no one idea of creativity that is appropriate for all endeavors. Creativity requires both cognitive and non-cognitive skills, inquisitiveness, intuition and determination. Creative solutions can be created or discovered immediately or over long periods of time. Creativity is not just a revolutionary changing product that comes from world-renowned innovators like Alexander Graham Bell, Thomas Edison, Albert Einstein, Sigmund Freud or more recently James Dyson, the late Steve Jobs or Mark Zuckerberg. Creativity is the ability to consistently produce different and valuable results.

Creativity is a process that can lead to incremental improvements or breakthrough innovations. While breakthrough innovations such as penicillin, the computer and the automobile are great, most innovations make incremental improvements to existing product lines rather than risk bringing something radically new to market.

Technological innovations such as voice and text messaging and the jet airplane occur more frequently than breakthrough innovations and are, in general, at a lower level of scientific discovery and advancement.

Incremental innovation is the form of innovation that occurs most frequently. It usually extends a technological innovation into a better product or service with a different and usually greater market appeal. American Express is always looking to extend, modify and enhance its services. Apple's successful innovations include the iPhone and the iPad. But the core innovation for Apple is the platforms that have facilitated an ecosystem of creativity – from gaming to finance to chip making.

Google Inc. was formed in 1997. Innovation (and enterprise) is at the core of their strategy.[1] Google has grown substantially. Initially providing single language search options, they now offer numerous products and services, as well as a variety of advertising and web applications for all task variations, in many languages. Google has been transformed from a single product into a diversified web power.

Facebook is a social networking site that created a breakthrough innovation by creating a new culture that changed the way people communicate. Facebook now has over 1.06 billion users worldwide. General Electric has a drive to invent and be innovative where it matters most in areas such as electronic medical records, innovative new power generation that reduces emissions and Water Explorer for Google Earth.

3M captures the essence of new innovative ideas and transforms them into ingenious products such as Post-It Notes, 3M stain-resistant additives and sealers, 3M Mobile Projector 225a and 3M Unitek Incognito Lite Appliance System.

Samsung combines innovation with green technology; they are moving fast and furious with innovative products such as Galaxy S Duos and Galaxy S III Mini. These companies have been able to continuously innovate and transform themselves to serve new and growing markets by developing innovative products and delivering them effectively.

Creativity and innovation does not just happen; it requires both general knowledge and field-specific knowledge, because creative individuals cannot know what is novel without an understanding of existing knowledge in any specific area. Additionally, without this knowledge, they cannot harness the creative energy and develop those ideas into realistic products, processes or services.

Creativity is a process of developing novel and useful ideas, processes or concepts. Being creative involves:

- open-mindedness and objectiveness
- perseverance and dedication to continuously seek and produce ideas
- an ability to put existing or new ideas together in different ways
- drive and ability to overcome obstacles or find alternative solutions
- moderate risk taker
- intrinsic motivation
- internal locus of control
- desire to achieve and grow
- driven by growth and development.

The creative process

The creative person uses a five-step process and alternating sequences of divergent (renegade, out-of-the-ordinary) and convergent (standard, conforming) thinking. The five steps are:

1. Fact finding: making sure that as many of the right questions as possible are asked to ascertain what the nature of the actual problem is.
2. Problem finding: defining the problem as effectively as possible, which affects the manner in which it is solved and the lasting validity of the solution.
3. Idea finding: developing as many different ideas as possible that solve the problem by using checklists, attributes and sub-groups.
4. Solution finding: evaluating the many ideas generated to find the optimal solution.
5. Acceptance finding: developing an appropriate specific, well-timed, action-inducing "sales pitch" for the idea through research, review of alternatives and a good presentation.

IDEO is a global design firm. The award-winning consulting firm assists in growth and innovation of organizations in both the public and private sectors. In addition to management consulting, IDEO works with firms to create brands and design and launch new products and services. They use a "design thinking" approach to solve problems and construct innovative strategies. IDEO is ranked as one of the most innovative companies in the world by Boston Consulting Group.

Design thinking

Design thinking is a new approach to create breakthrough innovation and promote high-performance collaboration.[2] It is quite different from analytical thinking and is a process for action. It is a method for discovering new opportunities and solving problems. While there are a variety of techniques and tools that can be used, the core process is somewhat universal.

It is generally understood there are five key elements in design thinking: (1) problem definition; (2) developing the options; (3) determining the direction; (4) selecting the best solution; and (5) execution. The steps have some degree of similarity to those in the scientific process. Each of these will be discussed in turn.

Defining the problem

This first step, correctly defining the problem, while sounding simple is often the most difficult of design thinking. If the right problem is not defined, then of course the solution, if obtained, is for something else. Defining the problem is usually a team effort with a significant amount of participation by each team member.

Defining the problem usually involves observation – discerning what individuals actually do versus what they may say they do. It also involves cross-functional thinking trying to find the real issues involved. Any preconceived notions or judgments need to be abandoned so that the right problem can be defined in such a way that creative solutions can occur. If the problem is a sitting apparatus, the problem is not to design a chair but to design something to suspend a person from the floor.

Developing the options

Once the problem is defined, the second element – developing the options – takes place. Care should be taken not to take the same approach as has been used in the past. Design thinking requires the creation of several solutions to the problem for consideration even when one solution seems obvious. For this to occur, multiple perspectives and team involvement are important. Multiple people involved develop a far richer range of solutions.

Determining the direction

This third stage – determining the direction – requires that the most promising solutions are carefully nurtured. An environment in the organization needs to be created so that each solution can be allowed to develop and grow. This environment of experimentation and testing allows the best solution to emerge. Often during this stage, ideas are combined to form an even better solution.

Selecting the best solution

From the many solutions maturing from the previous stage, the best solution can be selected. Prototypes of this solution are created and tested. This vigorous testing helps to ensure that the final solution is the best possible one.

Execution

Once the optimal form of the solution to the problem is found, the solution needs to be implemented. This execution element may prove difficult particularly when significant change is involved. Design thinking involves the acceptance of change and risk, which is often not easily embraced both by individuals and organizations. Execution also involves implementing design thinking on a continual basis as it is a repeatable process that will result in creative solutions to problems defined.

Classification of new products

New products may be classified from the viewpoint of either the consumer or the firm. Both points of view should be used by the entrepreneur to facilitate the success or failure of any new product.

From a consumer's viewpoint

There is a broad interpretation of what is a new product from a consumer's viewpoint. One attempt to identify new products classifies the

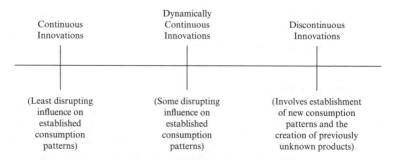

Source: Adopted from T.S. Robertson, "The process of innovation and the diffusion of innovation" (January 1967), *Journal of Marketing*, **31** (1), 14–19.

Figure 6.1   Continuum for classifying new products

degree of newness according to how much behavioral change or new learning is required by the consumer to use the product. This technique looks at newness in terms of its effect on the consumer rather than whether the product is new to a company, is packaged differently, has changed physical form or is an improved version of an old or existing product.

The continuum shown in Figure 6.1 contains three categories based on the disrupting influence that use of the product has on established consumption patterns. Most new products tend to fall at the "continuous innovations" end of the continuum. Examples are annual automobile style changes, fashion style changes, package changes or product size or color changes. Products such as compact discs, the Sony Walkman and the iPod tend toward the "dynamically continuous" portion of the continuum. The truly new products, called "discontinuous innovations", are rare and require a great deal of new learning by the consumer because these products perform either a previously unfulfilled function or an existing function in a new way. The internet is one example of a discontinuous innovation that has radically altered our society's lifestyle. Another is digitalization and digital media. The basis for identifying new products according to their effect on consumer consumption patterns is consistent with the marketing philosophy that "satisfaction of consumer needs" is fundamental to a venture's existence.

Some ideas are not accepted by consumers because they are ahead of their time. One was the electric car. Long before the Prius and other now popular electric cars by Volt and LEAF, in 1888 Nikola Tesla invented a workable AC auto engine. Another was an interactive TV product developed in 1983 by Microsoft. Even in 1996, when web TV was introduced, the concept floundered because consumers saw the TV and computers as two separate products.

Some technologies radically change the way consumers act and live. Online mapping technology resulted in Google Maps, social network technology resulted in Facebook and Twitter and VoIP technology resulted in Skype. Each of these ideas upended the way things were being done and established a new standard.

From a firm's viewpoint

The innovative entrepreneurial firm, in addition to recognizing the consumer's perception of newness, should also classify its new products on some dimensions. One way of classifying the objectives of new products is shown in Figure 6.2. In this classification system, an important distinction is made between new products and new markets (that is, market development). New products are defined in terms of the amount of improved technology, whereas market development is based on the degree of new segmentation.

The situation in which there is new technology *and* a new market is the most complicated and difficult and has the highest degree of risk. Since the new product involves new technology and customers that are not now being served, the firm will need a new and carefully planned marketing strategy. Replacements, extensions, product improvements,

Market Newness	Technology Newness		
Product Objectives	No Technological Change	Improved Technology	New Technology
No market change		**Reformation** Change in formula or physical product to optimize costs and quality	**Replacement** Replace existing product with new one based on improved technology
Strengthened market	**Remerchandising** Increase sales to existing customers	**Improved product** Improve products utility to customers	**Product life extension** Add new similar products to line; serve more customers based on new technology
New market	**New use** Add new segments that can use present products	**Market extension** Add new segments modifying present products	**Diversification** Add new markets with new products developed from new technology

Figure 6.2   New product classification system

reformulations and remerchandising involve product and market development strategies that range in difficulty depending on whether the firm has had prior experience with a similar product or with the same market.

Product planning and development process

Once ideas emerge from idea sources or creative problem solving, they need further development and refinement. This refining process – the product planning and development process – is divided into five major stages: idea stage; concept stage; product development stage; test marketing stage; and commercialization, which starts the product life cycle (Figure 6.3).

Establishing evaluation criteria

At each stage of the product planning and development process, criteria for evaluation need to be established.[3] These criteria should be all-inclusive and quantitative enough to screen the product carefully in the particular stage of development. Criteria should be established to evaluate the new idea in terms of market opportunity, competition, the marketing system, financial factors and production factors.

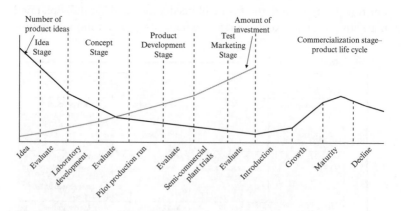

Source: From Robert Hisrich, *Marketing Decisions for New and Mature Products*, 2nd edn. Reprinted by permission of Pearson Education Inc., Upper Saddle River, NJ.

Figure 6.3   The product planning and development process

A market opportunity in the form of a new or current need for the product idea must exist. The determination of market demand is by far the most important criterion of a proposed new product idea. Assessment of the market opportunity and size needs to consider the characteristics and attitudes of consumers or industries that may buy the product, the size of this potential market in dollars and units, the nature of the market with respect to its state in the life cycle (growing or declining) and the share of the market the product could reasonably capture.

Current competing producers, prices and marketing efforts should also be evaluated, particularly in terms of their impact on the market share of the proposed idea. The new idea should be able to compete successfully with products/services already on the market by having features that will meet or overcome current and anticipated competition. The new idea should have some unique differential advantage based on an evaluation of all competitive products/services filling the same consumer needs.

The new idea should have synergy with existing management capabilities and marketing strategies. The firm should be able to use its marketing experience and other expertise in this new product effort. For example, General Electric would have a far less difficult time adding a new lighting device to its line than Procter & Gamble. Several factors should be considered in evaluating the degree of fit: the degree to which the ability and time of the present sales force can be transferred to the new product; the ability to sell the new product through the company's established channels of distribution; and the ability to "piggyback" the advertising and promotion required to introduce the new product.

The proposed product/service idea should be able to be supported by and contribute to the company's financial well-being. The manufacturing cost per unit, the marketing expense and the amount of capital need to be determined along with the break-even point and the long-term profit outlook for the product.

The compatibility of the new product's production requirements with existing plant, machinery and personnel should also be evaluated. If the new product idea cannot be integrated into existing manufacturing processes, more costs such as plant and equipment are involved that need to be taken into account. All required materials for the production of the product need to be available and accessible in sufficient quantity.

When dealing with competition and competitive situations, concerns regarding ethics and ethical behavior frequently arise.

Entrepreneurs need to be concerned with formally evaluating an idea throughout its evolution. Care must be taken to be sure the product can be the basis for a new venture. This can be done through careful evaluation that results in a go or no-go decision at each of the stages of the product planning and development process: the idea stage; the concept stage; the product development stage; and the test marketing stage.

Idea stage

Promising new product/service ideas should be identified and impractical ones eliminated in the idea stage, allowing maximum use of the company's resources.[4] One evaluation method successfully used in this stage is the systematic market evaluation checklist, where each new idea is expressed in terms of its chief values, merits and benefits. Consumers are presented with clusters of new product/service values to determine which, if any, new product/service alternatives should be pursued and which should be discarded. Many potential new idea alternatives can be evaluated with this method, with only the promising ideas further developed; resources are then not wasted on ideas that are incompatible with the market's values.

It is also important to determine the need for the new idea as well as its value to the entrepreneur/company. If there is no need for the suggested product, its development should not be continued. Similarly, the new product/service idea should not be developed if it does not have any benefit or value to the entrepreneur or firm. To accurately determine the need for a new idea, it is helpful to define the potential needs of the market in terms of timing, satisfaction, alternatives, benefits and risks, future expectations, price versus product performance features, market structure and size and economic conditions. Some factors help in this need determination. These factors should be evaluated not only in terms of the characteristics of the potential new product/service but also the new product/service's competitive strength relative to each factor. This comparison with competitive products/services will indicate the proposed idea's strengths and weaknesses and result in the unique selling propositions of the venture.

The need determination should focus on the type of need, its timing, the users involved with trying the product/service, the importance of controllable marketing variables, the overall market structure and the characteristics of the market. Each of these factors should be evaluated in terms of the characteristics of the new idea being considered and the aspects and capabilities of present methods for satisfying the particular need. This analysis will indicate the extent of the opportunity available.

In the determination of the value of the new product/service to the firm, financial scheduling – such as cash outflow, cash inflow, contribution to profit and return on investment – needs to be evaluated in terms of other product/service ideas as well as investment alternatives. The amount of each of the considerations important to the new idea should be determined as accurately as possible. The resulting figures can then be revised as better information becomes available and the product/service continues to be developed.

Concept stage

After a new product/service idea has passed the evaluation criteria in the idea stage, it should be further developed and refined through interaction with consumers. In the concept stage, the refined idea is tested to determine consumer acceptance. Initial reactions to the concept are obtained from potential customers or members of the distribution channel when appropriate. One method of measuring consumer acceptance is the conversational interview in which selected respondents are exposed to statements that reflect the physical characteristics and attributes of the product/service idea. Where competing products (or services) exist, these statements can also compare their primary features. Favorable as well as unfavorable product features can be discovered by analyzing consumers' responses, with the favorable features then being incorporated into the new product/service.

Features, price and promotion should be evaluated for both the concept being studied and any major competing products by asking the following questions: How does the new concept compare with competitive products/services in terms of quality and reliability? Is the concept superior or deficient compared with products/services currently available in the market? Is this a good market opportunity for the firm? Similar evaluations should be done for all the aspects of the marketing strategy.

Product development stage

In the product development stage, consumer reaction to the physical product/service is determined. One tool frequently used in this stage is the consumer panel, in which a group of potential consumers is given product samples. Participants keep a record of their use of the product and comment on its virtues and deficiencies. This technique is more applicable for product ideas and works for only some service ideas.

The panel of potential customers can also be given a sample of the product and one or more competitive products simultaneously. Then one of several methods – such as multiple brand comparisons, risk analysis, level of repeat purchases or intensity of preference analysis – can be used to determine consumer preference.

Test marketing stage

Although the results of the product development stage provide the basis of the final marketing plan, a market test can be done to increase the certainty of successful commercialization. This last step in the evaluation process, the test marketing stage, provides actual sales results that indicate the acceptance level of consumers. Positive test results indicate the degree of probability of a successful product launch and company formation.

Developing the business concept

The idea for the product or service is just one aspect of the business concept, which is a description of the entire opportunity. Besides the idea, the business concept contains three more parts: (1) the customer; (2) the benefit the product or service provides to the customer; and (3) how the customer will obtain the product or service being offered.

It is important for the entrepreneur to state the business concept in several clear and concise sentences so that anyone who asks about the new business can get the information quickly.[5] Some individuals call this the essence of the "elevator pitch".

When developing the business concept, it is necessary to know what business you are in. Do not make the error of defining your business so narrowly that you cannot grow your business beyond the initial product/service idea. In developing this broader business concept, the entrepreneur needs to describe the uniqueness of the product/service idea versus those products/services presently on the market. These are the unique selling propositions of your idea discussed in Chapter 5. These features or characteristics of the idea provide benefits to the customer, which are sometimes intangibles like convenience, reliability, better health or speed.

The business concept should be tested to make sure that it makes sense to invest more time and money in its development. While a large sample is not needed, several people, who are not your friends, should be consulted in terms of the appropriateness and quality of the concept.

Protecting the idea

Besides market protection, which means the idea is preferred by customers to other products/services available on the market, an idea can be protected through a patent, trademark, copyright or trade secret.

Patents

A patent is a contract between the government of a country and the global entrepreneur. In exchange for disclosure of the invention, the government grants the inventor exclusivity regarding the invention in the country for a specified amount of time. At the end of this time, the invention becomes part of the public domain.

The patent gives the global entrepreneur a negative right because it prevents anyone else from making, suing or selling the defined invention. Even if the entrepreneur has been granted a patent, he or she may find during the process of producing or marketing the invention that it infringes on the patent rights of others. There are usually several types of patents:

- Utility patents. A utility patent grants the entrepreneur protection from anyone else making, using and/or selling the identified invention; it usually protects new, useful and unobvious processes, such as chemical compounds or mixtures of ingredients, and articles of manufacture such as the toothpaste pump. A utility patent in the United States has a term of 20 years, beginning on the date of filing with the Patent and Trademark Office (PTO). The time period and filing process varies by country.

- Design patents. These patents cover new, original, ornamental and unobvious designs for articles of manufacture. A design patent reflects the appearance of an object and is granted for a 14-year term in the United States. Again, this time period varies by country. Like the utility patent, the design patent provides the entrepreneur with a negative right, excluding others from making, using or selling an article having the ornamental appearance given in the drawings included in the patent. Companies such as Reebok and Nike are very interested in obtaining design patents as a means of protecting their original designs. These types of patents are valuable for ventures that need to protect molded plastic parts, extrusions and product and container configurations.
- Plant (factory) patents. These are issued under the same provisions as utility patents and are for new varieties of plants. Few of these types of patents are issued in the United States.

Patents in the United States are issued by the PTO. In addition to patents, this office administers other programs such as the Disclosure Document Program, whereby the inventor files disclosure of the invention, gaining recognition that he or she was the first to develop or invent the idea. In most cases, the inventor will eventually patent the idea. A second program is the Defensive Publication Program. This gives the inventor the opportunity to protect an idea for which he or she does not wish to obtain a patent. It prevents anyone else from patenting this idea but gives the public access to the invention.

With international trade increasing each year, the need was recognized for an international patent law to protect firms from imitations by providing some protection in global markets. In response, the Patent Cooperation Treaty (PCT) was established in June 1970 to facilitate patent filings in multiple countries in one office rather than filing in each separate country. Administered by the World Intellectual Property Organization (WIPO) in Geneva, Switzerland, it provides a preliminary search that assesses whether the filing firm will face any possible infringements in any country. The company can then decide whether to proceed with the required filing of the patent in each country. There is a 20-month time frame to file for these in-country patents. There are some significant differences in patent laws in each country. For example, patent laws in the United States allow computer software to receive both patent and copyright protection. In the European Union, patent protection is not extended to software.

Trademark

A trademark is a word, symbol, design, slogan or even a particular sound that identifies the source or sponsorship of certain goods or services. Unlike a patent, a trademark can last indefinitely as long as the mark continues to be used in its indicated function. For all registrations in the United States, the trademark is given an initial ten-year registration with ten-year renewable terms. In the fifth year, the entrepreneur needs to file an affidavit with the PTO indicating that the mark is currently in commercial use. If no affidavit is filed, the registration is cancelled. Between the ninth and tenth years after registration and every ten years thereafter, the entrepreneur must file an application for renewal of the trademark. If this does not occur, the registration is cancelled. Trademark law in the United States allows the filing of a trademark solely on the intent to use the trademark in interstate or foreign commerce. The filing date often becomes the first date of use but this varies by country.

Generally, throughout the world, there are four categories of trademarks: (1) coined marks denote no relationship between the mark and the goods or services (for example, Mercedes, Kodak) and offer the possibility of expansion to a wide range of products; (2) an arbitrary mark is one that has another meaning in the language of the United States (for example, Apple) and is applied to a product or service; (3) a suggestive mark is used to suggest certain features, qualities, ingredients or characteristics of a product or service (for example, Halo shampoo) and suggest some describable attribute of the product or service; and (4) a description mark must have become distinctive over a significant period of time and gained consumer recognition before it can be registered. Registering a trademark can offer significant advantages or benefits to the entrepreneur in each country.

Copyright

A copyright protects original works of authorship. The protection in a copyright does not protect the idea itself, and thus it allows someone else to use the idea or concept in a different manner. Copyright law has become especially relevant because of the tremendous growth in the use of the internet, especially in downloading music, literary work, pictures, videos and software.

Copyrights in the United States are registered with the Library of Congress and usually do not require an attorney. To register a work, the entrepreneur sends a completed application (available online at www. copyright.gov), two copies of the work and the required filing fees (the initial filing fee). The term of the copyright is the life of the entrepreneur plus 70 years in the United States. This time period also varies by country.

Besides computer software, copyrights are desirable for books, scripts, articles, poems, songs, sculptures, models, maps, blueprints, printed material on board games, data and music. In some instances, several forms of protection may be available.

Trade secret

The entrepreneur may prefer to maintain an idea or process as confidential and to keep it as a trade secret. The trade secret will have a life as long as the idea or process remains a secret.

A trade secret is not covered by any laws, but is recognized under a governing body of common laws in some countries. Employees involved in working with an idea or process may be asked to first sign a confidential information agreement that will protect the entrepreneur against the employee giving out the trade secret either while with an employer or after leaving the venture.

The amount of information to give employees is a difficult decision and is often determined by the entrepreneur's judgment. Usually, entrepreneurs tend to protect sensitive or confidential company information from anyone else by simply not making the information available.

Most entrepreneurs who have limited resources can choose not to protect their ideas, products or services. This can become a serious problem because obtaining competitive information legally is easy to accomplish unless the entrepreneur takes the proper precautions. It is usually easy to learn competitive information through such means as trade shows, transient employees, media interviews or announcements and even websites.

Summary

This chapter has focused on creating and protecting the idea for the business. Following a discussion of creativity and design thinking, the different ways to classify new products/resources were discussed along with the product planning and development process. The chapter concluded with a discussion of developing the overall business concept and four ways of protecting the idea (patent, trademark, copyright and trade secret).

NOTES

1   John C. Lyons, "An innovator on the fast track", *BRW* (2011), **33** (30), 40.

2   Peter J. Denning, "Design thinking", *Communications of the ACM* (2013), **56** (12), 29–31.

3   Miia Martinsuo and Jarno Poskela, "Use of evaluation criteria and innovation performance in the front end of innovation", *Journal of Product Innovation Management* (2011), **28** (6), 896–914.

4   Paul Nieman, "In search of", *Inventors' Digest* (2011), **28** (8), 36–7.

5   Tennille M. Robinson, "How simple equals success", *Black Enterprise* (2011), **42** (1), 30.

Online sources

http://business.rediff.com/slide-show/2010/oct/19/slide-show-1-the-amazing-success-story-of-redBus.htm.

http://www.sramanamitra.com/2013/07/16/redBus-ride-to-success-and-its-implications/.

http://timesofindia.indiatimes.com/business/india-business/redBus-sold-to-Ibibo-in-one-of-the-biggest-overseas-internet-deals/article-show/20704509.cms.

PART III

The business plan

7 The business plan

Scenario: Sophia Amoruso – Nasty Gal

Sophia Amoruso is a perfect example of this generation's entrepreneurial moxie. Fittingly so, the word "moxie" is a dead-on description of Amoruso. Growing up as a rebellious youth, Amoruso spent most of her late teenage years and early 20s darting up and down the west coast, finding work in record stores and fancying such notions as anarchy and revolution. After dropping out of photography school in 2006, Amoruso, confident in her own edgy and vintage fashion tastes, began selling cheaply purchased thrift store finds on her eBay store, Nasty Gal. Her edgy, vintage tastes in clothes soon gained the attention of other young women willing to pay more for ethereal pieces too unique to be found in retail stores. Amoruso's business smarts did not end with her keen eye for clothes. While other eBay sellers commonly posted pictures of their pieces draped over dull, headless mannequins, Amoruso paid local California girls in either cash or hamburgers to model her pieces in front of different backdrops. Her fresh, personally styled eBay photos alone brought in even more visitors. Amoruso soon realized the amount her customers were willing to pay for her items and began marking up the prices of her finds, gaining margins to the tune of hundreds of dollars per piece. This barely slowed the growing mania of her followers for more, and Nasty Gal soon found itself the leader of a trend-hungry fashion cult.

Leveraging the unique value her own tastes have brought to her business, Amoruso has continued catering to her quickly expanding customer base. Her product lines, no longer dug up from thrift store bins, are now from specially picked, partnering designers. She has since bought the NastyGal.com domain from its previous owner, leased a 500000 square foot fulfillment center in Kentucky and finally decided to partner with a venture capital firm famous for its investments in now popular fashion sites such as Net-A-Porter and ASOS. The $50 million investment is now helping with expansions such as Nasty Gal's new and extremely successful in-house clothing line.

From its start-up in 2006 to the end of 2012, Nasty Gal has exponentially increased in size – its 2012 sales alone came close to $100 million. Most of its marketing and advertising is done through social media such as Facebook, Twitter, Pinterest and Instagram. Many of Nasty Gal's customers, rather than seeing a commercial on TV, are led to the company's website through word of mouth. And while the company can now afford to move into retail shops and larger advertising ploys, Amoruso has yet to budge in that direction. Her resistance to abandon the original personality of her business has been shown in the company's selective choices for expansion. Until her recent venture capital partnership, Amoruso had yet to take on any type of debt, reinvesting all of her profits back into the company. There was no need to invest in expensive advertising as Amoruso knew her target customers were already propelling the company's fame through social media outlets. Seven years after the start of Nasty Gal, Amoruso remains particular in what she chooses to sell, not letting any article of clothing deviate from her company's edgy charm. There seems to be no need to include other fashion styles – most of Nasty Gal's product lines sell out, sometimes within minutes.

Amoruso is staying true to her herself and loyal to her fan base. And while naysayers and competitors may shrug Nasty Gal off as a fashion movement destined to become the inevitable old hat, its continued sales growth and army of trend-setting devotees say otherwise. For now, Nasty Gal is not going anywhere (see Online sources).

Introduction

Successful entrepreneurs like Sophia Amoruso take the time to plan the future activities of their business. This often takes the form of a business plan as it provides a road map for implementing the entrepreneurial strategy established. While strategy can be defined as developing a plan for creating and operating a profitable new enterprise through the obtainment and development of internal and external resources in alignment with the environment,[1] it still exists at various levels in a new venture. These levels include: the enterprise, corporate, business, functional and sub-functional. This allows implementation to occur throughout the venture.

A key aspect of developing a strategy at each level is establishing goals. Goals need to be difficult to achieve and represent a challenge for the new venture and yet realistic enough to be achieved with effort. To accomplish the goals established and implement the strategy, a business plan covers the aspects of creating and starting a new venture. While the original plan developed will be modified and changed many times, still, "If you do not know where you are going, any road will get you there".

This chapter focuses on the business plan by covering the purpose of a business plan, its benefits and its aspects.

Vitamix originally started with the name The Natural Food Institute, which was focused on educating people about food and health. In 1937, the founder began selling blenders, realizing their use in efficiently preparing healthy meals. Their first blender product they named the "Vitamix". Since then, the company has focused exclusively on selling high-quality blenders to businesses and individual consumers, officially changing its name to Vitamix in 1955. The company continues to innovate and develop new products but remains narrowly focused on the high-quality blender industry.

Purposes of a business plan

Writing a business plan can be a difficult thing for an entrepreneur to do as they are usually individuals characterized as doers not planners. But it is not acceptable to hire someone to write the plan as the task needs to be done personally. While outsiders (accountants, consultants, lawyers) can be used for input in terms of numbers and pieces of the plan, the final business plan needs to be developed and written by the entrepreneur and any initial top management team members when appropriate. By doing this, the entrepreneur ensures that he or she is very familiar with all the details of the plan in order to be able to present the plan to outside sources of finance and make and be responsible for decisions that will affect the new venture. Every outside investor expects the entrepreneur to be knowledgeable about and totally involved in the proposed venture.

Developing the business plan takes energy, money and time with time being one of the most costly aspects. Since each business plan deals with an economy(s) and industry(s), a hidden cost of writing a business plan is a psychological one – understanding and knowing that anything can go wrong. This is particularly difficult for entrepreneurs who are overall optimistic and believe in themselves and their capabilities.

The main reasons for writing a business plan are:

* obtain finances
* determine resources needed
* establish direction for firm
* evaluate performance results
  * management by deviation
  * reporting results to stakeholders
* obtain a joint venture partner.

Of these, by far the reason most business plans are written is to obtain financing. Providers of debt or equity capital need a business plan to determine whether to loan or invest money in the particular new venture versus all the other investment options available.[2]

Another reason for writing a business plan is to establish the direction of the venture. Thus, what is often called focus is one of the main reasons some entrepreneurs are successful and others are not. When surveyed, to provide a basis for one of my books, entrepreneurs all over the world cited focusing as a critical aspect for success – focusing or establishing the direction of the firm. Staying focused allows a venture to stay on track and obtain the goals and objectives established.[3] One company that has done this very well since its start in 1921 by William Barnard is Vitamix Corporation. Even though changing its name from The Natural Food Institute, the company, headquartered in Cleveland, Ohio with 803 full-time employees worldwide, has stayed focused on providing blenders for the institutional and consumer markets. This focus has resulted in a consumer base that has increased by 500 percent in the last five years, recently adding a Vitamix model 5200 in Costco stores throughout the United States. According to the present management team of Jodi Berg, President, and John Barnard, Executive Chairman and CEO, it is highly doubtful that the company will ever deviate from staying focused on the blending business. The other purposes and benefits of a business plan are discussed in the next section.

Benefits of a business plan

Since a business plan details the entrepreneur's vision in writing and indicates the implementation strategy and the costs involved, it has several benefits and helps the entrepreneur avoid some of the problems identified by successful entrepreneurs.[4]

- Determining the amount and timing of resources needed. The business plan indicates the existing resources of the firm, the resources needed and some potential suppliers of these resources. This allows the entrepreneur to determine how much money is needed at various times to obtain these resources and what approach to develop and use to obtain the money as well as any other resources. The money will be obtained from outside capital providers.
- Establishing the direction of the firm. Since the business plan is a comprehensive document, it fully treats all the major issues facing starting and growing the venture. This enables the entrepreneur to develop strategies and contingency plans to reduce the impact of any problems.
- Guiding and evaluating. By setting goals and milestones for the new venture, the business plan lays out the intentions of the entrepreneur as well as his or her values. Accomplishments and results can be measured and any deviations to the plan corrected in a timely manner. These results can be reported to all interested stakeholders and to outside providers of financial resources at least four times a year if not more frequently such as every month in at least the first year.
- Avoiding conflicts. By being put together by the entrepreneur and the management team and being reviewed and revised frequently, the business plan can be used to guide decisions and help avoid conflicts among the entrepreneur, management, employees, outside vendors and financial providers. The amount of energy and resources needed to launch and grow something new are enormous and the new firm requires reinvestment and seems to always need more time and money. This requires significant sacrifice by the entrepreneur in terms of short-term income and people and family. There are often individuals hurt by the tough personal decisions that an entrepreneur needs to make.

Elements of the business plan

While there are some variations on what goes into a successful business plan, most have the same essential elements (aspects). These can be grouped into three sections as indicated in Figure 7.1.

Section 1

Section 1 contains the title (cover) page, table of contents and executive summary. The title (cover) page is an important part of every business plan as it has:

- The company name, address, telephone, fax, e-mail address and website.
- Name and position of each identified member of the management team and the contact person.
- The purpose of the plan, the amount of money needed and funding increments.
- At the bottom of the title page: "This is confidential business plan number –". Put in a low number and then keep track of when and who received this numbered plan for a 30-day follow-up.

The first page after the title (cover) page is the table of contents. This follows the usual format and lists at least the major subsections in each section and the corresponding page number as well as each figure, table and exhibit. Preferably each major subsection and smaller subsections should be labeled as 1.0, 1.1, 1.2, 2.0, 2.1, 2.2 and so on. The executive summary precedes the numbering and therefore either has no number or smaller letters or Roman numerals. The tables and figures should have a separate list as should the exhibits (appendices).

The last item in Section 1, following the table of contents, is the all-important two-page executive summary. This is by far the most important document in the business plan as it is the screening section. Most readers, especially potential providers of capital, never read beyond the executive summary. One head of a very successful venture fund, who is now managing his eighth fund, indicated that he receives about 1500 business plans a year, discards 1400 based on the cover page or executive summary and of the remaining 100, 80 will be discarded after the first 1–2 hour examination. Of the remaining 20, about four to six will receive investment from his fund. So the executive summary needs to be really well written to invite further reading of the business plan.

Section 1:	
Title Page	
Table of Contents	
Executive Summary	

Section 2:

1.0 Description of Business
- Description of the Venture
- Product(s) and/or Service(s)
- Mission Statement
- Business Model

3.0 Technology Plan
- Description of Technology
- Technology Comparison
- Commercialization Requirements

5.0 Financial Plan
- Sources and Applications of Funds Statement
- Pro Forma Income Statements
- Pro Forma Cash Flow Statements
- Pro Forma Balance Sheets

7.0 Organization Plan
- Form of Ownership
- Identification of Partners and/or Principal Shareholders
- Management Team Background
- Roles and Responsibilities of Members of Organization
- Organizational Structure

9.0 Summary
- Suppliers of Raw Materials
- Outsourcing Aspects

2.0 Description of Industry
- Type of Industry
- Future Outlook and Trends of Industry
- Analysis of Competitors
- Trends and Market Forecasts

4.0 Marketing Plan
- Market Segment
- Pricing
- Distribution
- Promotion
- Product or Service
- Sales for First Five Years

6.0 Production (Outsourcing) Plan
- Manufacturing Process (amount subcontracted)
- Physical Plant
- Machinery and Equipment
- Suppliers of Raw Materials
- Outsourcing Aspects

8.0 Operational Plan
- Description of Company's Operation
- Flow of Orders and Goods
- Exit Strategy

Section 3: Appendices (exhibits)
- Exhibit A: Résumés of Principals
- Exhibit B: Market Statistics
- Exhibit C: Market Research Data

- Exhibit D: Competitive Brochures
- Exhibit E: Competitive Price Lists
- Exhibit F: Leases and Contracts
- Exhibit G : Supplier Price Lists

Figure 7.1   Aspects of a business plan

The executive summary should have the name of the company and address at the top just as appears on the title (cover) page. It should begin with defining the nature and size of the problem existing. The larger and more critical the problem, the more interest there will be on the part of investors and others.

This needs to be followed by the proposed solution to the problem. TerraPower,[5] for example, is a technology company that is providing low-cost, clean electricity through a new traveling wave reactor (TWR) technology that runs on depleted uranium, solving a very large problem. In this section, all competitive ways to solve the problem should be discussed showing the uniqueness or the unique selling propositions of the solution. These would include nuclear, solar, cool and geothermal energy for TerraPower.

Following the solution is the size of the market, trends for at least three to five years and future growth rate. The market needs to be large enough and accessible to deliver the sales needed for the profits and returns expected by investors. The need for and increasing use of electricity make for a very exciting perspective for TerraPower.

The entrepreneur and team who will deliver these sales and profits then need to be described. The education, accomplishments and industry experience of each known member of the top management team needs to be described. The individuals involved in TerraPower are very noteworthy and include CEO John Gilleland, founder of Archimedes Technology Group, and founding members Bill Gates of Microsoft, Nathan Myhrvold, Microsoft's former chief technology officer, and Lowell Wood, a renowned astrophysicist.

The team needs to deliver sales and profits, which should be summarized over a five-year period in the following format:

	Year 1	Year 2	Year 3	Year 4	Year 5
Total revenue					
Cost of goods sold					
Gross margin					
Operating expenses					
Profit (loss) before taxes					

These numbers are taken directly from the pro forma income statement summary in the financial plan in Section 2. Note the exact calendar year is not used but rather year 1, 2, 3, 4 and 5 with 1 indicating the first year of company operations after the investment is received.

The two-page executive summary closes with a statement of the resources needed, the increments of capital accepted as well as contact information. An example two-page executive summary is indicated in Box 7.1.

Section 2

Following the executive summary, which is the end of Section 1 of the business plan, Section 2 starts on a new page with its first part – 1.0 Description of the Business. In this section, the nature of the venture is described to provide an understanding of how the venture will operate and deliver the products/services to solve the problem identified. Information on the products/services should be in enough detail to be easily understood; this will be expanded on in Section 3 if it is a technological product/service that employs a unique/new technology and in the product section of the marketing plan (Section 4). The mission statement of the company should be described as well as the business model – the entire picture of how the company does business – and if this business model significantly differs from the way business is presently being done in the industry today.[6] Some example mission statement summaries are indicated in Table 7.1.

Section 2.0 – Description of Industry – follows; this section discusses the type and size of the industry, industry trends for the last three to five years, future outlook and growth rate and a thorough analysis of competition presently fulfilling the same need as the new idea. This is a large section with significant use of data from authoritative sources. Sometimes the data is so much that only part of it appears in the body of the plan with the rest appearing in an appendix at the end of Section 3. Graphs, charts, histograms and other graphics should be used to thoroughly explain the industry, its growth projection and the competitors. A graph showing the market growing is important based on the trends of this market to date. The market, the market segment and target market for the first year will be further discussed in the first section of the marketing plan.

Following the description of the industry is Section 3.0 – Technology Plan. Some business plans where there is not a technological

BOX 7.1   EXAMPLE EXECUTIVE SUMMARY

Phoenix, Arizona
www.tidalpoint.com

Contact: _____

Stage

Pre-launch

Industry
Software Product
NAICS Code: 511210

Software Consulting
NAICS Code: 541512

Mission Statement

To empower our customers by providing them with better control of their IT systems through efficient, rational, and cost effective delivery of IT products and services. And do so by becoming our client's most trusted advisor and partner by sharing knowledge and best practices.

Problem Being Solved

Nature of Problem: When it comes to replacement of their legacy IT systems, insurance companies struggle with cost and effort overruns which makes the cost of transformation and cost of ownership significantly higher.

Market Segment: There are approximately 300 mid-sized to large insurance companies that need to replace their legacy IT systems. The segment growth rate is estimated to be 7 per cent CAGR and the total IT budget by year 2015 for COTS product and services is estimated to be US\$ 17.5 bn.

Importance: There is an unmet need for insurance software product providers who can combine the follow-up services required for product integration and implementation into insurance companies' operational landscape. We will offer a suite of services to the companies along with consultants and experts who can enable a smooth transition for insurance companies.

The Solution

We will provide a customized off-the-shelf product along with the services required to integrate this product into an insurance company's operational landscape. The product will be Tidal Point Policy Administration system which will cover all major classes/business lines and provide an end to end processing capability from which are distribution, new business, underwriting including rules engines, policy servicing, claims, and reinsurance. The services provided will include data migration, implementation, business analysis, process consulting, and IT strategy consulting.

USP

- Provide an integrated suite of services to the clients without having them organize different activities related to legacy system transformation.
- Overall cost and time will be reduced for the clients due to:
  - Reduced time and efforts in issuing multiple RFPs and RFIs.
  - Speed to start will improve as one vendor will provide all the services.
- More effective approach as all the services would be provided by a single vendor which will give clients better control and ease of managing the transformation.
- Lower cost of ownership for the customers.

Competition

IBM, CSC, Guidewire, Accenture (Duck Creek), MajescoMastek, Camilion, Exigen, Insurity, AQS, CGI, Cover-All.

Market

- 400 Property & Casualty (P&C), Specialty and Life Insurance companies in the U.S. market.

Market Segment

- Software (NAICS 511210): Insurance COTS product market estimated to be $17.5 bn by year 2015. Insurance software services including consulting market are estimated at $40.9 bn by 2015.

- Software Consulting (NAICS 541512): Insurance software consulting services are estimated to be $41.0 bn by year 2015.
- Approximately 300 insurance companies (direct carriers) need to replace their legacy IT systems for at least one class of business.

Marketing Plan

- Advertisements through industry publications such as Insurance and Technology.
- Participating in industry conferences and sponsorship of these events.
- Personal contacts and outside sales.

Price

- COTS Product: $1 250 000
- Business Analysis: $650 000
- Implementation: $700 000
- Process Consulting: $200 000
- Data Migration: $200 000
- IT Strategy: $ 150 000

Financial Summary

Year	2014	2015	2016	2017	2018
Revenue	1 950 000	5 641 000	5 949 762	7 603 796	11 953 167
Cost of Goods Sold	1 072 500	2 552 550	3 272 369	4 182 088	6 574 242
Gross Margin	877 500	2 088 450	2 677 393	3 421 708	5 378 925
Operating Expenses	779 500	1 738 590	2 050 380	2 392 271	2 923 929
Operating Profit	44 200	193 811	367 228	663 018	1 565 481

advancement in the product/service being offered would not have a technology plan. For example, one author founded a rainbow decal and sticker company with no significantly new technology so there was no technology plan in the business plan of the company. Whenever the

Table 7.1   Core of mission statements of selected US companies

3M	• Innovation; "Thou shalt not kill a new product idea" • Absolute integrity • Respect for individual initiative and personal growth • Tolerance for honest mistakes • Product quality and reliability
American Express	• Heroic customer service • Worldwide reliability of services • Encouragement of individual initiative
Ford	• People as the source of our strength • Products as the "end result of our efforts" (we care about cars) • Profits as a necessary means and measure for our success • Basic honesty and integrity
General Electric	• Improving the quality of life through technology and innovation • Interdependent balance between responsibility to customers, employees, society and shareholders (no clear hierarchy) • Individual responsibility and opportunity • Honesty and integrity

product/service has a patent, there will always be a technology plan as the patent adds value to the venture. A general rule is if you are having a hard time deciding whether to have a technology plan, then put one in as it is better to have one than not in this circumstance. The technology plan describes the state of the technology presently available and how the new technology revolutionizes the way things are done. This was the case for the TWR technology running on depleted uranium of TerraPower.

Section 4.0 – Marketing Plan, the next section, begins with a discussion of the market segment and target market for the product/service.[7] It defines the most appropriate market and its size, usually through using one or more segmentation techniques. Of the many available segmentation techniques (demographic, geographic, psychological, benefit, volume of use and controllable market elements), the two most widely used ones particularly for entrepreneurs and SMEs are demographic and geographic as this is the way secondary data is published. If the venture is a business to consumer (BtoC), then the most important market data is the demographics of the selected geographic market. The most widely used demographic variables are age, income and gender to determine the size of the market and a typical customer profile. For a business to business (BtoB) venture, then the business market needs to be identified using the classification (country) system of the country for the industrial (business) customer being served. The North American Industry Classification System (NAICS) code in the United States, the Standard Industrial Classification (SIC) code in Korea and the SIC code in China each uses a numbering system to classify each industry and specific products/services in that country. A sum of all the output of these numbers is the gross national product of the country. This procedure will provide the trends, size and growth rate of the particular industry market, which can be used to develop the typical customer profile.

Following the delineation of the target market, a marketing plan needs to be developed to successfully reach and sell to that target market. The marketing plan has four major areas – product/service, price, distribution and promotion. The market segment and marketing plan are the focus of the next chapter – Chapter 8.

Section 5.0 – Financial Plan, the next part of Section 2, focuses on a discussion of the created statements, which is the focus of Chapter 9. Chapter 10 follows and focuses on Section 7.0 – Organizational Plan, which describes the legal form of the organization.

Following the financial plan is Section 6.0 – Production or Outsourcing Plan, which indicates how the offering will be developed and produced. Some service ventures will not have this part in their business plan. Each individual cost needs to be specified so that an understanding is provided of the actual costs involved in the final offering and how much this can be reduced through economies of scale. All suppliers or outsourcing firms should be described in detail.

A short section, Section 8.0 – Operational Plan, describes in detail how the company will operate including the flow of goods and orders. An important aspect discussed here is the exit strategy by which investors will get their equity and a return on equity hopefully in a five- to seven-year period of time from the initial investment. There are only three mechanisms for having the capital to provide this exit and desired return: (1) retained earnings of the venture; (2) selling to another financial institution or firm; or (3) going public and being a public traded company. The most likely exit avenue is selling to another company and, if this is mentioned, then three to four likely exit companies need to be identified and discussed. Section 2 concludes with a brief summary, Section 9.0 – Summary, which completes this section of the business plan.

Section 3

Section 3 contains all the backup material to support areas in Section 2. This includes secondary support data, any research data, contracts or leases, the patent document and most notably the résumés of the entrepreneur and any known members of the management team. Nothing new should be introduced in this section.

Business plan development and update

The business plan is a very important document both for providing direction for the new venture and a tool for raising financial resources. It is important that it be well written and edited. The best way for an entrepreneur to proceed is to write down all the information in draft format and then go back and rewrite. During this process, the audience for the plan should be kept in mind and the material arranged in a way, such as the one suggested, that items flow smoothly from start to finish. Clear and concise writing is needed and all numbers need to be consistent. If possible, a friend or colleague should critique the final business plan. If needed, a professional writer could be paid at the end to make sure the plan flows smoothly.

A question frequently asked is how long (how many pages) should a business plan be. While of course that depends on the nature of the product or service, whether the business contains a technology plan and/or a production (outsourcing) plan and the extent of Section 3 (exhibits and appendices), most business plans are around 50 pages. There will be 12 pages of financial statements and several pages of résumés. Most importantly, all the necessary material should be covered in a clear, concise manner.[8]

Summary

Every new venture needs a business plan to set the direction for the firm and obtain financial resources. The essential elements of a business plan are contained in three sections with the main elements being in Section 2. The most important document in the plan is the executive summary as most business plans are not read beyond this by potential investors.

Each business plan needs to be well written and organized, and address as many anticipated questions as possible. It needs to flow smoothly and consistently without errors so that the reader has a clear understanding about the details and future success of the new venture. Time will tell whether TerraPower meets their plan of having a prototype ready for demonstration in 2022.

NOTES

1   As discussed in Gregory G. Dess and Alex Miller, *Strategic Management* (New York: McGraw-Hill, 1993); Henry Mintzberg and James Brian Quinn, *The Strategy Process* (Englewood Cliffs, NJ: Prentice Hall, 1991); John A. Pearce and Richard Braden Robinson, *Strategic Management: Formulation, Implementation and Control* (Homewood, IL: Irwin, 1992); Alonzo J. Thompson and Arthur A. Strickland, *Strategic Management: Text and Cases* (Homewood, IL: Irwin, 1992).

2   "Recent financings of start-ups . . .", *Start-Up* (February 2012), **17** (11), 43–8.

3   "Tapping in to the innovation ecosystem" (Three rules for start-up success), *Backbone* (June/July 2013), **30**, available at http://www.backbonemag.com/Magazine/2013-06/tapping-in-to-the-innovation-ecosystem.aspx (accessed 21 February 2014).

4   Robert D. Hisrich, *Small Business Solutions: How to Fix and Prevent the Thirteen Biggest Problems that Derail Business* (New York: McGraw-Hill, 2004).

5   TerraPower, Inc. website (n.d.), available at http://terrapower.com/ (accessed 5 June 2013).

6   Deborah Sweeney, "What's your mission?", *Smart Business Orange County* (2013), **8** (9), 8.

7   "Marketing plan template: exactly what to include", *Promotional Marketing* (2013), 3.

8   Marcia Layton Turner, "Short but sweet", *Entrepreneur* (2012), **40** (10), 105–9.

Online sources

http://online.wsj.com/news/articles/SB100014241278873243547045786378700865896 66.

http://www.inc.com/flash-steinbeiser/nasty-gal-raises-40-million.html.

http://www.inc.com/30under30/donna-fenn/nasty-gal-sophia-amoruso-2013.html. http://www.nastygal.com.

8 The marketing plan

Scenario: Claire Boonstra, Maarten Lens-FitzGerald and Raimo van der Klein – Layar

You are flipping through a magazine and turn to a one-page advertisement for hiking boots. The corner of the page asks you to download a free app on your smartphone and then point your camera at the page. You open the app, and then aim your camera phone at the ad. On your screen, you still see the table in front of you and the magazine is still resting on top. The only difference is the huge virtual, three-dimensional hiking boot popping out of the magazine. If you slide the magazine around the table, the boot moves with it. You can look at every side of the boot as if it were really there. Bring your camera in closer, and you can even see the boot's immaculate stitching.

Augmented reality is not a new idea – sci-fi movies and books have used this virtual notion for years. But thanks to firms like Dutch start-up, Layar, augmented reality is quickly becoming the global reality for businesses vying for consumer attention. In 2009, a team of tech-savvy colleagues came together in Amsterdam and launched Layar, a tech company centered around its augmented reality platform targeting mobile application developers. Claire Boonstra, Maarten Lens-FitzGerald and Raimo van der Klein had already shared their mutual infatuation with tech innovation during their formative years. The three had previously worked together in the Netherlands, setting up networking events for locals interested in wireless-related technology. Soon after, the group decided to pool their technology passion with their collective skills in civil engineering, marketing and web-related technologies to create Layar's platform software. Boonstra, Lens-FitzGerald and van der Klein used a mixture of funding, including venture capital funds for Layar's initial years. Layar provides use of its platform to companies revamping their marketing strategies to keep up with their technologically advancing customer bases.

One of the first companies to use Layar's platform developed an app that allows its users to aim their camera phones in any direction and see virtual bubbles pop up over homes marked for sale. Each bubble, when touched on the screen, is linked to the home's listing information. Another one of Layar's first customers was a local Dutch bank that allowed its customers to aim their phones in all directions and see virtual circles pop up over their ATM and branch locations. Layar now deals with hundreds of mobile app developers from different industries, guiding other companies in their search for more interactive and customer-engaging marketing ploys. Layar's platform and the app developers who use it are now coming up with new virtual advertising ideas. Magazine readers can view pop-up videos on magazine pages. Virtual three-dimensional furniture explodes out of its print ad and moves around to show how its pieces can be adjusted. Not only is Layar's software paving the way to a futuristic mode of marketing but it is also creating a resurgence in the lost art of print advertising, a strategy dumped by many companies due to its expense and growing obsolescence. And while other tech companies have jumped onboard to create their own similar platforms (some businesses are even developing their own virtual advertising platforms in-house), Layar prides itself as one of the first in its industry to successfully commercialize its technology, and remains a top international player in virtual mobile app development (see Online sources).

Introduction

The marketing plan is essential for every new venture as well as every business operation. As described in the scenario, the specifics of the all-important marketing plan rapidly change. The marketing plan serves as the essential part of the overall road map provided by the business plan indicating where the new venture is going and what it will accomplish along the way. It assists in the implementation and control of the strategy as well as obtaining and deploying resources. This chapter focuses on the marketing plan by first looking at the requirements for a successful plan. Then, the target market and elements and structure of the plan are discussed. The chapter concludes with a discussion of determining the sales force and forecasting sales.

Requirements for an effective plan

Since the marketing plan is the provider of sales and revenue for the new venture, it needs to be developed to achieve these as soon as possible so that the venture can reach positive cash flow, which will be discussed in the next chapter (Chapter 9). Some requirements for doing this are:

- Understand and satisfy target market needs.
- Know how various marketing variables perform separately and together in influencing the market.
- Clearly define organizational goals and objectives.
- Know the strengths and weaknesses of the organization.
- Understand the concept of newness: newness to the organization, consumers and the distribution system.
- Understand the market.
- Know the trends, growth rates and stages in the life cycle.
- Know the competition.

In order to create an effective marketing plan, it is essential that the target market be defined and well understood, particularly in terms of its acceptance of the new product/service. Understanding the market is essential to developing an effective plan to reach it and yet is often not given enough attention. Once the market is understood, then the essential elements of the plan can be designed, taking into account the goals and objectives of the new venture.

Understanding and selecting the target market

One of the most important aspects of the marketing plan is the selection of the best initial target market. This is particularly important since the initial sales are usually the most difficult to obtain due to the newness of the product/service being offered as well as the new venture. The target market is the group of potential customers the firm is going to focus on, which should be those most likely to need the new product/service being offered and have the ability for its acquisition. This group can be identified and selected through market segmentation.

Market segmentation

The process of market segmentation is extremely important. Once the target market has been correctly defined, it is much easier to develop a marketing strategy and the appropriate combination of product, distribution, promotion and price (elements of the marketing plan) to reach that market effectively. Even though a market is rarely over segmented, care should be taken to delineate a market only to the extent meaningful.

The overall segmentation techniques for all three types of markets (consumer, industrial and government) are indicated in Table 8.1. The basic segmentation criteria – demographic, geographic, psychological, benefits, volume of use and controllable marketing elements – can be effectively used to define a target market, whether the overall market be consumer, industrial or government.[1] It is particularly important to recognize and implement the capability of segmentation in the industrial and government markets. Firms in the consumer markets are generally much better at segmenting their markets.

Geographic segmentation

One of the most widely used segmentation techniques is dividing the market into separate geographic clusters such as nations, regions, states or provinces, cities or localities. Census information on businesses and consumers as well as data from trade associations and publications is broken down on a similar geographic basis, allowing data to be obtained. The market can also be evaluated in light of the distribution structure or market representatives either available or presently used in the market. In geographic segmentation, a firm can choose a market in which it enjoys a comparative advantage in terms of such marketing variables as distribution, advertising and company image. For example, one producer of specialty oil and fat products for commercial bakeries and restaurants expanded its marketing in the New England, New York and Pennsylvania area because of the cost advantages in transportation from a plan location close to this area.

Demographic segmentation

When you determine that there are particular types of individuals who will be more likely to use a product, you are defining a market through demographic segmentation.

Table 8.1 Market segmentation by type of market

Segmentation Criteria	Basis for type of market		
	Consumer	Industrial	Government
Demographic	age, family size, education level, family life cycle, income, nationality, occupation, race, religion, residence, sex, social class	number of employees, size of sales, size of profit, type of product lines	type of agency, size of budget, amount of autonomy
Geographic	region of country, city size, market density, climate	region of country	federal, state, local
Psychological	personality traits, motives, lifestyle	degree of industrial leadership	degree of forward thinking
Benefits	durability, dependability, economy, esteem enhancement, status from ownership, handiness	dependability, reliability of seller and support services, efficiency in operation or use, enhancement of firm's earning, durability	dependability, reliability of seller and support services
Volume of use	heavy, medium, light	heavy, medium, light	heavy, medium, light
Controllable marketing elements	sales promotion, price, advertising, guarantee, warranty, retail store purchased service, product attributes, reputation of seller	price, service, warranty, reputation of seller	price, reputation of seller

Even though demographics are not the only way or, in some cases, even the best way to define a market, it is the most widely used market segmentation method. This method is so frequently used because the demographic variables are closely associated with expenditure and preference patterns and the variables are easier to measure. In addition, the data is often already available in a published form from the census data of each country.

Controllable marketing elements segmentation

Another excellent segmentation technique is segmenting by where key market elements for product/service success are. For example, there are three levels of value for wristwatches: (1) some people want to pay the lowest price for a watch that works reasonably well; (2) some people buy to obtain a dependable watch for price paid; and (3) some people buy for prestigious reasons, for example, as a graduation gift that symbolizes prestige and success.

Since the low-price field had not been seriously entered by other manufacturers, it was the market chosen by Timex. The timely tactics of Timex proved very profitable in a market with relatively high brand loyalty.

Typical key elements used are value, usage of the product, degree of susceptibility to change, attitudes, individualized needs and self-confidence. Once the proper key element of segmentation is found, then the numbers or percentages of users in the entire market can be determined for each of the categories on the continuum reflecting the key element. From this, a category with sufficient potential that has not yet been developed by some other company can be selected.

Psychological segmentation

Psychological segmentation measures attitudes and lifestyles.[2] Sometimes clusters are identified and given names such as the contented housewife, the chic suburbanite, the retiring homebody, the devoted family man, the militant mother, the old-fashioned traditionalist, the elegant socialite and the frustrated factory worker.

Even though the named clusters are identified, the real question is whether a marketing plan for any of these clusters can obtain more sales than by marketing to all clusters. A large eastern candy manufacturer that manufactured products with low brand loyalty, and therefore experienced considerable shifting of consumer purchases to and from its brand, tried to identify separate clusters. Its research indicated that there might be two or three main clusters of candy eaters as well as many small clusters of candy eaters who prefer chocolate nut or chocolate coconut. Using a questionnaire and colored pictures of the product, a sample of respondents was personally interviewed. Based on conclusions reached through computer analysis of the data gathered, different product packages were designed and each brand was assigned its own advertising message. In some instances, brand name and the package were changed to identify more with the cluster. Each of the three products, the same but with a different package and advertising message directed to a different cluster, were put into a test market. In addition, a fourth test market was used in which the product, package and advertisements were directed at the entire candy-eating market regardless of clusters. The latter product sold so much better than the others that the idea of clusters was dropped.

Primary versus secondary data

One of the most important aspects of any market selection decision is the market and demographic information. This can be secondary data (data that is already published) or primary data (original data gathered specifically for the particular decision). Although primary data is generally more accurate, it is also more costly and time-consuming to collect versus data that already exists and has been collected by third parties. It is usually best for the entrepreneur to start the data-gathering process by first identifying the secondary data available.

The first step in obtaining secondary data is to identify the classification codes associated with the company's product/service. These include the Standard Industrial Classification (SIC) in some countries, the North American Industry Classification System (NAICS), the Standard International Trade Classification (SITC) and the International Harmonized Commodity Description and Coding System (Harmonized System), each of which is discussed in turn below.

The SIC code is appropriate for an initial appraisal of the extent and nature of the need in a foreign market, particularly for industrial products. Standard industrial classifications – the means by which the US government classifies manufacturing industries – are based on the product produced or operation performed. Each industry is assigned a two-, three- or, where needed for further breakdown, four-digit code.

To determine the primary market demand using the SIC method, first all potential customers that have a need for the product or service being considered are identified (see SIC code in Online sources).

NAICS is a system in the United States that replaced the SIC system. This newer system is based on a six-digit code and has new industries, particularly in the service and technology sectors, that were not included in the SIC system. NAICS is used in the United States, Canada and Mexico, allowing for greater country comparisons than previously available (see NAICS in Online sources).

Once the codes for the product/service have been obtained, these can be converted to the code system used in the European Union. Each NAICS Rev. 1.1 code is shown with its corresponding International Standard Industrial Classification (ISIC) Rev. 3.1 code on an easily accessible website (see United Nations Statistics in Online sources).

SITC, developed by the United Nations in 1950, is used to report international trade statistics. It classifies products and services based on a five-digit code, but frequently data is available at only the two- or three-digit code level. Each year, approximately 140 countries report their import and export trade statistics to the United Nations. The data is compiled and printed in the United Nations, *International Trade Statistics Yearbook* (and also available at the United Nations Statistics Division website, see Online sources).

The final system for obtaining international data is the Harmonized Commodity Description and Coding System, better known as the International Harmonized Commodity Codes. Each product or service is identified by a ten-digit number that is broken down by chapter (first two digits), heading (first four digits), subheading (first six digits) and the commodity code (all ten digits). Here are some sample codes:

Name	International Harmonized Commodity Code
Peanut butter	2008.11.1000
Grand pianos	9201.20.0000
Farmed Atlantic salmon	0302.12.0003

Care must be taken when using the International Harmonized Commodity Codes because there may be differences between countries, as well as variance within a country depending on whether the codes are used for exporting or importing products. In the United States, for example, the purpose of the commodity codes is different for importing and exporting. For importing, the code is used to determine the import duty (if any); for exporting, the primary use of the code is for statistical reporting. This results in two sets of commodity codes in the United States: one set for importing and one set for exporting. The exporting system of classification is labeled Schedule B, and the importing system of classification is called the Harmonized Tariff Schedule, maintained by the Office of Tariff Affairs and Trade Agreements.

There are several problems in collecting international secondary data. The first, and perhaps the most troublesome one, is accuracy. Often, countries are not particularly rigorous in their data collection, resulting in data not reflective of the true situation in a country. Sometimes, particularly in more controlled countries, the data is collected to satisfy a political agenda rather than statistical reliability.

The second problem is comparability – the data available in one country may not be comparable to the data collected in another country.[3] This may be due to the different methodologies used, errors in the data collection or differences in applying the commodity coding system.

Lack of current data in a country is a third problem. In many countries, the frequency of data collection is much more sporadic than in more developed countries. In dynamically changing economies, four- to five-year-old data is obsolete and not very valuable in decision making.

The final problem in secondary data is the cost. In many countries, the data may only be available at a fairly high price.

Finding useful, accurate data for your country selection decision can sometimes be challenging. There are several sources for both country market and industry data discussed in the following subsections.

Country industry market data

Economic and country data on such things as age, population, gross domestic product, inflation, literacy and per capita income is often available from a variety of sources depending on the country. The CIA's *World Factbook* provides data on various aspects of a country, such as demographics of the population, economic indicators, geography, military, politics and resources available. The Country Commercial Guides (CCG) are produced for most countries on a yearly basis. Each guide contains the following information on a country: executive summary; economic trends and outlook; political environment; marketing

US products and services; leading sectors for US exports and investments; trade regulations and standards; investment climate; trade and project financing; and business travel. It also has numerous appendices in such areas as country data, domestic economy, trade, investment statistics, US and country contacts, market research and trade event schedules. These are invaluable to the entrepreneur in understanding the numbers and trade possibilities in a country. Even though this data is mainly US-focused, the reports contain valuable information for entrepreneurs regardless of country. The National Trade Data Bank (NTDB), maintained by the US Department of Commerce, is also an important database available to the entrepreneur at virtually no cost. The NTDB comprises international reports, trade statistics, research and leads on trading opportunities.

Another source of country market data is STAT-USA. This international data source, managed by an agency of the US Department of Commerce, is enormous and includes the just-discussed NTDB, Global Business Opportunities (Globus) database and the State of the Nation database. Contributed to by many governmental agencies, the STAT-USA website has a multitude of international and national reports available.

One of the best sources of information is the World Bank, which uses various criteria to rank every country on the ease of doing business there. The World Bank index ranks countries (economies) from 1 to 189 and is calculated by averaging the percentile rankings on each of the ten topics covered in *Doing Business: Economy Rankings* (see World Bank in Online sources). The criteria being ranked include: ease of doing business; ease of starting a business; dealing with licenses; registering property; getting credit; protecting investors; paying taxes; trading across borders; enforcing contracts; and closing a business.

Trade associations in the United States and throughout the world are also a good source for industry data about a particular country. Some trade associations do market surveys of the members' international activities and are strategically involved in international standards issues for their particular industry.

There are numerous domestic and international publications specific to particular industries that are also good sources of information. The editorial content of these journals can provide interesting information and insights on trends, companies and trade shows by giving a more local perspective on the particular market and market conditions. Sometimes trade journals are the best and often the only source of information on competition and growth rates in a particular country.

If all the secondary data sources have been checked and the needed data has not been found, then the third aspect of a research project is commenced – the collection of data through primary research. Primary research can be best viewed in terms of four areas: research design; sample design; questionnaire design; and data collection.

Regardless of the research and sample design employed, the data-gathering form to be used in the research study needs to be carefully developed. The importance of this measuring instrument or question-naire as well as the difficulty of designing it properly cannot be over-stated. It is likely that you have seen poorly designed questionnaires. While the exact questions asked depend on the nature of the problem and the method of data collections to be employed, great care must be taken in choosing the types of questions and their wording so that there is minimal respondent bias. As indicated in Table 8.2, there is a wide variety of questioning techniques – dichotomous, multiple-choice, preference, rating, ranking and open-ended. Before the final question-naire is developed, the advantages and disadvantages of each should be carefully evaluated in terms of the problem being investigated.

Data collection

The most widely used methods of data collection are: (1) personal interviews; (2) mail surveys; (3) telephone surveys; (4) e-mail surveys; and (5) focus groups.

Primary research data is frequently obtained by personal interviews. For example, one might personally interview non-affiliated doctors to determine their views on a particular hospital, or personally interview wholesalers to determine their movement of specialized oil and fat products, or personally interview a few consumers to determine their views on a new line of merchandise for a small retail store.

Collection of primary data by a survey involves preparing a carefully worded and ordered questionnaire, mailing it to respondents and get-ting them to return the completed measuring instrument. To encour-age participation and ensure accuracy, the questionnaire has to be very carefully constructed and the introductory letter carefully worded. This

Table 8.2 Example questioning techniques

Questioning techniques	Example	Advantages	Disadvantages
Dichotomous	Do you usually like to try a new store? ___ yes ___ no	1. Easy to answer. 2. Can be used to screen before asking further questions. 3. Easy to tabulate. 4. Provides definite answer.	1. Forces a choice. 2. Provides no detailed information.
Multiple choice	Which of the following four stores do you like? ___ Store A ___ Store B ___ Store C ___ Store D	1. Usually avoids forcing an arbitrary choice. 2. Easy to answer. 3. Easy to tabulate.	1. Choices may not be all-encompassing. 2. Choices may not be clearly distinctive.
Preference	Which of these stores do you most prefer? ___ Store A ___ Store B ___ Store C ___ Store D	1. Gives information on preference. 2. Easy to answer.	1. Preferences may not reflect purchase choice. 2. Choices may present some confusion.
Rating	On a scale from 1 to 9 (with 1 being "did not like at all" and 9 being "liked it very much"), indicate your overall	1. Gives important information on relative feelings about various product attributes.	1. Distinctions on scale may not be clear to respondent.

Type	Example	Advantages	Disadvantages
	feelings about the overall store by circling the number that corresponds to your feeling. (did not like at all) (liked very much) 1 2 3 4 5 6 7 8 9 10	2. Does not force an arbitrary choice. 3. Provides a wide range of responses for comparative purposes.	2. Provides scale gradations that may not be commensurate with knowledge of respondent.
Ranking	Rank in order from 1 to 5 (with 1 being the best and 5 the worst) your opinion of the following stores. ____ Store A ____ Store B ____ Store C ____ Store D ____ Store E	1. Provides valuable information on relative consumer opinions on products or attributes. 2. Provides a definite answer. 3. Yields information quickly.	1. Is probably the most confusing type of question for the consumer to answer. 2. Provides no information on how good the best product is. 3. Provides no information on relative differences between ranks of products.
Open-ended questions	Why do you shop at this particular store?	1. Does not bias respondent's response with established answers. 2. Provides a wide range of information. 3. Provides information of more depth.	1. Interpretation of answers requires skill and may vary between interpreters. 2. Difficult to tabulate.

method avoids any interviewer bias and has a much lower cost than personal interviews. Also, more spontaneous and accurate responses may be obtained. Finally, it is easier to reach some groups of individuals, such as those in remote or inaccessible places, as well as to obtain combined reactions when a group such as an entire family is involved.

Information can also be obtained by telephone interviews. With the cost-effective, efficient telephone service available in the United States, this is probably the fastest and cheapest method for obtaining primary data, as any number of calls can be made to a specified area of the country for a fixed monthly rate. The interview process can be kept uniform by monitoring the calls on a regular or periodic basis.

In an effort to offer a more personalized service, Starbucks launched a "Names on coffee cups" marketing campaign in March 2012. The campaign involved addressing customers by their first names and writing the names on their disposable cups. Customers have responded by sharing images of their personalized coffee cups on social media sites. The popularity of sharing images of the cups on social media has increased to the point that there are now Flickr and Tumblr pages dedicated to showing the labeled cups.[4]

The marketing plan

Once the target market has been selected, the entrepreneur can develop the marketing strategy and plan. The marketing plan consists of four major areas: the product or service; the price; the distribution; and the promotion (Table 8.3).

Product or service

This element of the marketing mix indicates a description of the product or service to be marketed in the new venture. This product or service definition may consider more than the physical characteristics. For example, Dell's product is computers, which is not distinctive from many other existing competitors. What makes the products distinctive is the fact that they are assembled from off-the-shelf components and are marketed with direct-marketing and internet techniques promising quick delivery and low prices. Dell also provides extensive customer service with e-mail and telephone available to the customer to ask technical or non-technical questions. Thus, the product is more than

Table 8.3   Elements of the marketing plan

Product/ Service	Price	Distribution mix		Promotion
		Distribution channels	Physical distribution	
Quality	Price/consumer reactions relationships	Retailers	Storage	Advertising
Assortment	Price/cost relationships	Wholesalers	Inventory	Personal selling
Guarantee	Price/ competitive reactions relationships	Representatives	Transportation	Publicity
Servicing (if needed)				Sales promotion
Package				Social media

its physical components. It involves packaging, the brand name, price, warranty, image, service, delivery time, features, style and even the website that will be seen by most customers. When considering market strategy, the entrepreneur will need to consider all or some of these issues, keeping in mind the goal of satisfying customer needs.[5]

For example, in March 2013, Whole Foods Market announced that all GMO food products in their stores in the United States and Canada would require a GMO label by 2018. It is the first grocery store in the United States to enact this mandate.

PepsiCo teamed up with a fashion designer and used high-end apparel to promote its new Trop50 from its Tropicana line in the United Kingdom. London designer Richard Nicoll created a bright orange limited-edition dress with a floral print – only 50 of them were made. In support of its health mission, the brand donated all the proceeds from selling the 50 dresses to Fashion Targets Breast Cancer, an international charity that supports women diagnosed with the disease. PepsiCo also released a multichannel campaign dedicated to the launch that included a TV promotion, digital banners, in-store advertising and samplings.[6]

Perrier water introduced a new slim aluminum 250 ml single serve can in 2013 in Canada celebrating its 150th anniversary. The cans contain the French carbonated water in several flavors – natural, lime and pink grapefruit. Each flavor has no sugar and zero calories.[7]

Elevation Brands, LLC and Ian's announced their new products and packaging at the March 2013 Natural Products Expo West using a new brand tagline of "Friendly Foods for Life!" This new tagline and powerful brand promise to deliver allergy-friendly foods in its 34 SKUs of allergy-friendly convenience foods. This tagline combines product attributes – "allergy-friendly, family-friendly, convenience-friendly, taste-bud-friendly and health-friendly". The addition of a leaf as the apostrophe in Ian's logo emphasizes the all-natural aspect of its product line while also maintaining its friendly, approachable personality. This new packaging is clear and easy to read with descriptors such as "No Gluten, No Wheat, No Eggs, No Dairy". It saves shoppers from looking for the ingredients list, which is on the back of the product in small print.[8]

Appy Food & Drink Co. introduced a new line of juice drinks for children in 2013. Each drink features a reality technologically enhanced character from Nickelodeon. Each fruit drink is packaged in Tetra Pak cartons that allow consumers to scan the back of the carton with a smartphone to obtain props worn by a character. Consumers can download the free Appy Drink app, which is available from Google Play and Apple's app store. Digital props can be stored on phones and used to customize images.[9]

Pricing

Prior to setting the price, the entrepreneur, in the majority of situations, will need to consider three important elements: costs; competition; and the consumer. There are some exceptions, which are discussed at the end of this subsection on pricing. Also explained is the interaction of these elements in the pricing process.

One of the important initial considerations in any pricing decision is to ascertain the costs directly related to the product or service. For a manufacturer, this would involve determining the material and labor costs inherent in the production of the product. For a non-manufacturer, such as a clothing retailer, this would involve determining the cost of the goods from the suppliers. For a service venture, such as a student shuttle service, there are no manufacturing costs or costs of goods such as those that exist for a clothing retailer. Instead, the service venture's costs relate entirely to labor and overhead expenses.

Whatever the venture, the approximate costs need to be obtained for overhead (utilities, rent, promotion, insurance and salaries). Let us assume a manufacturer of a special oxygen-based rug cleaner incurs a materials and labor cost of $2.20 per unit (24 ounces). Estimated sales are 500 000 units, with overhead at this level of sales at $1 million or $2.00 per unit. Total costs would add to $4.20, and a unit profit of 30 percent of cost or $1.26 would mean a final price of $5.46.

For a retail example of pricing, let us consider a clothing store that sells T-shirts. Let us assume the company buys the T-shirts for $5.00 (cost of goods) from a supplier. Overhead costs are estimated to be $10 000, and the entrepreneur expects to sell 5000 units for a unit overhead cost of $2.00 per shirt. An additional $2.00 is added for profit, resulting in a final price of $9.00.

For the shuttle service example, the entrepreneur estimates that the cost per mile is approximately $6.00. This includes the depreciation of the vehicle, insurance, driver salary, utilities, advertising and all other operating costs. Each vehicle is expected to travel about 60 miles per day and service about 30 students. Thus, total cost per day would be $360 or $12 per student. Adding a profit of $3.00 would set the final price for this service at $1.00 per student or ride.

Whenever a distribution is used, there will be a chain of markups (margins) as indicated in Figure 8.1. Care must be taken to differentiate whether the channel member is using a markup on list or a markup on selling price.

Competition is the second C of pricing. Often when products cannot be easily differentiated, the entrepreneur is forced to charge the same price as the competition. A higher price may be appropriate for differentiated or unique products/services such as technology products (3D televisions or interactive games such as those for the Wii) or new drug products may warrant a higher price or skimming strategy for the new venture to recover some of its high development costs. In a non-differentiated product market (such as clothing or a portable radio), consumers may be willing to pay more if you offer service benefits such as free home delivery, guarantees on the life of the item

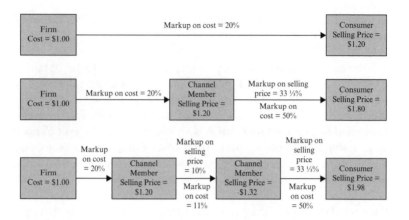

Figure 8.1   Channel members and the price

or free long-term repair. Although these services would increase the costs, they would establish a distinctive image for the product in a non-differentiated product category, allowing a higher price and, potentially, a higher quality image than that of the competition. Generally, in a non-differentiated product/service market, there is little room for price variations from the competition.

The final C in pricing is the consumer. The consumer makes the ultimate determination whether the price of the product/service is correct. In many instances, the consumer has a price limit above which they will not pay for the product/service offered. And each consumer judges the quality of the product/service by the price, which increases as the information on the product/service increases. In other words, you can charge too low a price that will negatively impact sales.

Distribution

Distribution provides utility to the consumer; that is, it makes a product convenient to purchase. This variable must also be consistent with other marketing mix variables. For example, a high-quality product will not only carry a high price but should also be distributed in outlets that have a quality image.

If the market for a new venture is highly concentrated, such as a major metropolitan area, the entrepreneur may consider direct sales to the customer or to a retailer rather than using a wholesaler. If the market is dispersed across a wide geographic area, the cost of direct sales may be prohibitive and the use of a longer channel with wholesalers and retailers may be necessary.

Attributes of the product also affect the channel decision. If the product is very expensive, perishable or bulky, a more direct channel would make sense because the costs of handling and shipping would drive the costs up to a prohibitive level.

Middlemen such as wholesalers and retailers can add important value to the product. They can provide functions such as storage, delivery, a sales staff, promotion or advertising and maintenance that would not be feasible for a start-up venture. Middlemen also have important experience in the marketplace that can support and assist the entrepreneur in his or her marketing strategy.

Environmental issues may also be important in channel strategy. Special considerations and regulations regarding such products as chemicals or food and drug products, to name a few, are too costly for a small start-up to absorb. Competitor strategy is also important to consider since alternative choices may help to differentiate the product. For example, Dell initially chose to use direct mail and the internet to distribute its products, creating a major differentiation from its direct competitors. Once it became established in the market, it then sought other channels such as electronics retailers.

A new venture may also consider brokers' or manufacturers' representatives to reach retailers or end users. Manufacturers' representatives do not take title or physical possession of any products. Their role is to act on behalf of a number of non-competing companies that will share the cost of their services. Manufacturers' representatives could also be used to market to the consumer or household market. In this case, the entrepreneur may look for those representatives that are presently marketing similar products to retail outlets. Orders then would be sent directly to the new venture and shipped from there to the end user. This saves on the costs of a sales staff, storage and multiple shipping points. Brokers are similar to manufacturers' representatives and are common in food or dry goods businesses. These types of representatives are also available in many international markets and represent an effective source of market data as well as a means to reach the target market with experienced sales people.

In some instances, it may be necessary to use more than one channel to service customers more efficiently as well as increase sales potential. Clothing retailers, for example, Sports Authority, L.L. Bean, Macy's, Walmart and Target, all sell their products using multiple channels such as retail stores, websites, catalogs and newspapers. Each of these may require a different communications channel to enable the customer to buy the desired products. These channels will also vary when engaged in international sales as the nature of these channels is sometimes culturally dependent. Channel decisions will also change over time. As the venture grows, the entrepreneur may find that hiring their own sales force is more efficient and is no longer cost prohibitive.

Having a strong marketing mix aimed at consumers at all levels of coffee consumption has been a key to the success of Starbucks. Even though competitors like McDonalds, Subway and Wendy's have significantly increased their emphasis on coffee and social media, Starbucks still outperforms and holds one of the leading positions in coffee. Starbucks has become such a lifestyle brand that people often say I am going to get a Starbucks fix not a caffeine fix, and at a premium price. Having over 33 million Facebook fans compared to 27 million fans each of McDonalds and Walmart, Starbucks does not post regularly on its site but when it does post, the photo or story attracts on average 150 000 likes and thousands of comments. The same results occur on the company's Twitter, Pinterest and Google+ accounts. These accounts have millions of followers with very little effort from Starbucks. This social media combined with a welcoming store atmosphere in each of its locations seemingly everywhere in the United States has built a strong brand loyalty position for the company. This presence and brand loyalty is growing significantly in China and India.[10]

Promotion

It is usually necessary for the entrepreneur to inform potential consumers about the product's availability or to educate the consumer using advertising, sales promotion, publicity, personal selling or social media. Usually, television is too expensive unless the entrepreneur considers cable television a viable outlet. A local service or retail company such as a pet store may find that using community cable stations is the most cost-effective method to reach customers. Larger markets can be reached using the internet, direct mail, trade magazines or newspapers. Each alternative medium should be carefully evaluated by considering not just costs but the effectiveness of the medium in meeting the market objectives mentioned earlier in the marketing plan. As previously stated, a website and social networks may also be valuable to create awareness and to promote the products and services of the new venture. Websites can now be easily designed with little experience using online services such as www.1and1.com or www.intuit.com.

With limited budgets, many entrepreneurs who need to be creative in their promotions are turning to social media. For example, Quintin Middleton was convinced that there was a market for American-made carving knives. Out of his home, this initial hobby of crafting high-quality knives has turned into a successful business that targets chefs. Invites on Facebook to about 800 people in the food industry resulted in 400 fans, many of whom were willing to pay Middleton $300 to $400 for a custom knife. He is now selling these custom knives as fast as he can make them.[11]

Tom First is not new to being creative, as he learned as one of the founders of Nantucket Nectars. Tom launched a new venture in 2004, Owater, a nutrient-enhanced water. Not able to compete with larger companies in this market, Tom promotes his product through an intensive sampling campaign. Owater may do as many as six or seven sampling events a day in key markets such as Boston, Chicago, Denver, Los Angeles, New York and Philadelphia. The ability to focus on specific large markets has enhanced sales at a rate that would have been much more costly using more traditional mass media.[12]

American Express has had a brand with admirable work in the social sphere, including initiatives syncing tweets to actual card purchases and discounts. The brand allows consumers to make an online purchase using only a tweet and a hashtag. Audi is also an early adopter of including Twitter hashtags in TV commercials. It is not only the big global brands that have this option. A New Zealand cookie company, Griffin's, listened to consumers who asked the company on Facebook to revive a discontinued brand, Choco-ades. The company brought back the brand and, in only a few months, became the number one biscuit brand in the country. Another example is Red Bull, which gets 100 to 200 tweets per day. These examples indicate where brands will go in the future.

Following the launch of "Operation Thunder" and a chicken-themed poetry contest, Kentucky Fried Chicken (KFC), part of Yum! Brands, appears to have recovered from a food safety crisis in one of its most important markets. KFC had to reposition itself following a report by the Chinese media in November/December 2012 that some suppliers were providing chickens to the company that had been injected with hormones and antibiotics that allow these chickens to mature in just 45 days. KFC responded by indicating that it was cooperating with the investigations but also that a 45-day maturity is the norm in the industry. This further upset consumers who stopped going to KFC. Finally, in January 2013, Sam Su, Chairman and CEO of Yum! China, issued an apology. The company began its repositioning by launching "Operation Thunder", which included a site that detailed the steps the company took to ensure the quality and safety of its chickens. The company pledged to use only the best quality suppliers and inform consumers about any product safety issues in the future. The company also had a poetry contest on social media. In addition, in an attempt to cement the repositioning, the company increased the amount and level of social media including increasing the activity on the company's own Weibo and RenRen accounts. The social media respond to questions about the crisis and obtain views from key opinion leaders.[13]

Forecasting sales

The marketing plan concludes with forecasting sales in units for the first five years. It is important to think in units even in a consulting firm where a unit can be a consulting contract, because then the number of units times price equals total revenue and the number of units times cost equals cost of goods sold, the first figures in the pro forma income statement discussion in the next chapter. This can be a difficult task, particularly when the new product/service is very unique.

Any forecast begins with defining the number in the primary market by focusing on the need that the product is going to satisfy and the number that have this need. In order to assess this need and the number possessing it, several methods are available. These can be generally classified as either top-down or build-up in orientation. Top-down methods use more of a deductive approach and start with an analysis of the total business system. Build-up methods for estimating primary demand start with identifying each individual segment sharing a common need and cumulating these to determine the total demand for the product. Specific techniques often used to determine the primary demand for the product are the survey of buying power method, the NAICS code method and the input-output method.

The primary demand for consumer products is often initially estimated by constructing an index of buying potential. Since there are so many final customers, there is a need to construct an estimating index from basic economic data. One approach for determining this is the "Buying Power Index" published each year. This index gives an indication of the ability to purchase in specific counties and cities in the United States. It is calculated by assigning a weight of 5 to the specific area's percent of US effective buying income, a weight of 3 to the area's percent of the US retail sales and a weight of 2 to its percent of US population as indicated in the following equation:

$$BPI_i = \frac{5EBI_i + 3RS_i + 2P_i}{10}$$

Where:

BPI_i = Buying Power Index (percentage of total national buying power) in area i

EBI_i = Percentage of national disposable income in area i

RS_i = Percentage of national retail sales in area i

P_i = Percentage of national population living in area i

Another market build-up method that is very appropriate for industrial products is the NAICS code method, the way by which the federal government classifies industries. To determine the primary market demand using the NAICS code method, it is necessary to determine all the possible industry categories that have a need for the product or service being considered. Once the groups have been selected, the appropriate base for the demand determination should be established and the published material on the industry groups obtained from the *Census of Manufacturers*.

Another technique for determining the primary demand for a particular product or product category is the input-output method. An input-output table is used to determine the number and size of the transactions occurring within specific sectors of the total economy. This table on a macro basis provides a summary of all exchanges between each industry grouping as well as between all industries and the final consumer. The total input-output structure of the US economy is determined each year on an 85-industry category basis. The relative primary demand among industries can be derived from input-output tables by allocating the proportion of total sales of an industry to each particular industry segment.

A company sales forecast for the new venture can be defined as the amount of sales a company expects to obtain during a given future time period in a specified area. While this sales level can be expressed in dollars or in physical units, it is usually better to forecast on a unit basis, therefore not reflecting price and price changes.

This overall primary demand must then be used to determine the sales for the first five years in units. The most difficult year is the first year. The sales for years 2, 3, 4 and 5 can be determined using a percentage higher than the growth of the industry in year 2 and then in year 3 and 4 accelerating the growth that will result in the J curve or accelerating sales curve expected for a new venture in years 3 through 5.

Summary

This chapter has focused on the marketing plan for the venture by first describing the requirements for an effective marketing plan. Following the discussion of market segmentation and target market, the major elements of a marketing plan were discussed – product/service, price, distribution and promotion. The chapter concluded by discussing how to approach estimating the sales in units that will be achieved in each of the first five years.

NOTES

1 B. Stuart Tolley, "Identifying users through a segmentation study", *Journal of Marketing* (1975), **39** (2), 69–71.
2 Gillie Gabay, Laurent Flores, Howard Moskowitz and Andrea Maier, "Creating technology-based merchandising ideas for hair coloring through weak signals, concept optimization and mind-set segmentation", *Journal of Consumer Marketing* (2010), **27** (3), 211–23.
3 Dong Ling Xu-Priour and Gérard Cliquet, "In-store shopping experience in China and France: the impact of habituation in an emerging country", *International Journal of Retail and Distribution Management* (2013), **41** (9), 706–32.
4 Mindi Chahal, "This is what my stuff says about me", *Marketing Week* (2013), (01419285), 20–21.
5 "Mandatory GMO labeling coming to Whole Foods", *Label and Narrow Web* (2013), **19** (3), 14–16.
6 http://popsop.com/2013/02/tropicana-has-collaborated-with-fashion-designer-richard-nicoll-to-launch-trop50-in-the-uk/ (accessed 27 March 2013).

7 http://popsop.com/2013/03/perrier-launches-slim-cans-in-canada-prepares-for-its-150th-anniv
   ersary/ (accessed 27 March 2013).

8 Rick Lingle, "Ian's package rebranding sensitive to allergens", *Packaging Digest* (11 March 2013),
   available at http://www.packagingdigest.com/article/523093-Ian_s_package_rebranding_sensi
   tive_to_allergens.php (accessed 24 January 2014).

9 Philip Chadwick, "Nickelodeon characters feature on augmented reality juice packs", *Packaging
   News* (15 March 2013), available at http://www.packagingnews.co.uk/design/markets/
   nickelodeon-characters-feature-on-augmented-reality-juice-packs/ (accessed 27 January 2014).

10 Sheila Shayon, "Why Starbucks' customer loyalty is more lucrative than any ad campaign",
   brandchannel (8 March 2013), available at http://www.brandchannel.com/home/post/Starbucks-
   Customer-Loyalty-030813.aspx (accessed 27 January 2014).

11 Margaret Littman, "A sharp idea", *Entrepreneur* (October 2011), **39** (10), 17, available at http://
   www.entrepreneur.com/article/220351 (accessed 28 January 2014).

12 Gwen Moran, "Try sampling", *Entrepreneur* (October 2008), **36** (10), 84.

13 Anita Chang Beattie, "How chicken poetry is helping KFC recover from China scandal after food
   safety crisis", *AdAge* (13 March 2013), available at http://adage.com/article/global-news/chicken-
   poetry-helping-kfc-recover-china-scandal/240319/ (accessed 1 May 2013).

Online sources

Scenario

http://www.businessweek.com/stories/2010-09-02/layar-augmenting-reality-via-smartphonebusinessweek-business-news-stock-market-and-financial-advice.

http://www.steamfeed.com/augmented-reality-for-print-using-layar.

Other

NAICS http://www.census.gov/epcd/www/naics.html.

SIC code http://www.osha.gov/oshstats/sicser.html.

United Nations Statistics http://unstats.un.org/unsd/cr/registry/regso.asp?Ci=26&Lg=1.

United Nations Statistics Division http://unstats.un.org/unsd.

World Bank http://doingbusiness.org/rankings.

9 The financial plan

Scenario: Clayton Christopher and David Smith – Sweet Leaf Tea

Clayton Christopher knew he would one day start his own business. He grew up in an entrepreneurial household and watched his father grow his own medical supply business. His parents supported his sense of adventure and raised him to crave challenges. The adventure was what attracted him first, and Christopher instead spent his young adult years physically challenging himself, cycling competitively against Lance Armstrong and soon after, chartering boats off the Florida coast. During a road trip through Alabama, Christopher met an enthusiastic tea merchant who serenaded him with charming tales and unchartered opportunities of iced tea brewing. This was a new challenge Christopher could not resist.

Deciding to brew and bottle his own homemade iced tea, Christopher returned to Beaumont, Texas in 1998 and enlisted his childhood friend, David Smith, to help start up Sweet Leaf Tea. Christopher's challenge was to find a way to bottle a great tasting homemade iced tea that he had encountered frequently at small mom and pop restaurants around the South, and bring it to the masses. While the market for bottled iced tea was already dominated by large beverage companies, Christopher felt that there had yet to be anyone to offer an iced tea with a homemade twist. Armed with his own $10000 in leftover savings and a matching loan from his parents, Christopher and Smith moved production into Christopher's father's warehouse with 50 gallon crawfish pots and pillowcases to use as giant tea bags. Acting like a couple of mad scientists, the partners tried hundreds of different teas before deciding on a mix to use for their recipe. Christopher de-chlorinated his own water with a makeshift carbon filter and used his grandma's famed iced tea recipe, steeping each batch strongly and for no more than five minutes before cooling it immediately to keep the bitter taste out. The pair filled each bottle themselves with garden hoses and capped the bottles off using electric drills.

Sweet Leaf Tea tasted great, but suppliers were not interested. Christopher and Smith could not afford to pay for shelf space in larger stores. Their first chance came from convincing a local convenience store to put their product on a bottom shelf. Barely any sold. However, their real break came from convincing ten small stores to place iced tubs filled with Sweet Leaf Tea near their cash registers. It was then that people began to notice, and more and more bottles began to sell. After five years, Sweet Leaf Tea finally made it to their target store, Whole Foods, and the rest was history.

While sales of the tea have continued to flourish, what stands out about the company is its loyalty to its original strategies and goals. Of course production has moved out of the warehouse and into an actual manufacturing factory. R&D remains in-house, and all decisions are still made by Christopher. Most of the company's marketing is currently done the way it originally had been. Christopher spends 8 percent of sales on freebies, chatting with patrons and giving away free tea at live music events. Sweet Leaf Tea also remains loyal to its charities, continuously donating much of its profits to several different organizations. Christopher still remains at the helm of Sweet Leaf Tea, trying out new flavor options and pushing the brand further out into the United States. And yet, while the success of the brand can be seen in its exponential growth compared to its humble beginnings, there is still a large way to go. Unfortunately for the company, larger brands like Nestea and Lipton are almost impossible to beat. Fortunately for the company, Christopher loves a challenge (see Online sources).

Introduction

As Clayton Christopher and David Smith experienced in their new venture – Sweet Leaf Tea – it is important to understand not only the sales but also the venue and cost side of your business. This aspect of a new venture can be best handled through developing and using a financial plan. The financial plan for a new as well as an existing business offers a way for investors and others to see the results of the business operations and provides the numbers needed by the entrepreneur to successfully launch and grow the business. This chapter focuses on the financial plan by identifying all the financial statements needed and then discussing the sources and uses of the funds statement, pro forma income statement, pro forma cash flow statement and pro forma balance sheet.

Mark Katz was a financial analyst on Wall Street before leaving in 2000 to start the online apparel retailer CustomInk. Today, the profitable CustomInk generates more than $70 million in annual sales and employs more than 250 people in its headquarters in McLean, Virginia. Katz's father, a three-time entrepreneur, thought it was a "terrible idea ... selling T-shirts on the web, I just didn't see how you distinguish yourself, so it would be a race to the bottom in terms of price ... It's amazing what you can do with a mediocre idea extremely well executed". Mark Katz's financial know-how propelled him to great success in a highly commoditized industry.

The financial plan

The financial plan is probably the most important part of the business plan for attracting any needed debt or equity capital discussed in Chapter 11 and of course is essential in effectively managing the new venture.[1] A complete financial plan has each of the statements in the order listed below.

• Sources and Uses of Funds Statement
• Pro Forma Income Statement – five-year summary
• Pro Forma Income Statement – first year by month
• Pro Forma Income Statement – second year by quarter
• Pro Forma Income Statement – third year by quarter
• Pro Forma Cash Flow Statement – five-year summary
• Pro Forma Cash Flow Statement – first year by month
• Pro Forma Cash Flow Statement – second year by quarter
• Pro Forma Cash Flow Statement – third year by quarter
• Pro Forma Balance Sheet – years 1, 2, 3, 4 and 5.

There are 14 statements under the general areas of: sources and uses of funds statement (1); pro forma income statements (4); pro forma cash flow statements (4); and pro forma balance sheets (5). Outside the need for the sources and uses of funds statement to obtain capital, the most important statements for a start-up and growing venture are the pro forma income and cash flow statements. As the company matures and has more assets, the balance sheets become more important.

Sources and uses of fund statement

The sources and uses of funds statement is developed by an entrepreneur when there is a need for capital to be infused in the firm.[2] As indicated in Figure 9.1, it is composed of two parts that must be equal in total – where the capital will come from (sources) and how the capital will be deployed (uses). Start by determining the amount of capital needed. Each business will need working capital, which is the total amount of capital used until the venture shows positive cash flows from the cash flow statements. Positive cash flow is indicated when the size of the negative cash flow position starts getting less (more positive) on the cumulative cash flow line. At the beginning, use a figure of two times this number for domestic ventures and three times for global ventures as it will probably take you a longer time to reach positive cash flow than you think. Other uses might be for equipment, renovations and/or inventory. You can put an average three months working capital figure in as a reserve for contingencies.

Once the total amount of capital needed for uses is determined, then that total number is the total source part of the statement. You will need to contribute some money so whatever capital you can invest goes on the "self" line. Other possible sources of capital are family and friends, private investors, grants or possibly a bank loan. Once the possible sources are considered, the uses total has to be adjusted downward. This is often done by first eliminating the reserve for contingencies and then not doubling or tripling the working capital number but using the actual number from the cash flow statement.

Pro forma income statements

The pro forma income statement reflects the profit and loss anticipated for the new venture on a yearly (five-year forecast), monthly (first year) and quarterly basis (Figure 9.2). It should be the first pro forma operating statement prepared as it provides the basis for all the pro forma cash flow statements and pro forma balance sheets. For example, it provides the profit and loss figures needed to determine the taxes in the cash flow statement. It contains the forecast revenue of the company (unit sales times price/unit), cost of goods sold (unit sales times cost/unit) and other operating expenses. It contains footnotes for the major items indicating how the number was obtained and refers to supporting material usually provided in other parts of the business plan. It is always

Sources

Self   _____

Friends and family   _____

Private investor   _____

Bank loan   _____

Grants   _____

Other   _____ _____

Total   _____

Uses (applications)

Equipment   _____

Renovations   _____

Inventory   _____

Working capital   _____

Reserve for contingencies   _____

Other   _____ _____

Total   _____

Figure 9.1   Sources and uses of funds statement

Five-year Summary

	Year 1	Year 2	Year 3	Year 4	Year 5
TOTAL REVENUE[a]					
Less: COST OF GOODS SOLD[b]					
GROSS PROFIT (Margin)					
OPERATING EXPENSES:					
Management Salaries					
Fringe Benefits					
Other Salaries					
Other Fringe Benefits					
Consultant					
Advertising and Promotion					
Delivery					
Bad Debts					
General Administration Expense					
Legal Expenses					
Rent					
Utilities					
Insurance					
Taxes and Licensing					
Interest					
Outsource Accounting and Payroll					
Depreciation					
Miscellaneous					
TOTAL OPERATING EXPENSES					
PROFIT (LOSS) PRE-TAX					
TAXES (leave blank)					
NET PROFIT (LOSS) (leave blank)					

Notes:
a. The calculation for the Total Revenue should be shown with reference to the marketing plan.
b. The Cost of Goods Sold should be broken down into its components on a separate table.

Figure 9.2 Pro forma income statement

important to footnote the revenue figure in the first year showing its calculations with references to the section of the marketing plan that shows the costing, price determination and the sales forecast.

An example pro forma income statement calculation is shown in Figure 9.3. The figure indicates the typical expenses for a new venture. The usual four areas are footnoted: total revenue; cost of goods sold; manufacturer's representative commission and costs; and advertising.

Total Revenue	$56 000[a]
Less: Cost of Goods Sold	14 000[b]
Gross Profit (margin)	$42 000
Operating Expenses	
Salaries	$60 000
Fringe Benefits (25% of salary)	15 000
Rent and Shared Office Answering Service ($300/month)	3600
Electricity ($70/month)	840
Gas ($20/month)	240
Legal (start-up expenses)	4000
Manufacturer's Representative	2800[c]
Advertising (from advertising budget)	40 000[d]
Telephone (unlimited cell phone – $100/month)	1200
Consultant ($3000/month)	36 000
Outsourcing Accounting and Payroll ($75/month)	900
Total Operating Expenses	$164 580
Net Profit (loss)	($122 584)
Taxes	$0
Net Profit (loss)	($122 584)

Notes:
a. This reflects 1400 units sold at a price of $40/unit. See sections of marketing plan.
b. This reflects 1400 units sold at a cost of $10/unit. See sections of marketing plan.
c. This reflects a 5% commission paid on a sales price to retail of $40 or 1400 x 40 x 5%. See marketing plan.
d. See marketing plan for the allocation of the advertising expenditures.

Figure 9.3   Pro forma income statement calculation

On a first-year pro forma income statement, any other areas that are large and need explanation should be footnoted showing its calculation with a reference provided to the area of the business plan where it is discussed. This area is most frequently the marketing plan.

Once the first-year statement is done, it needs to be broken down by month. Care should be taken not to have revenue occur too early such as in the first three months as it generally takes longer to obtain the first sales in a new venture, particularly when the product is discontinuous or radically new. For most new ventures, there will be a loss for most if not all the months and often for at least the first and often the second year.[3]

Pro forma income statements for years 2, 3, 4 and 5 then need to be calculated. The total revenue figure needs to reflect an increase more than the growth rate of the industry indicated in Section 2 of the business plan in at least year 2. Sometime in year 3 or 4, if equity is raised, investors expect to see a significant acceleration in sales called the J curve effect. In year 2, most costs except for cost of goods sold and the manufacturer's representative commission that always follow sales remain the same and costs such as rent, electricity, gas and telephone except in periods of significant inflation could remain constant over all five years. Usually the consultant, unless replacing a salaried position, and legal expenses only occur in the first year. Once these pro forma income statements have been determined, years 2 and 3 need to be broken down into quarters.

Pro forma cash flow statement

The bottom line for any new venture is cash as cash pays the bills and provides the means to grow. Cash is the lifeblood of the business making the pro forma cash flow statement very important.[4] As indicated in the example pro forma cash flow statement in Figure 9.4, the cash flow statement records all the cash flow inflows and outflows of the new venture. As such, it records all the items in the income statement except those that are non-cash ones such as depreciation. Note that the pro forma cash flow statement indicates the amount the new venture was capitalized. It appears in the total cash flow of year 1 and month 1. In month 1, it may be the only thing offsetting cash disbursements as cash from revenue often does not occur in the first month for a new venture. As previously mentioned, the pro forma cash flow statement indicates the amount of working capital needed as seen when the negative cumulative cash flow becomes less negative and continues this trend. It is not its only use particularly in the first year when the monthly pro forma cash flow statement indicates where the deviations occur with the actual cash flow statement. This use of cash flow, though crucial for the first year, should be done throughout the life of the new venture.

There are two generally accepted accounting methods to project cash flow. The first one is the indirect method where the objective is not to repeat what is in the income statement but to understand any adjustments that need to be made to the pro forma income statement as actual cash may or may not have been received or disbursed. In this method, even though a $5000 sale is recorded as income, if the payment has not been received (the cash), it will not appear in the cash

Five-year Summary

	Year 1	Year 2	Year 3	Year 4	Year 5
Receipts – Sales (total revenue)	_____	_____	_____	_____	_____
Disbursements					
Equipment purchase	_____	_____	_____	_____	_____
Cost of goods	_____	_____	_____	_____	_____
Salaries	_____	_____	_____	_____	_____
Rent	_____	_____	_____	_____	_____
Utilities	_____	_____	_____	_____	_____
Advertising	_____	_____	_____	_____	_____
Sales expense	_____	_____	_____	_____	_____
Insurance	_____	_____	_____	_____	_____
Payroll and misc. taxes	_____	_____	_____	_____	_____
Office expenses	_____	_____	_____	_____	_____
Inventory	_____	_____	_____	_____	_____
Total disbursements	_____	_____	_____	_____	_____
Cash flow	_____	_____	_____	_____	_____
Cumulative cash flow	_____	_____	_____	_____	_____

Figure 9.4   Pro forma cash flow statement

flow statement for that period of time. Since this is difficult to predict, most entrepreneurs, particularly at start-up, use the second method, which uses the same numbers as occur in the income statement at least in developing the initial pro forma statements. This avoids the most difficult problems in projecting cash flows – determining the exact monthly receipts and disbursements.

For management control purposes, it is often good to develop several scenarios of both the pro forma income and cash flow statements based on different levels of success of sales and the business in general. These scenario projections provide insight into the factors affecting the sales and operation of the new venture.

Pro forma balance sheet

The pro forma balance sheets indicate the condition of the venture in terms of its assets, liabilities and net worth of the owners at the end of each period of time. Unlike the other two sets of statements, the pro forma balance sheets indicate the operations of the venture at the end of a time period, usually a year. The pro forma balance sheets for years 1, 2, 3, 4 and 5 in providing a financial profile indicate whatever financing will be needed in the future to support growth.

The numbers for the pro forma balance sheet indicated in Figure 9.5 come from the pro forma income statement and cash flow statements.

By indicating the position of the venture at the end of the year, the pro forma balance sheet provides a measure of the solvency of the venture. It is composed of three major areas: assets (everything of value owned by the venture); liabilities (everything owed to creditors by the venture); and net worth owner equity (the excess of all assets over all liabilities).

Current Assets		Current Liabilities	
Cash	$_____	Accounts Payable	$_____
Accounts Receivable (net)	$_____	Current Portion LTD	$_____
Merchandise Inventory	$_____	Other	$_____
Supplies	$_____		
Pre-paid Expenses	$_____		
Total Current Assets	**$_____**	**Total Current Liabilities**	**$_____**
Fixed Assets		**Long-term Liabilities**	
Fixtures	$_____	Notes Payable	$_____
Vehicles	$_____	Bank Loan Payable	$_____
Equipment	$_____	Other Loans Payable	$_____
Leasehold Improvements	$_____		
Building	$_____	**Total Long-term Liabilities**	**$_____**
Land	$_____		
		Total Liabilities	**$_____**
Total Fixed Assets	**$_____**	Net Worth (owner's equity)	$_____
Total Assets	**$_____**	**Total Liabilities/Net Worth**	**$_____**

Figure 9.5   Pro forma balance sheet example

Software

There are a number of good software packages that can be used to track financial transactions and prepare the three pro forma statements discussed. It is often easier and cost-effective for the entrepreneur, particularly at start-up, to outsource this function as there are not a lot of transactions to record.[5]

The basis of each of these is usually a spreadsheet program with a commonly used one being Microsoft Excel. Software packages vary in price and complexity. A widely used accounting software package is Intel's Quickbooks.

Summary

This chapter has focused on the financial plan, an important part of the business plan. After discussing all 14 financial statements, the chapter focused on the sources and use of funds statement (1), the pro forma income statements (4), the pro forma cash flow statements (4) and the pro forma balance sheets (5). The chapter concluded with a discussion of outsourcing and software packages available to track and collect financial transactions and prepare the statements.

NOTES

1 Sean Wise, "The impact of financial literacy on new venture survival", *International Journal of Business and Management* (2013), **8** (23), 30–39.

2 Patricia Cox, "Master budget project: analyzing the pro forma statements", *Strategic Finance* (2010), **92** (5), 56–7.

3 Gavin Cassar, "Are individuals entering self-employment overly optimistic? An empirical test of plans and projections on nascent entrepreneur expectations", *Strategic Management Journal* (2010), **31** (8), 822–40.

4 Hsin-hui I.H. Whited, "Constructing a cash budget and projecting financial statements: an exercise of short-term financial planning for entrepreneurs", *Review of Business and Finance Studies* (2014), **5** (1), 99–101.

5 Michael T. Lee and Spencer R. Cobia, "Management accounting systems support start-up business growth", *Management Accounting Quarterly* (2013), **14** (3), 1–17.

Online sources

http://www.actonhero.org/celebrating-heroes/stories-of-heroes/clayton-christopher.php.

http://www.inc.com/magazine/20090701/how-to-start-a-beverage-company.html.

http://www.inc.com/ss/7-start-success-stories#3http://www.inc.com/ss/7-start-success-stories#3.

10 The organizational plan

Scenario: Gilad Japhet – MyHeritage

Believe it or not, but online genealogy tracking is a booming business. Several online companies have emerged offering browsers the chance to uncover information about long-gone ancestors or discover long-lost relatives in other places. One company that has made a name for itself is Gilad Japhet's MyHeritage. Gilad Japhet has much to brag about. MyHeritage is close to reaching 1 billion online profiles, connects over 60 million registered users and has grown over 18 million family trees. And yet, perhaps Japhet's biggest bragging right can be seen in his company's perilous rise from meek beginnings to online juggernaut.

Gilad Japhet was raised in Israel and, according to him, had been interested in genealogy since "forever". But genealogy was not his immediate career choice. Japhet attended Technion, a renowned Israeli engineering school, and worked night shifts for computer security companies. Soon after, Japhet married and started a family. However, Japhet was still captivated by genealogy tracking and he eventually sold his stock options to take time off to study his own family's roots.

During this time, Japhet realized that the existing genealogy software was not up to par. In an act of pure entrepreneurialism, Japhet started his own business that provided the type of program he had been searching for. Unfortunately, 2002 was a bad year for any start-up. On top of the lack of public knowledge on the growing consumer interest in genealogy, most funders were still too shaken from the previous dot-com bust to invest in any new business. Japhet stuck to his idea, ignoring the lack of outsider funding, and instead decided to hire a small team to create MyHeritage's first software. The free software soon became a hit, but not enough to convince investors. Japhet ran out of money, stopped paying himself and eventually took out a loan on his house.

MyHeritage survived through 2005; Japhet took the software online and began offering paid premium accounts for access to extra services. However, it was the free account that fast became one of the company's strongest points. Many web-goers were logging in to try the program, and once convinced of its superior and easy-to-use software, continued on, sometimes upgrading to premium accounts. MyHeritage also excelled as the only company in the business to truly call itself global. From the company's start-up, the program offered its services in six different languages and now is up to 40. While larger, well-funded competitors created swankier looking programs, MyHeritage allowed its users to search for and connect to family from all across the globe. Many countries still consider MyHeritage as its go-to family tracking site.

Their next successful social networking is geared toward families. Customers of MyHeritage are using the site to meet up and chat with newly found family. And now that tracking, finding and connecting with family has become so much easier and accessible, Japhet's website has a new purpose – providing DNA testing (see Online sources).

Introduction

The organizational plan presents the legal form of the organization and the organizational structure of the new venture, which is the major focus of this chapter. The chapter begins with a discussion of how to develop the plan followed by a presentation of the reasons for selecting one legal form over alternative forms. Then, the chapter focuses on the legal forms of business available in the United States. The chapter concludes with a discussion of the organizational structure and operations of the new venture, a factor in the scenario on MyHeritage.

Developing the organizational plan

It is important for an entrepreneur to establish the right legal form of business as well as organizational structure as both will impact the culture of the new venture as well as its possibility for success. Investors prefer certain legal forms due to tax and liability and expect the new venture to operate efficiently and effectively. Not only must the entrepreneur be able to make the decisions necessary to launch and grow the business successfully but he or she also needs to have in place a management team that has the background and skills to create value. Often some of these skills and knowledge needed are provided by members of the board of advisors/directors.

The biotech company Progenitor Cell Therapy was organized as a limited liability company (LLC). Albert L. Sokol, a partner at the business law firm Edwards Wildman Palmer, says some biotech companies find that organizing themselves as an LLC rather than a corporation works better to maintain funding. By organizing as an LLC, they are able to sell each drug in their business separately to investors. This way, a biotech firm can gain more profit out of each individual drug and the investors do not need to concern themselves with therapies that do not attract them. Progenitor Cell Therapy was acquired by the cellular therapy firm Neostem in 2011.

Selecting a legal form

In selecting which legal form of business to establish, several factors need to be considered: (1) the legal forms available in the country; (2) the ownership and capital requirements; (3) distribution of profits and losses; (4) legal liability; (5) transferability of interest; and (6) taxes.

It is necessary to know and then consider the types of legal forms of organizations that are available in the country. This sometimes requires legal advice particularly in countries in transition where the forms available and their composition vary over time. In the United States, as discussed in the next section, there are three basic legal forms: (1) proprietorship; (2) partnership; and (3) corporation. A proprietorship is one owner; a partnership more than one owner; and a corporation has the business and not the individual take on the legal liability. There are of course some options with each of these basic legal structures, particularly in corporations. In most countries, comparable legal form alternatives are available but may have different features than occur in the United States.[1]

Ownership and capital requirements also need to be considered in selecting the best legal form for the new venture. Ownership means of course who owns the business and takes in any new venture anywhere in the world. Sometimes, as was the case in China, foreign ownership in a country is restricted to none or no percentage of the venture in order to ensure that local ownership has the most say and control.

The amount and timing of any needed capital affects the legal form of the venture an entrepreneur should use.[2] In the United States, for a proprietorship any new capital can only be obtained from loans or additional money put in by the entrepreneur. When a loan is obtained in this type of organizational form, a bank or other lending institution may require some additional form of guarantee to further secure the loan and reduce the risks. Partnership and most types of corporation can take infusion of money more easily either in the form of debt or equity as discussed in the next chapter. An S corporation, for example, has a limit of 100 shareholders while an LLC and C corporation do not. If you are going to be a publicly traded company on one of the stock exchanges, the venture will need to be some type of C corporation.

Distribution of profits and losses

The distribution of the profits and losses is a major factor in determining the organizational form particularly in the United States.[3] In proprietorships, the proprietor (owner) secures all the profits and is responsible for any losses. In a partnership, the distribution of the profits and responsibility for the losses depends on the agreement but is usually based on the percent of ownership of each of the partners involved. In a corporation, usually only some part of the profits are distributed to the owners (shareholders) in the form of dividends.

The legal liability of the owner(s) is also an important part of the decision to form one form of organization over another. In the United States, this is probably one of the most significant reasons to form some type of C corporation over the proprietorship and partnership. In a C corporation, the corporation or venture itself becomes the legal entity in case of a lawsuit whereas in a proprietorship or partnership, the individual owner(s) is the legal entity. This means that any lawsuit is filed against the corporation not the individuals, which occurs in the other two forms of organization. The individuals are only liable if they do not make the best decisions for the value of the venture and its owners in light of the information available or in the case of an LLC to the amount of the money invested in the venture. Individuals of course can be a part of the lawsuit if they do not use good judgment in their decisions as occurred in the case of Enron when the management team and board of directors were also found legally liable as well as the company itself.

The transfer of interest aspect refers to the right and ease of a present owner to transfer his or her ownership to someone else. This is very easy in a sole proprietorship as there is one and only one owner who can sell for any price any part or all of the new venture to anyone. In a partnership, LLC, S corporation or B corporation, the interest of the owner is dependent upon the specifics of the operating agreement of the venture. The transfer of interest (ownership) is easiest in a C corporation, particularly those publicly traded as the shares of the company can be exchanged at any time. There is often a restriction on the entrepreneur and management team from selling their shares during at least the first year when their company becomes a publicly traded one to help support the initial offering price of the shares of the company when listed.

The final aspect that needs to be considered in what form of organization to establish is taxes. The tax laws of the country need to be carefully evaluated to determine the form of organization that will minimize the taxes paid.[4] In some countries, if a citizen of the country has a specified level of ownership, then the venture has a different (usually lower) tax rate than if not. In the United States, the different forms of organizations have different tax attributes. In terms of a proprietorship, the taxes are treated as for the individual owner as the business is treated like the individual owner. The taxes then will be levied at the particular individual's tax level. For a partnership, the income is distributed to each partner according to the percentages in the agreement so the taxes are paid by each individual based on their individual tax rates and the income received. Since a corporation is viewed as its own legal entity (as was discussed in terms of legal liability), the profits of the corporation are taxed at the tax rate established. Any distributions of income usually in the form of dividends to individual owners (shareholders) are taxed at the tax rate of the individual. For the LLC and S corporation, usually preferred by individual investors, they are taxed like a partnership unless otherwise specified in the operating agreement of the LLC or S corporation. In other words, all income is not taxed at the entity level but at the level of the tax rate of the individual based on the income (profit) received.

Legal forms of organization

The general legal forms of organization in the United States are:

- proprietorship
- partnership
- corporations

- LLC
- S corporation (Subchapters)
- C corporation
- professional corporation
- non-profit corporation
- hybrid corporation.

Since the legal liability shifts from the individual to the business unit, most entrepreneurs prefer to start corporations. There are six basic types of corporation available.

One of the most widely used forms of organization to start a business is a corporation versus a proprietorship, which means nothing more than doing business as (DBA) if the owner does not use his or her name for the business or partnership when two or more people share the assets, liabilities and profits. A corporation is a separate legal entity that may sue or be sued, own property, make contracts, have its own employees, have liabilities and pay taxes. The owners (shareholders) in a corporation have the risk limited to their capital investment as long as management decisions are made to the best of their abilities. Unless limited by the certificate of incorporation, the life of a corporation is perpetuity. Ownership in a corporation is represented by shares of stock that can be freely transferred to others unless restricted in the articles of incorporation. To form a corporation in the state of choice the following three-step process is followed:

- Check name availability – include "company", "co.", "corporation", "corp.", "incorporated" or "inc".
- File "Certificate of Incorporation" with the secretary of state (including statutory agent) of the state incorporating in.
- Apply to the Internal Revenue Service (IRS) for Employer ID Number – Form SS-4.

Once you receive your certificate of incorporation, you will need to apply for worker's compensation, unemployment, sales tax and other necessary licenses or permits. In a corporation, you need to adopt bylaws, elect directors and officers, issue certificates of ownership (stock certificates) and open a bank account with appropriate resolutions and signature cards.

An LLC is just like a corporation and can, for the purposes of legal forms of organization, be considered one. It can be a highly creative

Table 10.1   US tax system (a very simple example)

	C Corporation	S Corporation	LLC
Income	200000	200000	200000
Corporate tax	(61250)	0	0
Net profit	**138750**	**200000**	**200000**
Dividends to owner A	69375	100000	150000
To owner B	69375	100000	50000
Personal income tax	20813*	42300**	42300**
* = 15% dividend rate			
** = ordinary rate			
Net to owners	**117937**	**157700**	**157700**

form of business organization and can have one member (owner). Interests in an LLC are represented by "units" and management is either by "members" or by "designated managers". Even though the legal terminology is different, an LLC operates just like any corporation and can have a board of advisors or board of directors and officers of the company. The biggest advantage of an LLC like a Subchapter S corporation is its tax savings due to its pass-through feature of the US tax code. The gains, losses, income, deductions and any tax benefits flow directly to the member owners on a pro rata basis according to the terms of the agreement. This can result in tax savings and substantial increase in the amount of money flowing to members. The following are steps in forming an LLC:

- Name availability check – include "Limited Liability Company", "L.L.C." and "LLC".
- File "Certificate of Formation" with the secretary of state (including statutory agent) of the state incorporating in.
- Single member LLC: Written Declaration.
- More than one member: LLC Agreement.
- Apply to IRS for Employer ID Number – Form SS-4.

The flow-through feature, which is similar to an S corporation due to absence of corporate tax, is substantial (Table 10.1).

A Subchapter S corporation, usually called just an S corporation, is also a pass-through corporation avoiding the corporate tax of a corporation. This corporate structure has the same limited liability as an LLC or C corporation and conducts business as a corporation. It only has one class of stock but this may be voting or non-voting. Its limitations are that these individual stock owners must be resident citizens of the United States not non-resident aliens that are allowed in other legal organizational forms. Also, there can be no more than 100 shareholders.

A C corporation is the most well-known and common legal form of organization particularly for publicly traded companies. It is a separate legal entity and has the most flexibility in terms of capital structure such as the ability to create different classes of stock such as Common A, Common B and Preferred. Each of these can have different voting rights. The C corporation, as discussed previously, does have double taxation – taxation at the corporate level and taxation on any income distributed to its owners at the individual income tax rate.

There are several other legal forms of corporations available: professional corporation; not-for-profit corporation; and hybrid B corporation. A professional corporation is for doctors, lawyers, accountants and certain licensed professionals to establish a legal organizational structure. This is a legal entity for liability purposes and has some tax benefits. However, each participant in the professional corporation still has personal legal liability.

A non-profit corporation, as the name implies, is granted tax exemption status from the IRS, the taxing authority in the United States. While the organization can still make a profit, there are limitations and the majority of the income needs to be used for the purpose the organization was founded. Contributions to a non-profit corporation are also tax deductible by the issuing entity usually an individual or corporation. It has similar features to most legal forms of organizations: a certificate of incorporation; a statutory agent; bylaws; and a board of directors. The biggest difference is that it has to be granted non-profit status upon filing, which extends the time of formation.

The last and newest legal form of organization is a hybrid B corporation, which is a combination profit and non-profit organization. Made famous by companies like Ben & Jerry's (ice cream) and The Body Shop (body accessories), this type of organization pledges to distribute a certain percentage of the income (tax free) before the income is taxed for distribution to shareholders (owners). As such, it is receiving an increase in formation rate in many states.

Organizational structure and operations

The organizational structure of the new venture needs to be carefully developed and filled with people with the necessary background and skills so that value of the venture can be created through successful sales and profits. A typical organizational chart is indicated in Figure 10.1. The structure of the company includes the owners (shareholders), board of directors or board of advisors, president or chief executive officer and the next level of management. In this case, there are only three positions at the level indicated – vice president of marketing, vice president of finance and accounting and vice president of information and operations. You want to start your company with as few people as possible to minimize the salary costs. Investors are not particularly interested in paying high salary costs particularly at startup when the venture is not receiving revenue or has reached positive cash flow.

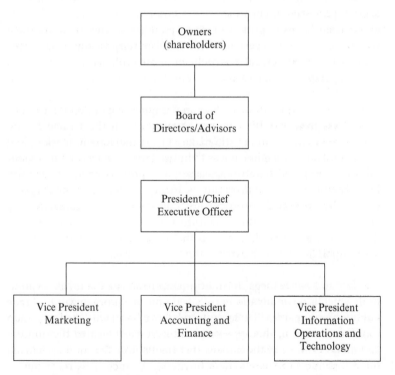

Figure 10.1 Organizational structure example

Since the board of directors/board of advisors is discussed in the next subsection of the chapter, the management team needs to be spelled out in detail along with the responsibilities, in this case for the four positions indicated. This is an important consideration of investors in deciding to put money into the company. To obtain money not every position has to be filled with an individual as long as the need for the activities in the position is noted. At start-up, these can be covered by part-time "consultants" or outsourced like accounting.

While there are no perfect founding teams, there are some good things to keep in mind. Make sure that someone on the management team or if necessary the board of directors/advisors has experience in the field of the industry of the venture. This is one criterion closely looked at by investors as there is some indication that this helps success to occur. Make sure that all the expertise needed in each functional area for success is identified and when appropriate filled with a team member who has expertise, experience and skills in this area. Make sure each team member is knowledgeable about his or her functional area and the venture and is passionate about their area and the success of the venture. Finally, make sure each person selected to be a part of the management team is willing to spend the necessary time needed and has this amount of time available. As the business expands, more team members will be needed as well as different functional areas. A chief financial officer (CFO) is not usually needed at start-up as there are few if any transactions and the assets of the venture are limited. Similarly, a director of human resources is not needed until there are enough positions and people working for the company to warrant the costs (salary plus fringe benefits) of the position.

Board of directors/board of advisors

Each start-up needs a board of directors/advisors; not having a board of advisors reflects the legal liability and costs associated with a board of directors. Operationally, the difference is that a board of directors has fiduciary (legal) liability for the operation of the venture and a board of advisors does not. As implied, a board of advisors gives advice to the venture without any legal liability. It is important to distinguish between privately owned and publicly owned companies as publicly owned companies are required to have a board of directors, the majority of which may not get their major source of income (be an employee) from the company.

When developing a board of directors/advisors, be sure to have represented all the needed talent/skills relevant to the business. The typical skills/talent needed include marketing, finance, distribution, technology and legal. A good board member has had successful experience and has the skills and experience in an area needed.[5] It is often desirable to have this skill and experience in the entrepreneurial/SME sector. If possible, a successful, seasoned entrepreneur often adds a lot to a board. A good board member is creative, a good problem solver and has the connectivity needed in the areas identified. As one entrepreneur stated, "I want a board member who can think and has the honesty and integrity to engender mutual trust".

At start-up, a board member is usually not compensated but is involved with the venture due to interest in the area of business and the desire to "give back". He or she can be compensated by giving them a small equity position. It is usually better that they vest over time so that continuity occurs. A typical situation is 1.5 percent equity in the company vested over a three-year period. In this way, a board is incentivized to help make sure the venture including his or her shares increases in value, in a sense a performance-based pay.

Summary

This chapter has focused on the organizational plan, a document that indicates the legal form of the organization and how it will operate. After concentrating on developing the plan and reasons for selecting one legal form over another, the basic legal organizational forms in the United States were discussed, that is, proprietorship, partnership and corporation. Six types of corporation presented are LLC, Subchapter S corporation, C corporation, professional corporation, not-for-profit corporation and the newest type – hybrid B corporation. The chapter concluded with a discussion of organizational structure and operations and the board of directors/advisors.

NOTES

1 "Types of company", *MEED: Middle East Economic Digest* (2012), 28–30.
2 Rebel A. Cole, "What do we know about the capital structure of privately held U.S. firms? Evidence from the surveys of small business finance", *Financial Management* (2013), **42** (4), 777–813.
3 Jaana Lappalainen and Mervi Niskanen, "Financial performance of SMEs: impact of ownership structure and board composition", *Management Research Review* (2012), **35** (11), 1088–108.
4 Karin Edmark and Roger H. Gordon, "The choice of organizational form by closely-held firms

in Sweden: tax versus non-tax determinants", *Industrial and Corporate Change* (2013), **22** (1), 219–43.

5 "Recruit board members with 'networks'", *Board and Administrator: For Administrators Only* (2012), **29** (S3), 1.

Online sources

http://www.businessinsider.com / myheritage - family - social - network-2011-7.

http://www.businessinsider.com/myheritage-story-gilad-japhet-2011-7.

http://www.myheritage.com/.

PART IV

The venture

11 Obtaining capital and other resources

Scenario: Kelly Flatley and Brendan Synnott – Bear Naked

It was not until the past decade that many US citizens began to agree with one growing reality – America is getting fat. The growing concern for our national health, however, provided a stepping stone toward the fight against obesity. Fearful that this epidemic would plague our younger generations, Americans launched multiple initiatives ranging from fitness camps to fast-food laws. Not only were these changes great for American individuals but they opened up a slew of opportunities for American companies. Health foods sprang up in neighborhood supermarkets. One health aisle could provide five different brands of organic, gluten-free cereal, four different brands of natural juice and seven different brands of granola. The surge in health foods brought on a quick concentration of businesses and brands into the market. So what in the world was Kelly Flatley thinking when she decided one more granola business was a good idea?

To Kelly Flatley, having seven brands of granola to choose from did not mean that any of them were good. Flatley kept granola with her every day to fuel her active lifestyle, fitting yoga and running in between her job as a sports marketer. But instead of choking down any of the store options, Flatley mixed and baked her own batches. Using whole ingredients and controlling the baking process let Flatley create granola batches that came out soft and tasty, rather than commercial brands that were typically jaw-shattering and bland. In 2002, with the support of her family and friends, Flatley started Bear Naked.

Unable to produce enough batches in her small Connecticut kitchen, Flatley pulled her savings and rented out a commercial kitchen, baking through the night and delivering batches to target grocery stores and health markets. Soon after, she took on an old friend, Brendan Synnott, who cooked up bigger ideas for the small granola company. Synnott pushed Flatley to think about expanding to a factory and applying to Walmart for distribution. However, the first couple of years proved too meager to seriously consider these bigger dreams, and the pair survived mainly by driving most of the company's operations themselves. They drove a van full of granola to give out at sports events. They used a small business accounting program to keep track of their books. They labored into the night, baking and packaging granola, and making sure that all batches contained overly generous portions of whole nuts and fruits. And to ensure the company stayed afloat, neither of the two paid themselves.

The company's first break came from utter determination and a bit of luck. After having unsuccessfully hounded a local grocery chain buyer for months, the team (including several new employees) decided to show up at the buyer's office with a fancy breakfast including their granola and the chain's own yogurt. The buyer was out of town, but the owner of the chain was in and walked right past them. He loved the granola and the group's enthusiasm, and put their bags on his shelves. This gave Flatley and Synnott a foot in the door, and the pair continued to expand Bear Naked eventually to a larger chain that pushed Bear Naked into grocery stores throughout the entire East coast.

In 2006, almost five years after the company's start-up in Kelly Flatley's home kitchen, global cereal giant Kellogg took notice of Bear Naked's soaring popularity and offered to buy the brand. Flatley and Synnott accepted and relinquished Bear Naked for $60 million. Since then, Bear Naked granola has spread nationwide and now graces the shelves of health food and supermarket mammoths, such as Whole Foods, Central Market, Walmart and Target. While the scale of their company is now far outreaching the meager size it once inhabited, Flatley and Synnott continue to head up the brand's management, overseeing strategies that sell tens of thousands of granola bags per day. Bear Naked, starting from selling in a mere local chain, has now expanded to over 10 000 retail stores. It is safe to say they will be needing more nuts (see Online sources).

Introduction

As occurred for Kelly Flatley and Brendan Synnott when they created and grew their company Bear Naked, a new venture is constantly in need of resources. This chapter addresses obtaining these with particular attention on the one needed the most – financial. The chapter first focuses on the sources of financing, with a discussion of bank loans and the three sources of private equity (enterprise capital) and then of venture capital firms and going public. The chapter concludes with a description of obtaining other resources for the venture.

Kickstarter is a paradigm-shifting way to fund projects. The website provides a platform where regular people can help fund projects in anything from films and music to design and technology (see Table 11.2). Since its inception in April 2009, almost $950 million has been pledged by over 5.5 million people, helping fund more than 55 000 projects. Kickstarter does not get involved in the projects, only the funding. Kickstarter is open to anyone with a project that fits its guidelines. The project creators make their own goals and deadlines for receiving funds. If the funding goal is met by the set deadline, then the full amount will be given to fund the project.

Sources of financing

From the start of a business through its sale, a new venture is always in need of money. Two things an entrepreneur tends not to have enough of are money and time. Throughout this period of time, different types of financing become available depending on the amount of capital needed and the size of the venture in terms of sales and profits. Early-stage financing is often the most difficult to obtain and costs the most in terms of equity give-up and/or interest. In this stage, the financial resources usually come from the entrepreneur (self), management team, family and friends, crowdfunding and bank loans. Expansion (development financing) comes from a variety of sources depending on the stage of financing (first, second or third) and the amount of capital needed. In this stage, capital often comes from bank loans, private equity financing, venture capital financing and government grants.[1] The funding at this stage, due to the sales, profits and track record of the venture, is usually less costly than in early-stage financing. The last stage of financing, usually less costly than the previous stage, typically involves acquisition financing, leveraged buyouts or going public. The alternative sources of financing are indicated in Table 11.1. There are three aspects of any source of financing shown in the major column headings – length of time, cost and any covenants or control features. Each of the alternative sources indicated in the table that are available should be evaluated on these three bases with ideal source of capital

Table 11.1 Sources of financing

Source of financing	Length of time		Cost				Control	
	Short term	Long term	Fixed rate debt	Floating rate debt	Percent of profits	Equity	Covenants	Voting rights
Self								
Family and friends								
Crowdfunding								
Suppliers and trade credit								
Commercial banks								
Angels (private investors)								
Venture capital								
Private equity placements								
Public equity offerings								
Private equity funds								
Government programs								

being available forever, having no cost and having no covenants or loss of control aspects. Of course, this source of capital is not available except when it comes from yourself or perhaps a relative such as a grandparent who is providing the capital because of the relationship, not as an investment. Sometimes an entrepreneur, for example, is better paying a slightly higher interest rate or going up a higher percentage of equity, both of which are costs to avoid having on too restrictive covenant in the terms of the financing. Similarly, to have the capital for a large period of time (length of time) can require a higher interest rate (cost).

In order to attract other equity, and sometimes even debt financing, often requires that you as the entrepreneur have some capital (investment) in the venture as discussed in Chapter 9 on the financial plan. Usually, the easiest source of capital to obtain is from family and friends as they know you the best and believe in you and your idea. Crowdfunding has emerged as a good way to obtain capital particularly at an early stage for capital up to $1 million.[2] While the final rules and regulations on this source of capital are still being developed, there are several mechanisms for a venture to use to obtain small amounts of capital per individual investors using this source. Sometimes suppliers, particularly those who have excess capacity or view the venture as having the potential to be an excellent growing new customer, will extend the terms of payment or retailers who want to help a new venture or small or medium-size business grow will pay in a shorter period of time. Both of these sources provide capital by extending the terms of payment or reducing the time of collection. Whole Foods is known for its prompt payments and wanting to help new ventures, particularly in the organic or health food areas, by paying in 30 days versus the sometimes 90-day norm in some sectors of the food industry. Banks and private investors in the private equity market as well as venture capital are discussed in separate subsections in this chapter. Private equity placement is a very lengthy process that allows a venture to raise capital through stock sale to accredited investors and avoid being listed on a public stock exchange.

Public equity offerings are when a venture issues an initial public offering to shareholders and is then traded on a stock exchange. This form of capital as well as private equity funds occurs usually at the last stage of financing or when the entrepreneur wants to exit the business. Private equity funds almost always buy the entire venture as occurred when KK&R, a private equity fund in New York, purchased Miller Brewing Company. Finally, in almost every country, there are usually government programs to stimulate technology development, new venture starts and growth or employment. These occur at the local, regional (state) or federal government level. For example, the city of Phoenix (Arizona) has several programs to help finance new ventures. The state of Massachusetts has a state venture capital fund to finance ventures in the state.[3] And the US government has a small business investment program (SBIR) to stimulate innovation and new product/ service development in selected areas. Similar types of programs can be found in such countries as Austria, Germany and the United Kingdom. For example, the city of Vienna, the Bundesland region of Austria and the country itself each have programs to stimulate technology, new product/service development and venture creation.

Bank loans and lending decisions

Every business will want to have some debt in its capital structure. This takes the form of a short-term or long-term loan, which is most frequently provided by banks in most countries, although some private investors, family and friends and venture capitalists provide loans or a combination of loan/equity financing. This debt is provided to the business in return for payment of interest and the return of the capital (principal repayment). Since banks provide the majority of this debt, it is important to understand how bank lending decisions are made as well as the types of loans available.

Bank lending decisions are made according to the five Cs of lending, that is, character, capacity, capital, collateral and conditions. Past financial statements (balance sheets and income statements) are reviewed in terms of key profitability and credit ratios, inventory turnover, aging of accounts receivable, the entrepreneur's capital invested and commitment to the business. Future projections on market size, sales and profitability are also evaluated to determine the ability to repay the loan. Several questions are usually raised regarding this ability. Does the entrepreneur expect to be carried by the loan for an extended period of time? If problems occur, is the entrepreneur committed enough to spend the effort necessary to make the business a success? Does the business have a unique differential advantage in a growth market? What are the downside risks? Is there protection (such as life insurance on key personnel and insurance on the plant and equipment) against disasters?

Although the answers to these questions and the analysis of the company's records allow the loan officer to assess the quantitative aspects of the loan decision, the intuitive factors, particularly the first two Cs – character and capacity – are also taken into account. This part of the loan decision – the gut feeling – is the most difficult part to assess. The entrepreneur must present his or her capabilities and the prospects for the company in a way that elicits a positive response from the lender. This intuitive part of the loan decision becomes even more important when there is little or no track record, limited experience in financial management, a non-proprietary product or service (one not protected by a patent or license) or few assets available.

Some of the concerns of the loan officer and the loan committee can be reduced by providing a good loan application. While the specific loan application format of each bank differs to some extent, generally the application format is a "mini" business plan that consists of an executive summary, business description, owner/manager profiles, business projections, financial statements, amount and use of the loan and repayment schedule. This information provides the loan officer and loan committee with insight into the creditworthiness of the individual and the venture as well as the ability of the venture to make enough sales and profit to repay the loan and the interest. The entrepreneur should evaluate several alternative banks, select the one that has had positive loan experience in the particular business area, call for an appointment and then carefully present the case for the loan to the loan officer. Presenting a positive business image and following the established protocol are necessary to obtain a loan from a commercial bank.

The different types of loans are:

- accounts receivable loans
- equipment loans
- inventory loans
- real estate loans
- character loans
- installment loans
- long-term loans
- straight commercial loans.

The ones most commonly used by entrepreneurs are equipment loans, inventory loans and accounts receivable loans. Equipment loans are perhaps the easiest to obtain and is one way to secure longer-term financing, usually over a three- to ten-year period depending on the nature of the equipment, its depreciation and resale value. If it is new equipment, a lender will often loan up to 50 to 80 percent of its value using the equipment as collateral. The same loan agreements can be obtained on real estate (land and buildings). Since a new venture needs to minimize its cash outlays in the beginning, the loan can take the form of a sale-leaseback arrangement.

An inventory loan is using the inventory of the venture as an asset. Depending on the state of the inventory from raw materials to finished goods, a loan can be secured for usually up to 50 percent of the value.

The most frequent loan used by a new venture is based on accounts receivable. Accounts receivable are a good asset for a loan depending on the reputation of the buyer and type of product/service. Often a loan amount up to 80 percent of the value of the accounts receivable can be obtained. If a customer has a particularly strong reputation, factoring accounts receivable can be used where the bank actually buys the account receivable (invoice) for up to 80 percent of the value and collects the money from the customer.

When a new venture has too much risk and fails to receive a loan from a commercial bank, many governments have a guaranteed loan program. The government assumes a percentage of the loan risk, sometimes up to 70 percent, reducing the bank's risk to 30 percent of the loan amount with the bank assuming the role of primary lender and obtaining their loan amount before the government in the case of loan default by the new venture. These guarantees are available in such countries as Austria, Germany, Hungary, Poland, Russia, the United Kingdom and the United States. The percentage of the loan varies by country and is highly dependent on the nature of the asset and the industry of the venture. In the United States, these loans are done through different programs of the Small Business Administration.

Private equity market

The private equity market, which is better called the enterprise capital market, provides capital for privately held ventures. The market is composed of three verticals as indicated in Figure 11.1 – individuals, venture capital firms and private equity funds. While the size of the investment increases from individuals to private equity funds, the number of deals done decreases. While the individual market is the least understood with limited information, in the United States the total amount invested in smaller amounts is equal to the total amount invested by the venture capital industry.

The largest number of investments made in this market is done by individual investors, often called angel investors, acting alone without any group affiliation.[4] In the United States, these individuals are accredited investors, which means they have either a $200 000 per year income and/or net worth, excluding their primary residence of $1 million or more. Their individual investment usually occurs in the range of $10 000 to $500 000 with an average investment of $220 000. Sometimes this individual gets other individuals involved so that the

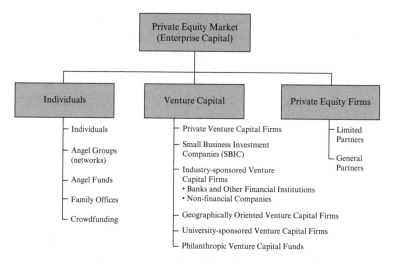

Figure 11.1   Private equity market

amount of capital per individual is reduced as well as the risk. These individuals have no formal identification and are often found by referrals from accountants, bank officials, lawyers and university professors teaching in the entrepreneurship/venture finance area.

Some of these angels belong to a group or network of other individual investors and meet together periodically throughout the year. These angel groups or networks occur all over the world with the largest number being in the United States. Most of them are listed by geographic area and the head of the group or network by the Kauffman Foundation (see Kauffman in Online sources). Each angel group has a somewhat different format and meeting times but most use a similar software program for access. For example, one angel group, the Thunderbird Angel Network (TAN), meets five times each year and looks at three to four deals per meeting, screened from 75–100 applicants. Each invited firm has 12 minutes to present their idea, market, financials and management team followed by a ten-minute question and answer period and then by a five-minute initial due diligence done by Thunderbird School of Global Management students. Those ventures of interest by the investors and the group interested then receive further evaluation (due diligence) to determine the investment potential and valuation. The hosting group itself has no investment money and charges a small annual fee for hosting the meeting and securing the possible investment deals.

When the private individual investors put money into a fund, which usually has a manager, then this becomes an angel fund. An angel fund operates much like a small venture capital fund except the private investors or their designated representatives make the investment decisions. Since most private investors prefer to invest on a deal-by-deal basis without this upfront commitment as occurs in angel groups or networks, there are very few angel funds operational.

When an entrepreneur is very successful in previous call-outs of ventures, he or she often establishes a family office to manage their affairs and assets particularly upon passing. A portion of these assets are often invested in private ventures along with real estate, stocks and bonds.

The final type of individual investing is crowdfunding. This is occurring in the United Kingdom and more recently in the United States. It is different to traditional funding models in that it is based on networks and individuals and sometimes companies. It can be used to actually pre-test an idea for a product/service. Often the individuals involved in the crowdfunding idea are very interested in the idea and its potential for success. Sometimes, as in the case of LawBite, the idea is oversubscribed when listed on crowdfunding.

While the laws have yet to be finalized, according to the US Securities and Exchange Commission (SEC) Chair, Mary Jo White, at the 41st Annual Securities Regulation Institute, this will be done in a thoughtful way to implement one of the mandates of the JOBS Act passed by Congress in 2012. Even though the laws have not been finalized, business owners and entrepreneurs have successfully raised capital using one of two basic models. One, the donation-based model, the start of crowdfunding, is when money is raised by donations from donors in a collaborative process in return for perks, products/services or rewards. The second more recent model, investment crowdfunding, raises money by selling ownership in the business venture in the form of equity or debt. When this occurs, the crowdfunding individuals become owners or shareholders and can have financial returns or losses depending on the success of the venture.

There are various crowdfunding sites to choose from (Table 11.2) depending on what you are trying to achieve and the nature of your product/service and venture. Kickstarter is a site where creative products can raise money through donations. Crowdfunder offers a blend of donation-based and investor-based funding and is often the plat-

Table 11.2   Crowdfunding sites

Website	URL
AngelList	https://angel.co
Appbackr	http://www.appbackr.com
Crowdfunder	https://www.crowdfunder.com
Crowdrise	http://www.crowdrise.com/
Indiegogo	http://www.indiegogo.com
Investedin	http://invested.in
Kickstarter	https://www.kickstarter.com
Quirky	http://www.quirky.com
RocketHub	http://www.rockethub.com
SoMoLend	https://www.somolend.com

form for small businesses with a growing network of investors, tech start-ups and social enterprises. Crowdfunding will continue to play a role in financing ventures and testing new product/service ideas in the future.

Venture capital

Another area of enterprise capital providing money for privately held firms is venture.[5] There are a variety of venture capital firms and funds available, particularly in the United States – private venture capital firms, small business investment companies (SBIC), industry-sponsored venture capital firms, regionally oriented venture capital firms, university-sponsored venture capital funds and philanthropic venture capital funds.

Venture capital is a professionally managed pool of equity capital. Frequently, the equity pool is formed from the resources of wealthy individuals or institutions who are limited partners. Other principal investors in venture capital limited partnerships are pension funds, endowment funds and other institutions, including foreign investors. The pool is managed by a general partner – that is, the venture capital firm – in exchange for a percentage of the gain realized on the investment and a fee. The investments are in early-stage deals as well as second- and third-stage deals and also leveraged buyouts. Venture capital can best be characterized as a long-term investment discipline, usually occurring over a five- to seven-year period that is found in the creation of early-stage companies, the expansion and revitalization of existing businesses, and the financing of leveraged buyouts of existing divisions of major corporations or privately owned businesses. In each investment, the venture capitalist takes equity participation through stock, warrants and/or convertible securities and has an active involvement in the monitoring of each portfolio company bringing investment, financing planning and business skills to the firm. The venture capitalist will often provide debt along with the equity portion of the financing.

The types of venture capital firms vary in terms of size of investment, number of deals, geographic area, objectives and mission. A private venture capital firm is a large pool of capital with a high minimum investment. It is generally composed of a managing partner (the venture capital firm) and limited partners, like most of the other venture capital firms that are discussed except for industry-sponsored venture capital firms. Small business investment companies have smaller pools of capital and smaller minimum investments and are more geographically focused. Industry-sponsored venture capital firms are either in the financial or the non-financial industry. Those in the non-financial industry are usually part of a large corporation who invest in entrepreneurial ventures inside the company (corporate entrepreneurship) or enterprises outside the company but in the industry focus area of the firm. Regionally sponsored venture capital firms focus at least the majority if not all of their investments in a specific region of a country such as the lower region of Austria or in most states in the United States. University-sponsored venture capital funds, such as the standard venture fund, focus on the technologies and ventures developed by alumni, faculty, staff and students of the university. Philanthropic venture funds, as the name implies, focus on some philanthropic need. These funds frequently only pay a higher interest on the money invested in the fund but do not return the principal amount of the investment as most funds do.

Private equity firms

Private equity firms, the last area of capital for the privately held firm, are the largest pools of capital and generally buy the entire company, thus providing one way for the entrepreneur to exit the company. There are basically two types of private equity firms – limited partners and general partners. General partners invest mostly in limited partner venture firms who then invest large pools of capital usually in buying the entire company or funding the entire project. In some countries, these take the form of large national pools of capital.

Table 11.3   Advantages and disadvantages of going public

Advantages	Disadvantages
Ability to obtain equity capital	Increased risk of liability
Enhanced ability to borrow	Expense
Enhanced ability to raise equity	Regulation of corporate governance
Liquidity and valuation	Policies and procedures
Personal wealth	Pressures to maintain growth pattern
	Loss of control
Prestige	Disclosure of information

Going public

Going public occurs when the entrepreneur and other equity owners of the venture offer and sell some part of the company to the public through a registration statement filed with the securities commission of the country. In the United States, this is the SEC pursuant to the Securities Act of 1933. The resulting capital infusion to the company from the increased number of stockholders and outstanding shares of stock provides the company with financial resources and generally with a relatively liquid investment vehicle. Consequently, the company will have greater access to capital markets in the future and a more objective picture of the public's perception of the value of the business. However, given the reporting requirements, the increased number of stockholders (owners) and the costs involved, the entrepreneur must carefully evaluate the advantages and disadvantages of going public before initiating the process (Table 11.3).

Obtaining other resources

Other resources needed by a new and growing firm include distribution channels, sources of supply and manufacturing and human resources. These are often identified in the business plan and are needed at different stages of the firm's development. One firm, La Bella Terre, in the flavored organic sugar market, increased its production capabilities by adding additional outsource suppliers as it increased its distribution channels throughout the United States through Whole Foods as well as with a tea and spirits company.

Human resources are also added as a firm grows. Initially, there is often not enough capital involved or transactions occurring to warrant a CFO or enough employees to justify hiring and paying the salary of a human resources director. These positions are added when the firm size warrants.

Summary

This chapter has focused on obtaining financial and other resources for the venture. The chapter started by identifying the sources of financing available and the three reasons for selecting one source – cost, length of time and covenants and control. Then bank loans, the lending process and the private equity (enterprise) capital market were discussed. Following a discussion of venture capital and going public, the chapter concluded by a discussion on obtaining other resources.

NOTES

1 Eric M. Adams, "Tips to financing start-up companies", *Northern Colorado Business Report* (2011), **16** (20), 5.
2 Susan B. Garland, "Investing in start-ups is risky business", *Kiplinger's Retirement Report* (2013), **20** (12), 7.
3 "Follow the money trail", *Entrepreneur* (2013), **41** (6), 75.
4 Carolyn M. Brown, "Hooking investors", *Black Enterprise* (2012), **42** (11), 76–80.
5 "Life science start-ups: venture funding", *Start-Up* (2014), **19** (1), 50–56.

Online sources

Scenario

http://money.cnn.com/2008/02/05/smbusiness/bear_naked.fsb/index.htm.

http://www.forbes.com/2009/07/13/bear-naked-start-up-forbes-woman-entrepreneur-kelly-flatley.html.

Other

Kauffman http://www.kauffman.org.

12 Launching the venture

Scenario: Chase Adam – Watsi

Two years prior to starting his business, Chase Adam worked as a Peace Corps volunteer in Costa Rica. As endearing as it would have been to hear of his experience as a fulfilling, life-affirming dream come true, Adam's own recount of his stint was more along the lines of disgusted. Non-profit work, as he had come to experience, was messy, poor and highly inefficient. It was a wonder that non-profit organizations were surviving while constantly hurdling government regulations only to receive small funds that seemingly disappeared overnight.

Although his volunteer assignment had rendered Adam miserable and disheartened, one small encounter had piqued his interest. While Adam was riding a public bus through a Costa Rican town named Watsi, a woman jumped on and began asking riders for money for her sick son. Adam was surprised when most of the people on the bus began giving her cash. The interaction between the bus riders that day was eye-opening for Adam. After hearing the mother's story and looking at medical records she had brought with her, people trusted enough to give her the funding she asked for. Was that similar to crowdfunding? It reminded him of a familiar start-up, Kiva, an online site that managed and organized crowdfunding from willing benefactors to small start-ups in developing countries. If only there was something like that for people in underdeveloped countries with medical needs.

His passion for helping others, coupled with this revelation, induced Adam to start his own crowdfunding website, Watsi. Inspired by Kiva, Adam geared Watsi to allow site visitors to donate small to large amounts of their own personal funds toward patients in developing countries who cannot fund their own life-threatening medical needs. Adam worked out of his Mountain View, California apartment using his free time to develop a business plan. Much of his initial start-up time was also spent on connecting and partnering with medical practitioners around the world who all had patients needing funding for different medical issues. Adam formed a team of local doctors and medical professionals who looked through patient records and provided third opinions for patients entering the pool of Watsi participants.

One characteristic that gave Watsi fresh appeal was the pure transparency it gave to the funds that began to come in. While very few non-profits would offer public disclosure of their operations, Adam and his team made sure that every aspect of documentation was provided online for anyone to see. An online spreadsheet was launched on Google Docs to provide information for each financial transaction. Just as Adam believed that the bus riders had trusted the mother after she showed her son's medical records, so would the benefactors trust that Watsi would direct donations straight to the patient. Alongside the company's strategy of full disclosure, the website also keeps track of each patient's progress. Even after a patient receives the funding and the care, Watsi continues to monitor their health, posting pictures, stories and updates each step of the way.

Adam had despised non-profit organizations for their lack of efficiency and transparency that would often give non-profits a bad reputation. And yet, here he was launching his own non-profit. However, what Adam really hated was the inefficiencies and not the organizations. By uprooting those characteristics that led non-profits into corruption or early graves, Watsi has continued to grow its amount of donations quicker than it can find patients. Since its launch in 2011, Watsi has received seed money from an incubator program, raised over $200 000 and received enough donations to contribute to over 450 medical procedures. There still are issues to be hashed out, such as dealing with fraudulent credit card donations and adjusting to an exponentially growing patient database. But, as long as there are funds to give, Adam will continue to give them (see Online sources).

Introduction

Probably the most critical strategy for success as an entrepreneur is the one for launching the venture. No matter how much effort has gone into the venture to this point, the launch strategy affects whether or not the market will accept the idea for the new product/service and decide to purchase it. This chapter focuses on the aspects of developing and implementing a successful launch of the new venture. After discussing situation analysis and the adoption process, the chapter describes four market entry positionings – stressing the unique aspects of the new idea, comparing the new idea with those presently on the market, leveraging the government and government regulations, and focusing on the customer. Following a look at the strategies for launch, the chapter concludes by discussing the first mover advantage and developing contingency plans.

Situation analysis

A key component of the launch plan is the assessment of the current situation, which provides the basis for the customer focus and target market selection. One of the most important aspects of this assessment is the situation analysis. The situation analysis involves several parts including: (1) defining the category (the NAICS or country code of the country) of the new product/service; (2) analyzing the features of attractiveness of the category and those products being successful in it; (3) analyzing the customers; (4) analyzing the competition; and (5) doing an analysis of the resources. Each of these are discussed in turn.

It is critical that the entrepreneur determines the nature of the need being filled and the product/service category doing that. The category can be assessed on the basis of aggregate category factors and more specific category factors. Aggregate category factors include: technological; social; regulatory; category size and growth; stage in the life cycle of the category; and sales and profits. More specific category factors include: category capacity and sustainability; number of new entrants; bargaining power of buyer and suppliers; and degree of competition. These are related to the industry analysis, which is Section 2 of the business plan previously discussed in Chapter 7.

Customer analysis results in knowing the customer and having the customer as the focal point of the launch. Customer analysis helps ensure that the marketing plan for the launch has the customer orientation necessary to secure sales as quickly as possible. A basic question that needs to be answered is: What are the benefits desired by the customers and who are the customers buying (and not buying) the products/services in the category? Potential customers should be queried to provide the needed marketing information and all secondary data carefully searched. Customers can be evaluated and categorized based on behavioral and descriptive variables. Behavioral variables describe how the customers act toward the product/service category including: degree of loyalty; purchase quantity; and benefits desired and obtained. Descriptive variables include: demographic variables (age, income and gender); geographic location; and psychological variables (lifestyle, personality and degree of risk taking). Aspects of the buying process that need to be considered are the initiation of the process, the purchase decision maker, the influence(s) of the purchase and the final user. What do customers buy, how they buy, where they buy and when they buy are important to know.

There are four general benefits of competitive analysis: generic competition (all products/services that satisfy the same need); budget competition (all products/services competing for the same part of the budget); product form competition (products/services most similar to the new product/service); and product category competition (all products/services directly filling the same market need). Competitive analysis involves two major activities: data collection and data analysis. Data collection is much easier today due to the large amount of information available on the internet. The analysis of this data provides the basis for the market positioning and plan.[1] Competition should be assessed in terms of their objectives, current strategies, capabilities and likely future activities in response to the new product/service launch.

The final aspect of situation analysis is resource analysis. This analysis compares the new product/service and the company to those of the competitors. This results in a determination of the strength and weakness relative to what it takes to be a success on the market.

Adoption process

Forecasting initial sales through adoption of the new product/service is one of the most difficult tasks of the entrepreneur.[2] This becomes increasingly difficult in some foreign markets and as the technology advancement of the new product/service increases. One helpful way to view this customer acceptance is by using the adoption process indicated in Figure 12.1.

As indicated in Figure 12.1, since potential customers adopt (accept) the product/service at different times, there are different categories of customers doing so over time. These categories range from individuals who are the first to purchase the new product/service – the innovators

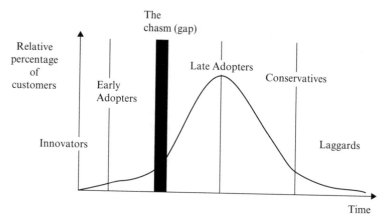

Figure 12.1 The adoption process

– to the last ones going through the process – the laggards. It is helpful to know the characteristics of and benefits desired by the first two categories – innovators and early adopters – and focus the initial marketing efforts in the launch on them as they would be more likely to adopt the new product in the initial introductory period. This allows sales to occur more quickly and the venture to reach positive cash flow in a shorter period of time.

From the point in time when a customer first hears of an innovation to the point in time when adoption occurs there can be five sequential stages:

- Awareness stage. The individual is exposed to the innovation but lacks complete information about it. The individual is aware of the innovation but is not yet motivated to seek further information.
- Interest stage. The individual becomes interested in the new idea and seeks additional information about it. The innovation is favored in a general way but is not yet judged in terms of its utility to a specific situation.
- Evaluation stage. The individual mentally applies the innovation to his or her present and anticipated future situation and then decides whether or not to try it.
- Trial stage. The individual uses the innovation on a small scale in order to determine its utility in his or her own situation.
- Adoption stage. The individual decides to continue the full use of the innovation.

Any new product/service may be rejected at any stage of the adoption process. For example, a housewife may hear about Bounce, but she does not own a clothes dryer, so she would reject the innovation at the awareness stage.

Rejection of an innovation can also occur after an individual has adopted it. This behavior is referred to as a discontinuance. A discontinuance is the cessation of using an innovation after previously adopting it. Discontinuances in marketing are quite common, especially since consumers often purchase everyday items without any special loyalty to one brand. Thus, in marketing, the importance of defining adoption as a function of the commitment to the product/service becomes very critical.

A consumer could conceivably move through several of these stages simultaneously, such as in an impulse decision or when a free sample of a new product is received.

Increased understanding of the sequencing of these stages and the types of communication most effective in each stage will enable the new venture to develop a promotional campaign consistent with the behavior of the consumer. Initially, generally more mass media should be employed to relay product awareness and information on the product/service utility. As time passes, the appeal should be modified to include a more personal appeal, since the consumer generally becomes more dependent on others for evaluating, trying and adopting the new product/service. The characteristics of the new product/service affect the adoption process and it may be a necessary part of the promotional considerations to alleviate any negative characteristics of the product that may deter its rate of adoption.

In marketing a new product/service, special emphasis must be given to particular product/service attributes and the image created by the new venture. The perceived attributes or characteristics of the innovation affect the rate at which diffusion occurs. These characteristics are: (a) relative advantage; (b) compatibility; (c) complexity; (d) divisibility; and (e) communicability.

Relative advantage is the degree to which an innovation is superior to one it supersedes or competes with in the market. Removal of phosphates from detergents represented a likely perceived relative advantage over the old product it replaced or any competitive product that still maintained its traditional formula. However, the addition of green crystals to a detergent was less likely to be perceived by the consumer as having any relative advantage. The strategy used by most new ventures is to seek product differentiation by employing tactics that would result in a relative advantage over any existing products. A new wonder drug that could cure a sore throat within hours certainly has a superior edge or advantage over any other available products, thus likely increasing the rate at which this product would be adopted. The relative advantage of an innovation depends extensively on the perception of the members of a given social system. Aspects of advantage such as quality, convenience (easier and faster) and avoidance of bad aspects of a competitive product/service may have a greater advantage in one group versus another in increasing the rate of adoption.

Compatibility refers to the degree to which a new product/service is consistent with existing values and experiences of the target customers. A new product/service that has a perceived image that is not consistent with cultural norms will diffuse less rapidly than one that is consistent. Also, new products/services that are similar to other products that have been failures will negatively affect the rate of diffusion. Instant coffee experienced some initial barriers in achieving its predicted success. Since the product was promoted as a time saver, during this period some target customers often associated the use of time-saving products with lazy people and tended to reject the product. Research revealed this error and advertising was corrected to be more compatible with existing norms and values.

Complexity refers to the degree of difficulty in understanding or using an innovation. A new product/service that is confusing to the target customers, making it difficult to evaluate (evaluation stage) its utility will generally take longer to diffuse in a given market. Products/services that require new knowledge also take longer to diffuse. One reason that the videocassette recorder (VCR) and television diffused at different rates was the difference in complexity of the two ideas. The VCR required some personal explanation, whereas television usage was relatively simple and required little explanation.

Divisibility is the degree to which a new product/service may be tried on a limited basis. The ability of consumers to purchase small, trial-size packages of new products at a low cost may encourage the rate of adoption. The amount of risk associated with such a small-scale purchase is minimal and allows consumers to examine an alternative to their present brand. Other products that are sold with the added feature of a ten-day, free home trial attempt to accomplish the same effect as the small trial size. Free samples have also shown substantial increases. New ventures must make it as easy as possible for the consumer to try a new product/service with little or no risk so that the rate of diffusion may be enhanced.

Communicability refers to the degree to which information regarding a new product/service may be easily communicated to other people in the marketplace. Products/services that are visible to others, such as clothing and automobiles, and products that can be easily demonstrated, such as televisions and other small appliances, usually fall into the high communicability category. Generally, products/services that are more complex will be more difficult to communicate, thus having a slower adoption process.

Concept of newness

The newness of the new product/service to the consumer and to the distribution system affects its launch. The newness to the consumer in its discontinuity to the present way things are being done both in the business to business and business to consumer market was discussed in Chapter 4. The more discontinuous or the more radical the new product/service is to the present, comfortable way of doing things, the harder it will be to accept it and the longer the time for adoption and the adoption curve.

Those products/services requiring a new distribution system or that are radically new (discontinuance) to the present distribution system will have the same problems. Just think of the difference in acceptance of new apps. At first there was only one platform – Apple, which in itself reduced the speed of adoption as the customer had to have an Apple product to be able to purchase and use the app. Now that apps have been more accepted and are available on multiple platforms, new apps are adopted at a much higher rate, encouraging an increasing number to be developed as the costs of production go down as well. Similarly, new distribution methods of communication such as Facebook, Twitter and blogging and social platforms took time to catch on and be a regular part of most people's lives.

In some distribution systems, a new product needs to be packaged in a manner and consistent with the size limitations imposed by the channel member carrying and stocking the product. A new dog treat developed by a Swedish company that was odorless to humans but very attractive to dogs had to be packaged in a smaller size to meet the requirements of the shelf space allocated to dog treats by major supermarket chains, such as Kroger and Walmart. Similarly, sometimes a more radically new package can help a product/service stand out among alternative competitive products/services in the channel system. Nature Brothers, a new venture with a salt and salt-free seasoning of excellent, almost "addicting taste", made its product stand out in supermarkets by having a cylindrical package with red on yellow and yellow on red in the spice section dominated by the usual white rectangular container or bottles of spice alternatives.

TaskRabbit is an online market for outsourcing tasks and small jobs, founded by IBM software engineer Leah Busque in 2008. The idea originally came about for small errands that could be outsourced online for a mutually agreed upon price. The firm started as RunMyErrand.com in Boston with about 100 errand runners.[3]

In 2009, the firm acquired $1.8 million in seed funding. The firm grew quickly, officially changing its name to TaskRabbit in 2010 and launching a mobile phone app in 2011. By that year, TaskRabbit had moved into several major cities and received an additional $17.8 million in funding. Today, the company has received just under $40 million in venture capital funding and boasts over 20 000 "TaskRabbits". It is a unique player in the temporary hiring industry, which is estimated to be valued at $230 billion annually.

Market positioning

Another aspect of the new product/service launch is the market positioning strategy adopted.[4] Market entry positioning is not a fully developed strategy but a way an entrepreneur can obtain an initial foothold in a market. The first sale and then the sales to follow are the hardest to obtain but necessary to get as quickly as possible up the revenue curve so that positive cash flow is achieved. This needs to be a major if not *the* major focus of the entrepreneur. Most new ventures employ one or more of four major positioning strategies: focusing on aspects of the new product/service; parallel competitive parity; customer orientation; and/or government information.

Stressing the unique aspects of the new product/service is usually the best entry strategy. A new product/service employing a new technology that has distinctive features will at least get the attention of potential customers. Such was the case of the RED camera that used digital technology to record movie screen-quality pictures. Typically, new products have a lower failure rate than new services due to their higher barriers to entry. A winning combination is to offer the new product/service with its unique selling propositions and follow up with a related service.[5] With this entry positioning, often a prominent and sometimes permanent leadership position can be created. The RED camera had this opportunity if it had delivered on time at the price point originally offered. Having this position gives the new venture market position, which can lead to significant awareness and recognition, and eventually brand loyalty.

A parallel competitive parity positioning strategy can also be used to effectively launch a new product/service.[6] This strategy can be employed when the features of the new product/service while different are not radically unique from the features of the products/services presently on the market. This is an attempt to fill a niche, a position in the market not presently being served. Such was the case for TaskRabbit as there were already service providers on the market filling the same need – hiring someone on a short-term basis to do a certain task. An entrepreneur who attempts to make present unhappy customers of a particular product/service of another venture happier when buying his or her product/service is employing a parallel competitive parity strategy. This entry strategy of course usually does not receive the same potentially strong market leadership positioning; some other venture will more than likely employ a similar strategy later.

The third market entry positioning strategy – customer orientation – focuses on the customer and their changing attitudes and purchasing behavior.[7] The new Lincoln automobile is now geared toward a younger, more trend-setting customer.[8] Gone are the days when a significant segment of the population is satisfied with a steakhouse. Sometimes customers can be obtained by the venture becoming a second source of supply. When a customer is having difficulty with their present supplier, starting off as an alternative supply source if done correctly can lead to being the primary supplier. This strategy worked for Arnolite Pallet Company who started off with its present customer base by being the alternative supplier of choice for the needed pallets used by several Fortune 500 companies. This can be an excellent entry strategy when there is not significant, radical uniqueness in the product/service being offered and there are delivery problems in the industry.

The final market entry positioning strategy is government information. Often, information on new rules/laws of the government can provide the launch opportunity and entry strategy.[9] The government can provide assistance, favored purchasing states or rule changes. Such government agencies as the Small Business Administration, National Aeronautics and Space Administration (NASA) and Sandia National Labs have programs that particularly assist the launch of technology ventures. Some of these are in conjunction with specific states. The US federal government, as well as some state governments, has procurement policies that set asides and quotas for small technology ventures. Some of these procurement policies and practices have been incorporated into other government agencies and throughout large corporations. Also, as government regulations change and new laws are enacted, new launch opportunities often occur. Pressure and rule changes have mandated that utility companies encourage their customers to become more energy efficient and give credit for new appliances or the use of solar energy. One technology firm, R&H Safety Sales, launched by offering specific first aid kits that met the United Services Automobile Association (USAA) requirements for specific industries. Similar firms started by supplying the mandated exit signage and safety devices.

Strategies for launch

One particularly good strategy for launch is a market penetration strategy. This strategy focuses on the venture's existing capabilities and contacts in one market. The goal is to penetrate the market with the new product/service by encouraging customers to buy and through satisfied customers and word of mouth advertising have more customers in the market to buy more. The marketing effort in the launch can encourage more frequent usage (purchasing) as well as reward customers who get others in the market to purchase through their referrals. Once a market is saturated, follow-up products/services can be offered in the existing market or the same product can be introduced into a new market (market rollout). One company using regenerative medicine to cure arthritic hips in dogs, such as golden retrievers, is launching its medical product in San Diego through veterinarians and then plans to roll out into the veterinary/dog owner market in Phoenix and then Dallas/Fort Worth.

Another company successfully satisfied its customers in the Boston area with quality delivered bark mulch. The customer then received one free cubic yard of bark mulch if they referred another customer who purchased three or more cubic yards of the delivered bark mulch. When market saturation was reached, the company then offered other delivered products such as crushed clam shells to these same satisfied customers.

One company, Color Lines Clothing, started manufacturing and exporting high-quality children's clothing using such a strategy. Bela Katrak, a young woman with two young children, moved to Bengaluru, India in 1988. She could not find affordable, comfortable, durable ready-to-wear clothes for her kids. All the clothes available in the market were fussy, highly embroidered and over-adorned. Bela started her own clothing business with an investment of Rs 40 lakh (US$80000). She first started her own retail outlet that sold high-quality kids clothes. Soon she realized that the Indian market was not ready for her clothes. Indian mothers were not ready to buy "all cotton" clothes as maintaining vis-à-vis polyester was difficult. So she started exporting to other countries that were ready to accept these clothes and her business flourished.

Even though the international market was large, to start from one location and be successful was difficult. Bela started her international sales in Australia. She made numerous cold calls but did not get any leads. She got her break when one large group was at a Target (US chain) store. Her customer was more concerned with quality clothes rather than quantity, which was a perfect match. Today, Color Lines focuses on variety and styles. It prefers to have numerous orders with smaller runs than small orders with longer runs. This helps Color Lines to maintain unique product designs and styles. It is unique in India as it provides high fashion for children with quality for those sensitive to dyes. Color Lines has its own in-house studio and design team that works closely with buyers to provide garments that are high quality at an affordable price. The company takes high fashion adult wear from international designers and converts them into children's clothing. Color Lines remains the only export venture in India that deals almost exclusively in children's wear.

Apple has been incredibly successful at being the first mover in innovative technologies over the last decade. In 2001, they released the first iPod mp3 player, which sold over 100000 units in its first year. In 2003, they launched the iTunes store, allowing consumers to purchase digital music online legally. They created the original smartphone, the iPhone, which was originally released in 2007 and has been a remarkable success. Building on this technology, Apple launched the first tablet, the iPad in 2010. All of these products were the first of their kind on the market and have been able to maintain their advantage over the competition that quickly followed. Apple's proprietorship technology allows it to maintain greater entry barriers by increasing consumer switching costs and promoting brand loyalty.

First mover advantage

A well-planned launch of a new product/service can provide the entrepreneur with the first mover advantage – being the first with the product/service category on the market. Being first can result in a number of advantages that can enhance sales and profits of the new venture such as: (1) developing a cost advantage; (2) having less competition; (3) developing better supply and distribution channels; (4) gaining experience; and (5) switching costs.[10] An entrepreneur who is first to launch a product in a market means that his or her venture will be the first to start achieving a cost advantage through economies of scale and experience. The experience factor of producing more and more units enables the new venture to produce each unit more cost-effectively. More units allows the new venture to spread its overhead costs, such as R&D costs, over more units and purchase in larger quantities, reducing the unit cost of component parts and equipment and other supplies.

Also, being the first on the market (the first mover) means there is less competition in the market at launch. In a growing market, this advantage is lost as competitive products/services enter the market. The first mover is usually more than compensated by the increasing sales from a growing market.[11] These growing markets and increasing sales often result in less direct competitive actions such as price cutting.

Being the first mover provides the entrepreneur with the opportunity to receive the best position in the supply chain both with suppliers and sellers. The best suppliers and distribution channel members can be selected and strong relationships developed. This can become a barrier to entry for competing products.

First movers gain the experience of participation by being in the market. This can lead to improving the first generation of products/services and provide opportunities to develop new products for the satisfied customers obtained. The networks and satisfied customers provide knowledge and insight that can be very valuable to the entrepreneur.

Finally, the first mover may provide a barrier to entry by imposing switching costs on buyers. These switching costs can be established through marketing or contractual obligations. When customer satisfaction occurs leading to brand loyalty, the high buyer learning and evolution costs that is needed to purchase a competitive product may inhibit a buyer from even considering another alternative. It is much easier, safer and quicker to buy the brand loyal product.

Develop a contingency plan

Regardless of the quality of the launch strategy employed, there is no crystal ball that will indicate success. Since it is imperative that the entrepreneur set up the revenue curve as quickly as possible while maintaining or reducing costs to achieve positive cash flow, he or she should consider many different scenarios and contingency plans in case changes in the launch strategy are needed. Problems can occur with downturns in the economy, other new products/services being introduced and/or changes in consumer tastes and preferences that can radically alter the market and industry and disrupt the planned launch strategy of the venture.

One thing that the entrepreneur needs to maintain in this turbulence is the quality of the product/service. A high-quality standard can be sustained and used as a competitive advantage through continuous improvements (process of setting higher standards of performance with each interaction of the quality cycle), benchmarking (identifying and imitating the best in the world at various tasks and functions) and outsourcing (procuring the best quality from outside organizations).

Summary

This chapter has described the all-important launch strategy that is focused on obtaining sales as quickly as possible while maintaining or lowering costs in order to achieve positive cash flow as soon as possible. The chapter started by introducing situation analysis and the adoption process. Following a discussion of the concept of newness, the chapter turned to market entry positioning. Discussion of strategies for launch, the first mover advantage and developing contingency plans concluded this important chapter.

NOTES

1   Magdalena Krzyżanowska and Jolanta Tkaczyk, "Identifying competitors: challenges for start-up firms", *International Journal of Management Cases* (2013), **15** (4), 234–46.

2   Mark E. Parry, Qing Cao and Michael Song, "Forecasting new product adoption with probabilistic neural networks", *Journal of Product Innovation Management* (2011), **28** (s1), 78–88.

3   Danielle Sacks, "The purpose-driven startup", *Fast Company* (2013), **177**, 92–106.

4   Cristina Cardona, Nile M.Khanfar and Jim Clauson, "Cargus: a case study", *Journal of Business Studies Quarterly* (2011), **2** (4), 53–61.

5   Somesh Dhamija, Amit Agrawal and Amit Kumar, "Place marketing – creating a unique proposition", *BVIMR Management Edge* (2011), **4** (2), 95–9.

6   Lien-Ti Bei, Chia-Hsien Chu and Yung-Cheng Shen, "Positioning brand extensions in comparative advertising: an assessment of the roles of comparative brand similarity, comparative claims and consumer product knowledge", *Journal of Marketing Communications* (2011), **17** (4), 229–44.

7   Paula Hortinha, Carmen Lages and Luis Filipe Lages, "The trade-off between customer and technology orientations: impact on innovation capabilities and export performance", *Journal of International Marketing* (2011), **19** (3), 36–58.

8   Laura Clark Geist and Amy Wilson, "Lincoln Zephyr attracts younger buyers", *Automotive News* (17 April 2006), **80** (6198), 62.

9   Stuart Nathan, "Innovation for the nation", *Engineer* (00137758) (2011), **296** (7830), 16.

10 William P.Barnett, Mi Feng and Xaioqu Luo, "Social identity, market memory and first-mover advantage", *Industrial and Corporate Change* (June 2013), **22** (3), 585–615.

11 Jungho Kim and Chang-Yang Lee, "Technological regimes and the persistence of first-mover advantages", *Industrial and Corporate Change* (October 2011), **20** (5), 1305–33.

Online sources

http://thenextweb.com/insider/2013/10/20/inspiring-story-behind-crowdsourcing-platform-watsi-y-combinators-first-non-profit/.

http://www.nytimes.com/2013/04/14/business/watsi-a-crowdfunding-site-offers-help-with-medical-care.html?_r=0.

http://www.redcross.org/charitable-donations.

http://www.westsoundwildlife.org/.

https://watsi.org/.

http://www.cnn.com/interactive/2013/06/tech/tech-list-startups/.

13 Growing the venture

Scenario: Father Greg Boyle – Homeboy Industries

Wilfredo had a difficult childhood, one that most children had never seen, but one that many in his neighborhood were well familiar with. Raised as one of five children by a single immigrant mother in the depths of San Fernando Valley, Wilfredo had not even hit puberty before he got into trouble. By age 11, he had joined a gang. For the next 14 years, Wilfredo was in and out of juvenile detention and state prisons. It was not until his last jail stint when his wife became pregnant that he realized he had to make a change. When he got out, he went to Homeboy Industries and asked for a job.

The birth of Homeboy Industries began in 1988 by Father Gregory Boyle originally as a gang intervention program ("Jobs for a Future") that found jobs for local Los Angeles gang members wanting a way out. Boyle, or Father G as many locals call him, had been preaching at a church in the midst of Boyle Heights, one of Los Angeles' most dangerous neighborhoods. While his evening walks and bike rides through Boyle Heights had, at first, rendered people speechless, his compassion and acclimation to the neighborhood eventually gained him the trust of the whole community. His rides through the projects gave him insight into the neighborhood. If these teens and adults could not find work, then what was the point of leaving their gang? The job program could not find enough jobs for everyone, so Father G decided that Homeboy Industries would create them.

In 1992, Father G officially founded Homeboy Industries and, with the program's donation money, bought a small, closed-down bakery. Later on, Father G opened Homegirl Café and Catering and Homeboy Silkscreen and Embroidery. Ex-felons and gang members wanting a second chance could now walk into Homeboy's Los Angeles office and ask for help and a job without fear of judgment or rejection. Aside from jobs, Homeboy also offered consulting, educational classes, tattoo removal and other services that helped clients re-enter society. As the non-profit's motto stated, "Nothing stops a bullet like a job".

As much as Homeboy had grown in effectiveness and reputation, little had been done about its equally growing debt. Homeboy's donations and businesses had amounted to millions in revenue. But the organization's expenses had outpaced its revenues to the tune of $5 million. Without a restructure and a miracle, many "Homies" would lose their jobs. Ironically, it was a fellow ex-convict who stepped in to turn Homeboy around. Former KB Homes CEO Bruce Karatz had recently been convicted of multiple felonies concerning stock manipulations of the home-building titan and was awaiting sentencing. After hearing about Homeboy's claim to fame and current fall into hard times, Karatz grew fascinated with the program and reached out to Father G to help. Karatz moved into the office and used his probation hours to rebuild Homeboy. While pulling in more funding, Karatz developed a financial plan and cut spending down to feasible amounts. After bringing in a new financial officer, Karatz then pushed the Homeboy brand into other opportunities. Homegirl Café began to sell jars of Homeboy Salsa to a local grocery chain. Homeboy Tortilla Chips soon followed. Homeboy Diner opened on the second floor of the Los Angeles City Hall. And in early 2013, Homeboy Café and Bakery opened in Terminal 4 of the Los Angeles International Airport. Thanks to Karatz, Homeboy is turning around its deficit and will hopefully continue pulling in jobs and positive revenue streams for years to come.

Similar to the story of Wilfredo, felons and gang members wind up in jail for a variety of crimes and many end up going back. However, what Father G saw was not a hopeless cause but an open opportunity to display his faith and unconditional love for anyone willing to take it. Homeboy continues to give hundreds a second chance at life, instilling a renewed sense of hope among those who thought they had ruined their lives forever. But as Father G still continues to repeat to those at the end of their rope, "You are so much more than the worst thing you have ever done" (see Online sources).

Introduction

As Father Boyle needed to do for Homeboy Industries for survival, each new venture needs to think about growing or at least reinventing a part of their business as remaining at a certain constant stage rarely occurs. This chapter focuses on this important aspect of growing the venture by first looking at identifying its core capabilities and benchmarking. Characteristics of fast-growing companies and management actions enabling growth are then discussed along with four major growth strategies – market penetration, market development, product development and diversification. The chapter concludes with a presentation of some methods for growing a venture – going global, strategic alliances/acquisitions, joint ventures, franchising/licensing, attracting and retaining employees, managing cash and going public.

Identifying core capabilities

In order to grow a venture, its core capabilities need to be identified. Core capabilities are independent systems of content and process knowledge and capabilities that have been built up over time. It is best when these core capabilities, sometimes referred to as core competencies, are not easily imitated or transferred. They are strategic and are a particular competitive advantage of a venture.

The core capabilities of a venture are usually composed of most if not all of four dimensions: knowledge and skills; managerial systems; physical systems; and/or values or norms. The skills and knowledge of employees of a venture is a key ingredient of a core capability and is one that is not easily duplicable. As discussed at the end of this chapter, attracting and retaining skilled, knowledgeable employees is perhaps one of the most important things in successfully growing and even launching a venture. A portion of this needs to be tacit knowledge – that know-how in the minds of individual employees that cannot be codified or captured in a transferable form. It can relate to any activity of the venture and may be in one, few or diffused among many employees. The skills and knowledge to successfully obtain the best distribution channel would exemplify this, which is very important particularly for consumer goods.

All of the knowledge of the venture is guided by its managerial systems – its system of hiring, education, rewarding and modes of interaction together and with the market. Sometimes, when looking at these as competitor advantages, they are referred to as the culture, organizational assets or routines. Procter & Gamble is known for using sophisticated marketing research techniques to identify gaps in the marketplace and positioning its brands.

Some of the knowledge of the venture that is built up over time is incorporated in its infrastructure particularly its software and hardware. The history or database of the venture needs to be maintained as people's skills and knowledge formation should be maintained even when they leave the venture. Employee, customer and vendor knowledge, proprietary/adapted machinery, old product/service prototypes and even how things are done are important capabilities that need to be systematized and retained. Some of these can become patented to protect the core capability and competitive advantage. Even tag lines like "You can't eat just one" (Lay's potato chips) or "Where's the beef" (Wendy's) should be copyright protected as they are an asset reflecting a core capability.

The attitudes, accepted behavior, values and norms also affect and in some instances become core capabilities. These impact corporate activities, the way things are done and how knowledge is sought, ventured and maintained. Of course, except for the core values of the mission statement, these should not be rigid (as discussed in the next chapter on building a lasting venture).

Of course, the relative importance of each of these dimensions varies from venture to venture reflecting the characteristics and competition of the industry. Because they become deeply ingrained in a venture, they are difficult to manage and become difficult to change if needed because of their rigidity.

Benchmarking

Besides identifying the core capabilities of a venture, it is important to ensure that the products/services and processes are competitive and meet industry standards as well as the needs of the customer.[1] This can be done by comparing the process and performance of the venture with other companies or standards, that is, benchmarking. This continuous process of comparison and searching for best practices that lead to superior performance basically falls into four major types of benchmarking: performance benchmarking; product/service benchmarking; process benchmarking; and strategic benchmarking.

Performance benchmarking typically covers venture-wide measurements such as current ratios, asset test ratios, debt to assets and/or sales per employee. The benchmark calculated for the venture in each of these areas should be compared against previous times as well as against those of comparable companies where available.

Product/service benchmarking compares the features and performance of the actual product/service with the same venture measurement in a previous period or with those of competitive products/services. Sometimes independent product test data is available from commercial sources. St Elizabeth Hospital in Boston commissioned a survey of patients every six months concerning their satisfaction with various services of the hospital and provided and compared the results with those of previous surveys.

Process benchmarking typically refers to comparisons between discrete business and other functional aspects of the venture. Manufacturing, distribution and human resource processes are typically the ones done. Noteworthy Medical Systems monitors staff costs per employee and absentee figures per time period.

Finally, strategic benchmarking is the one least done and is more controversial. Strategic benchmarking compares strategies of the venture with those of competing companies in order to better compete in particular markets. Since they usually measure patterns and not specific precise comparisons, they are not done as frequently.

Growth cycle of the venture

Identifying core capabilities and benchmarking should occur throughout the growth of the venture as indicated in Figure 13.1. The sales, revenue, profit and productivity of a new venture typically goes through stages in this growth process – launch, early growth, rapid growth, maturity and innovation decline, similar to the stages in a product life cycle. Different strategies and management techniques need to be employed at each stage in order to make the venture successful. Besides launch, perhaps the most difficult stage in this life cycle is the rapid growth stage where failure frequently occurs due to insufficient funding, inability to obtain enough suppliers or produce product and lack of skilled management. The characteristics of fast-growing ventures and sound management actions for growth are particularly a part of this stage and are discussed in the next sections of the chapter.

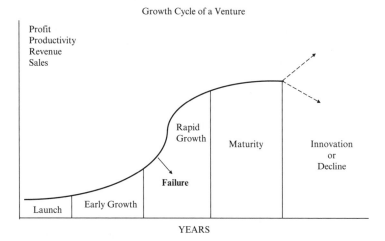

Source: Robert D. Hisrich, *How to Fix and Prevent the 13 Biggest Problems that Derail Small Business* (New York: McGraw-Hill, 2004), p. 144.

Figure 13.1   Growth cycle of a venture

Characteristics of fast-growing ventures

Typically, fast-growing companies, often called "gazelles," have all or many of the following characteristics:

- leaders with a clear vision
- retention of small company traits
- market-driven behavior
- belief in customer service
- shared focus
- being flexible.

These companies have a leader (usually the founder/CEO) who has a clear vision for the venture in mind. He or she has a passion for this vision and communicates it throughout the organization. One entrepreneur had the company's vision and the basic aspects of its mission statement on a card the size of a business card and encouraged all employees to carry it with them.

Fast-growing ventures try to maintain as much as possible desirable traits in the new venture in pre-start-up, launch and early stages. These traits include: a friendly cordial environment; a strong culture; and everyone knowing each other as much as possible and willing to do whatever it takes to get the job done. Some of these traits are hard to keep as the venture grows larger and larger and strong control and reporting systems are needed to support the growth.

A market-driven behavior is essential at all stages of the life cycle of the venture but perhaps more than any time to foster and stimulate growth. Developing a marketing plan that informs and allows the customer to understand and purchase the product/service with as little effort as possible is one aspect for achieving fast growth. Magna-Lock developed an automobile safety device that shut off the gas supply to the engine when engaged. To make the purchase and needed installation as easy as possible, the purchaser would set up a time for the device to be installed at home or in the parking lot at work through a fleet of mobile vans.

Belief in customer service

Fast-growing, well-run ventures make sure the customer is the focal point of all activities in the firm and not just the marketing ones.[2] Making sure that the customer is king allows the correct return policies, right distribution policies and the correct marketing message, to mention just a few, to be developed and used. William Sonoma allows the return of any merchandise regardless of when purchased and sometimes without a receipt. Pepsi/Frito Lay has the policy of no store, regardless of the volume of sales, will be without stock for more than 24 hours. No wonder these companies are so successful in their market space.

Most fast-growth companies like to share their mission and needs with other firms. This can provide resources and other support for the growing venture. Nature Brothers, a start-up seasoning company, was able to grow by sharing with key distributors who helped finance the inventory in the stores and even invested in the company itself.

Finally, every venture needs to be flexible in order to grow. No matter how well planned and executed the launch and growth strategies are, everything you think will not happen will. It is hard to successfully launch and grow a business. Even Facebook, once it went public, had to face the reality that newness and income were important and necessary for shareholders to be happy and either keep the stock they purchased or buy new shares.

Management actions enabling growth

While solid management decisions are necessary throughout the life cycle of the venture, they are particularly critical in the rapid growth stage as the venture continuously needs more time and money. Some critical management actions enabling growth are:

- increasing human resources
- increasing production capabilities
- increasing raw material sources
- adding distribution channels
- accessing additional private capital financing
- going public
- implementing growth activities.

One of the hardest, but necessary, actions is increasing human resources, particularly hiring individuals at the management level. All too often the founder/entrepreneur has been taking a below market salary, putting the money back into the venture to create value. It is hard to hire someone at the vice president level and pay the market rate salary plus, in the United States, a 25 percent fringe benefit package. Yet the venture becomes stifled by the inability of the entrepreneur to make timely decisions. Sometimes below market salaries can be negotiated with stock in the venture that should be vested over a three-year period to help ensure the individual will stay and grow the venture. Jameson Inns knew they had to hire a high-level marketing manager to grow the hotel chain from 40 hotels. The addition of this manager and other resources allowed the chain to grow the number of hotels substantially before selling to a private equity firm.

Growth of a venture almost always puts strain on its ability to produce/supply the amount of product/service needed. This is not particularly the case for business to consumer ventures and consumer non-durable goods where a single store will take 12 of one item. Illumination Inc., a venture producing and selling Rainbow decals and stickies, needed to scramble to be able to supply the quality demanded by the 320 stores in the Zayre Corporation chain as well as the Toys R Us toy chain nationwide. Similarly, La Bella Terre, producer of flavored organic sugars, will have to be able to supply 12 of each of six flavors when the distribution expands nationally throughout the United States from the six stores in Arizona it is currently in.

When increased production capabilities are needed for growth, this is often accompanied by an increased need of supply for the production. Dumas Markt H.K. needed to increase its supply of lower grade Tokaji wines when the distribution system to Moscow expanded to other cities in Russia as well.

Particularly in growing a business to consumer venture almost always requires adding distribution channels. This of course requires management time and resources such as slotting allowances and increased inventory. Polymer Technology, the maker and distributor of the Boston Lens and more importantly the Boston Lens cleaning and soaking solutions, needed to expand its distribution in drugstores and large box stores as the company rolled out its lens throughout Canada and then the United States before being purchased by Bausch & Lomb.

The last two management decisions involve accessing additional capital as a growing business never has enough money. This is often done through accessing additional sources of private capital and in fewer cases going public – having an initial public offering and becoming a publicly traded company. The latter will be covered as a growth activity later in this chapter. Often, a variety of private enterprise capital is obtained to fund the growth. This can be in the form of debt and equity as discussed in Chapter 11. Frequently, this takes the form of borrowing on factory accounts receivable particularly if they are from well-known distributors/retailers and obtaining equity from private investors (angels).

Growth strategies

The successful launching of the venture, discussed in Chapter 12, frequently provides an opportunity to grow the venture through one of four growth strategies: increasing sales in the existing market (market penetration strategy); increasing sales by entering new markets (market development strategy); increasing sales by developing and selling new products/services (product/service development strategy); and/or selling a new product(s)/service(s) to new markets (diversification strategy).

A market penetration strategy for growth focuses on the existing product(s)/service(s) of the venture in its existing market(s). This means concentrating on getting the customer to buy more of the product by taking more market share from competitors. It is often employed in business to business markets where a supplier has less than 100 percent of the order of a particular product from a customer. Arnolite Pallet Company, maker of quality plastic molded pallets for production and/ or shipping, always attempted to secure more than supplying just one third to one half of the pallets ordered by a customer after the customer was satisfied with the quality and delivery of the product.

Growing by selling the existing product(s) to new customers is employing a market development strategy. These new customers may be on a demographic or geographic basis. A new geographic basis means selling existing products in locations instead of a new customer group based on age, gender or income in the present market.[3] Selling to a new geographically based customer group is a frequent strategy employed by business to business and business to consumer ventures and is frequently referred to as a market rollout strategy. This is a strategy employed by Vet-Stem, Inc., a venture producing a method for treating joint, particularly hip, problems in dogs by injecting a stem cell-based therapy. After successfully launching to veterinarians in its home city, San Diego, it then launched in Phoenix and then Dallas to successfully grow the venture at a good pace.

The third strategy for growth, product/service development, involves developing and selling new products/services to presently satisfied customers. The experience with satisfying a particular customer group often makes it easier to develop and market a new product/service to this group. Arthur Schofield, Inc. attempted to employ this strategy by marketing crushed oyster shells as a potential outside decorating option to satisfied customers of its delivered bark mulch. However, in this case, the satisfied bark mulch customers did not have an interest in the new product being offered.

The final strategy, diversification, the one usually most difficult to implement, is to sell a new product(s)/service(s) into new markets. Often, this is accomplished by developing a new product(s)/service(s) in the same industry that is vertical and just closer to the customer (forward integration in the value chain) or back toward the production of the present product(s)/service(s) (backward integration in the value chain). These provide growth opportunities related to the existing knowledge of the venture and in the case of backward integration, actually being the supplier to one's present venture. Green Mountain Digital employed a forward integration strategy by building Yonder, a social platform for nature lovers to help promote and sell its nature apps such as Birds of North America and Owls.

When IKEA opened its first retail store in China in 1998, it quickly faced strategic problems. While IKEA is focused on low-end consumers in developed markets, its prices were relatively high for Chinese consumers where Western brands were seen as aspirational products. The company had formed a joint venture in accordance with local laws, which helped it adapt its designs to better meet local apartment sizes. Furthermore, it changed its target customer to the young middle class. IKEA marketed itself as a high-quality, aspirational Western brand through social media rather than through its typical store catalog, which had easily allowed imitators to create local knock-off products. It also built factories and obtained more resources from within China to cut down on high import taxes. This and other cost saving measures enabled the firm to cut costs by more than 60 percent to further appeal to the price-sensitive Chinese consumer. IKEA was able to adapt and become profitable in China and has learned valuable lessons as it plans to enter Indian markets in 2014.

Methods for growing a venture

There are several methods for growing a firm:[4]

- going global
- strategic alliances/acquisitions/joint ventures
- franchising/licensing
- attracting and retaining employees
- managing internal cash
- going public.

One method frequently employed with the shrinking of the world and the age of the internet and online sales is going global. Some ventures are born global, meaning their company headquarters is in one national state and their initial market in a different one or, in other words, they cross a national boundary. Polymer Technology, the maker of the Boston Lens and the Boston Lens Solution, was located and manufactured in the Boston area but sold for the first years in the Canadian market starting in Toronto, that is, born global. The biggest factor that needs to be taken into account is the cultural climate of the country. Country tax policies on companies and individuals, import duties, government attitude toward businesses, government support available (grants, incubators, training), the banking and distribution systems, and the differences in the customer and their purchasing behavior all impact the new culture the venture is entering and need to be taken into account before deciding on this method of growth as well as the country selection decision.[5]

There are several methods for going global and doing international business. These center around exporting, non-equity arrangements and equity arrangements (direct foreign investment). The risk involved in going global is reduced with exporting. Often, a new venture can test the validity of a new market by exporting before deciding to set up a corporate office or investing in a particular country. Exporting can take the form of indirect exporting or direct exporting. Indirect exporting, the easiest way to do global business, involves selling to a foreign purchaser in your present market who then does everything necessary to move the product/service into new markets or using an export management firm who represents many non-competing new ventures in specified foreign markets. They do not take title (ownership) of the product/service but sell to a customer on a percentage basis in that market similar to a manufacturer's representative in the home country of the venture. Direct exporting involves more international knowledge and involvement as it is done through selling the product(s)/service(s) either through an independent foreign distributor(s) or the company's sales person in that country. Sometimes a mixed policy occurs in direct exporting as was employed by Polymer Technology in going global. The company used a company sales person of German origin and background in Germany to sell its Boston Lens and Boston Lens cleaning and soaking solutions due to its large market potential and an independent foreign distributor in Italy.

Another method of going global is using some type of non-equity arrangement such as licensing, franchising, turn-key operations and management contracts. Franchising and licensing are discussed later in this chapter. Fiat employed a turn-key operation when it sold, set up and operationalized a manufacturing plant of one of its older car lines it was no longer producing in the Soviet Union. The Lada was then successfully produced and marketed by the Soviet Union until production ceased in 2013.

Direct foreign investment, such as investing money in a foreign operation, is the riskiest way of going global as there is capital investment involved that often cannot be fully recouped if problems occur. One way to reduce the risk is by forming a joint venture, which is discussed later in this section. When making a direct foreign investment two issues need to be addressed – ownership and control. Particularly in developing economies, it is better to take control at the start and invest over time so that the government of the country is aware that new direct foreign investment may be forthcoming depending on the degree of success achieved. The amount and timing of the new investment that increases the ownership can be specified in the original purchase agreement. General Electric acquired Tungsram, a manufacturer of light bulbs in Budapest, Hungary, in three stages over a period of time but had complete control of operations on its initial investment.

The second method of growth is through strategic alliances or acquisitions.[6] Strategic alliances can be based on internal transactions or market transactions and typically involve long-term suppliers, marketing/distribution partners or joint ventures. A strategic alliance involves cooperation between two or more ventures with the arrangement going beyond price and top-down orders. It is basically an agreement between two or more ventures to cooperate versus competing by sharing the costs, risks and benefits of addressing a market condition or constraint. The success of the strategic alliance relies on the ease of information exchange and sharing, the amount and level of joint activities and joint problem solving, and the decision making balance of power. A venture (company) can have alliances with competitors, suppliers, customers, governments or universities. Some of the unique characteristics of alliances are: immediate presence and size; immediate and externally improved performance expectations; a common domain or experience base of the participants in the alliance backing; and frequently involves crossing industry boundaries as well as national boundaries. A strategic alliance can take a variety of forms and different levels of degree. There are two basic types – partial ownership and contractual control (joint ventures and partially owned subsidiary) and contractual control only (R&D partnerships, exchange of personnel, research contracts, technical assistance, joint bidding/purchasing activities and long-term contracts).

An often used form of strategic alliance is a joint venture, an organizational form of cooperation between two or more sponsoring ventures that creates a separate entity with the sponsoring entities remaining. It is sometimes referred to as an equity-joint venture as the sponsoring partners of the new entity own it according to their respective pro rata shares. This ownership percentage split varies by the cultures, national laws, tax incentives and the purpose and objectives of the joint venture. While a joint venture usually develops its own organization structure and goals, a typical joint venture formation involves the partners agreeing on purpose, resources to be provided by each partner, identification of activities to be performed and the reporting partner(s), identification of activities with substantial joint venture autonomy, expected duration, specific milestones to be accomplished and the benefits to be received by each partner. Many joint ventures do not succeed because the objectives and therefore the benefits received by each partner are not clearly defined. General Electric's acquisition of Tungsram, previously described in this chapter, was called a joint venture even though it was not because a new entity was not formed due to political and cultural reasons.

The third method for growing a firm is through franchising or licensing. The basic premise behind the two is the same but one (franchising) involves the distribution system and the other (licensing) involves the manufacturing area. Franchising is a method for growing a venture that involves expanding the distribution or services of the product(s)/service(s) of the venture through independently owned distribution establishments (franchisees) who will use the logos, trademarks, marketing materials and operating procedures of the existing venture (franchisor). A venture decides to grow by franchising when it does not have sufficient capital, management talent or marketing techniques to expand the distribution of its product(s)/service(s) on its own. There are many advantages of growing through franchising including: (1) a strong possibility for rapid market expansion with minimum capital expenditures; (2) direct managing responsibilities become the franchisee's obligation, allowing the franchisor more freedom to do other things; (3) the franchisee has pride of ownership and self-motivation because of his or her capital investment and stake in future profits, resulting in lower costs and higher profit margins; (4) more national and local advertising dollars being available; (5) an increase in buying power resulting in lower purchase prices; (6) R&D facilities being available; (7) the franchisor having a steady cash flow from royalties; (8) the franchisor enjoys control over franchisees through the established contract provisions; and (9) some limits of liability as franchisees generally are not held to be agents of the franchisor in the event of injuries due to negligence.

There are several disadvantages to franchising as a growth method including the independence of the franchisee, relinquishing the rights to the market specified in the agreement, high costs and decreased net benefits to the franchisor that would not occur in developing the distribution channel on their own.

Licensing is similar to franchising but focuses on the manufacturing/ production side of the business as well as the market side. As such, it is a much broader agreement between two partners but provides a nice way to grow a venture. Favorable circumstances for licensing include: (1) venture lacks capital, managerial resources, knowledge or commitment in a market; (2) venture wants to test the viability of a market; (3) technology is not central to the venture's core business; (4) strong possibility of acquiring new technology; (5) market too small to warrant any other activity; (6) laws of country restrict other options; (7) risk of nationalization in country too great; (8) licensee could become a future competitor; and (9) rapid rate of technological change.

The next method for growth is growing by attracting and retaining employees. For a new venture at any stage in its life cycle, attracting and retaining good, strong employees is important but it is perhaps particularly key when growing the venture. A venture needs to establish a process for finding and recruiting the best possible candidates. This process has four basic steps: finding candidates; interviewing; hiring; and an employee handbook.

The process starts by finding the right candidates, which is usually best accomplished through contacts and word of mouth. The entrepreneur and management team should aggressively use their own personal contacts as well as those of their network, that is, board of advisors, fund providers, suppliers, customers and professors. While this usually produces the most suitable candidates, advertisements in appropriate trade outlets and postings on job boards can also be used.

In order to fund and hire the right candidate, a proper job description needs to be developed defining the skills, expertise and experience of the ideal candidate. This profile is then used to establish the questions to be used in the interview for each job. The key to a good interview is developing the thoughtful questions that will reveal the strengths and weaknesses of each candidate along the profile developed within the legal limits of the country. The legal side in the United States means staying away from such topics as age, religion, ethnicity, sexual orientation and marital status. Throughout the interview, the vision and the mission of the venture needs to be precisely shared as well as performance expectations.

The actual hiring process involves developing the compensation package and having the right forms. A compensation package is more than money and includes economic and non-economic aspects as indicated in Figure 13.2. The elements of the economic package include: cash; equity; pension; risk program; vacation; working hours; and the medical/dental plan. Using these elements, the economic part of the compensation plan tailored to the extent possible should be developed to fit the needs of the ideal candidate. Providing equity that vests over a period of time, usually three years, not only attracts a good candidate but motivates them to stay for at least the time of the vesting period. Where possible, the economic part of the compensation plan should be based on performance, which nicely meets the requirements of any strong candidate.

The non-economic parts of the compensation plan might actually be the factors that are very attractive to a candidate. These include the environment, career potential, training and professional development and image. Noteworthy Medical Systems was able to attract a strong candidate due to its Cleveland, Ohio location, which had a lower cost of living and very affordable lower-cost quality housing than would be the case if the candidate took an offer in Silicon Valley or Boston. Similarly, the vision of the firm and the entrepreneur can provide an exciting opportunity for a strong candidate. Besides the compensation package in the hiring process, in the United States, forms such as non-disclosure agreements, non-compete agreements, W2, social security, 401K and insurance benefits must be executed.

The final part of the hiring process is the employee handbook. This part of the process is often overlooked by the entrepreneur and is perhaps most easily developed by the first or second employee hired. Having the employee develop the handbook will ensure that the important issues will be addressed, making the handbook a useful tool. It is an essential aspect when growing the venture and adding new employees at a faster rate as it spells out performance standards, codes of behavior and general terms and conditions of employment. It needs to be reviewed and updated on a regular basis.

The last two methods for growth focus on financial issues – managing the cash flow and going public. Since one of the biggest problems in

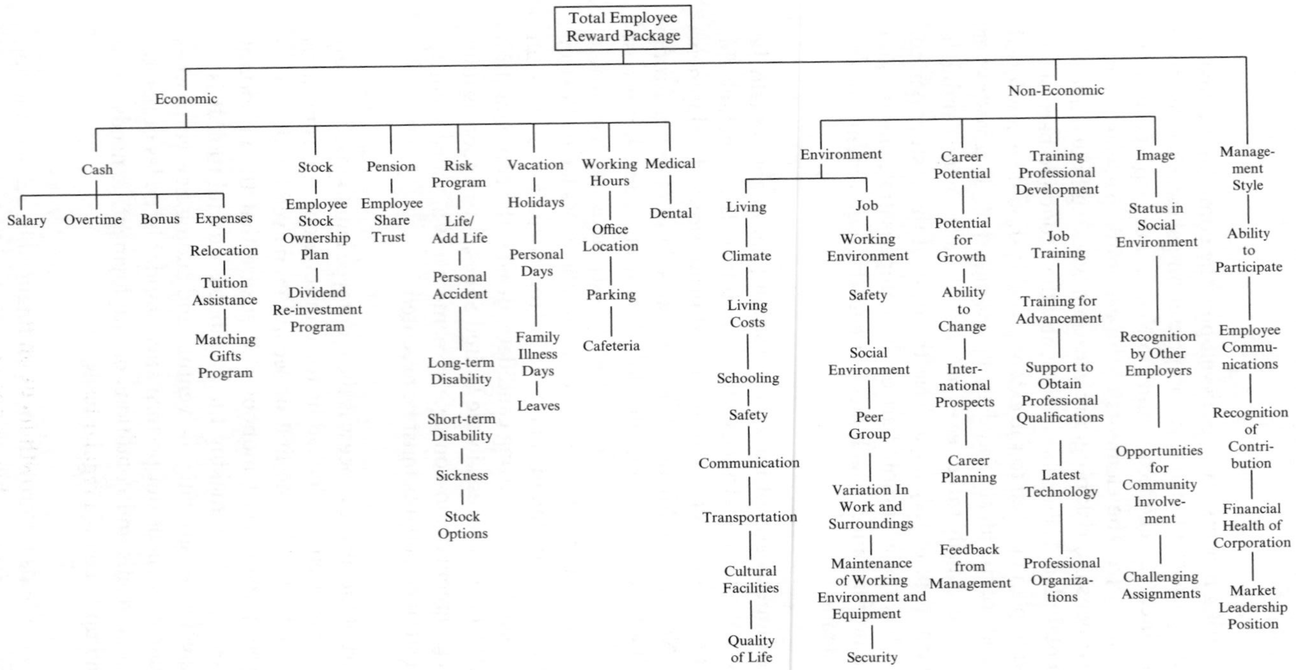

Source: Adapted from material by Gerard Torma, Director of Compensation and International Human Resources, Nordson Corporation, in Robert D. Hisrich, *How to Fix and Prevent the 13 Biggest Problems that Derail Small Business* (New York: McGraw-Hill, 2004), pp. 55–6.

Figure 13.2 Compensation package options

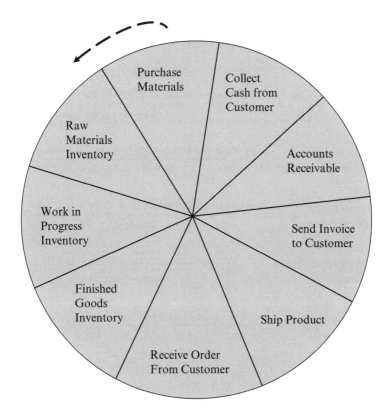

Source: Robert D. Hisrich, *How to Fix and Prevent the 13 Biggest Problems that Derail Small Business* (New York: McGraw-Hill, 2004), p. 188.

Figure 13.3   The cash cycle

growing a venture is money, managing the cash is crucial for growth. Monitoring the cash requirements and understanding the cash cycle (Figure 13.3) and reviewing at least weekly the cash flow statement (discussed in Chapter 9) are essential.

The cash cycle shows the length of time that cash can be tied up before being collected. While not every business has all these stages, the goal, no matter how many stages, is to make the cash cycle be as short as possible. The key is to free up cash for the venture in every way possible by minimizing the days in the cash cycle. Make sure there is the minimum number of days possible in such areas as the raw materials inventory, work in progress inventory, finished goods inventory and accounts receivable. Have the maximum number of days possible that is acceptable to suppliers in accounts payable. These can be calculated and monitored through the following ratios:

Days in raw materials inventory:

$$\frac{\text{average raw materials inventory} \times 365 \text{ days}}{\text{cost of raw materials}}$$

Days in work in progress inventory:

$$\frac{\text{average work in progress inventory} \times 365 \text{ days}}{\text{cost of goods sold}}$$

Days in finalized goods inventory:

$$\frac{\text{average finalized goods inventory} \times 365 \text{ days}}{\text{cost of goods sold}}$$

Days in accounts receivable:

$$\frac{\text{average accounts receivable} \times 365 \text{ days}}{\text{credit sales}}$$

Days in accounts payable:

$$\frac{\text{average accounts payable} \times 365 \text{ days}}{\text{cost of goods sold} - \text{labor}}$$

Managing these days helps to improve the liquidity and activity ratios, that is, current ratio, acid test ratio, average collection period and inventory turnover indicated below:

Current ratio:

$$\frac{\text{current assets}}{\text{current liabilities}}$$

Acid test ratio:

$$\frac{\text{current assets} - \text{inventory}}{\text{current liabilities}}$$

Average collection period:

$$\frac{\text{accounts receivable}}{\text{average daily sales}}$$

Inventory turnover:

$$\frac{\text{cost of goods sold}}{\text{inventory}}$$

Another method impacting the finances as well as the financial structure of the venture, the last method for growing the venture, is going public. Going public occurs when the equity owners of the venture offer for sale all or part of the company to the public through a registration statement filed according to the laws of the country and the rules of the particular exchange. In the United States, this is done with the SEC pursuant to the Securities Act of 1933 and can involve any of numerous exchanges, with the three most known ones being the New York Stock Exchange, the American Stock Exchange and NASDAQ.

The resulting capital infusion to the venture from the sale of stock increasing the number of shareholders provides the venture with financial resources and a relatively liquid investment forum. The advantages of using this method to finance growth are ability to obtain equity capital, enhanced ability to borrow, enhanced ability to raise more equity in the future, liquidity, higher valuation and wealth for the founders and early investors. The disadvantages include increased risk of liability, expense, regulation of the governance policies and procedures of the venture, disclosure of information on a regular basis (usually four times per year), potential loss of control and increased pressure to grow and perform.

Summary

Focusing on growing the venture, the chapter began with a discussion of identifying core capabilities of the venture and benchmarking these against other firms and the venture itself on previous measurements. Then the growth cycle of the venture and the characteristics of growth companies were presented followed by four overall growth strategies – market penetration, market development, product development and diversification. The chapter concluded with a discussion of growing through going global, strategic alliances/acquisitions/joint ventures, franchising/licensing, attracting and retaining employees, managing cash flow and going public.

NOTES

1 Sherry Sidwell, "Benchmarking for success", *Executive Housekeeping Today* (2012), **34** (11), 14–17.

2 Stephanie Nall, "Customer focus drives growth at the GPA", *Journal of Commerce* (15307557) (2013), **14** (2), 2A–6A.

3 Stephen Wunker, "Achieving growth by setting new strategies for new markets", *Ivey Business Journal* (2011), **75** (6), 1–4.

4 For a complete discussion of the process of going global and doing international business, see Robert D. Hisrich, *International Entrepreneurship*, 2nd edn (Thousand Oaks, CA: Sage Publications, 2010).

5 Kjell Toften and Trond Hammervoll, "International market selection and growth strategies for niche firms", *International Journal of Entrepreneurship and Innovation Management* (2011), **13** (3), 282–95.

6 Jang Yi, "Decisions for growth", *Smart Business Northern California* (2012), **5** (6), 28.

Online sources

http://www.cnn.com/2013/08/23/us/gang-rehabilitation-program/.

http://www.fastcompany.com/1826868/house-second-chances.

http://www.homeboyindustries.org/life-at-homeboy/history/.

http://www.homeboyindustries.org/life-at-homeboy/stories/P2/.

14 Building a lasting company and ending the venture

Scenario: Alexis Ohanian and Steve Huffman – Reddit

Reddit has continued to grace the internet with its somewhat controversial, yet impactful, presence since 2005, when it was co-founded by Alexis Ohanian and Steve Huffman. The website calls itself the "front page of the internet", allowing users to post news or other links and then democratically "upvote" links to the top of the page. Also in 2005, the pair caught the interest of start-up funder Y Combinator and received $100 000 to continue kick-starting their site. Success did not happen overnight. In fact, most of Reddit's first links were posted from fake accounts by Ohanian and Huffman themselves. But by the end of 2006, Reddit was bringing in over 500 000 daily views. That year, Reddit accepted a buyout offer from Condé Nast for $20 million.

From the outside looking in, Reddit's story from start to sell is almost pure success. However, personal hardships during the site's start-up provide a more telling story of what it really was like for the founders, particularly Ohanian, during the company's launch. Huffman and Ohanian had hit the ground running with Reddit, most days working on it and all other days thinking about it. Life soon got in the way. A month after starting work on Reddit, Ohanian received a call that his girlfriend had fallen out of her five-story apartment window in Germany and was rushed to the emergency room in critical condition. The next months consisted of Ohanian traveling to Germany to support his girlfriend with Huffman back in Boston holding the fort. Ohanian's girlfriend fortunately recovered and returned with her family to the United States.

No more than two months after his girlfriend's fall, Ohanian received another call, this time from his mom in Maryland. The family dog, who had been suffering from Cushing's syndrome, had to be put down. It was a blow to Ohanian who was living in Boston at the time, but even more so for his mom who was there when he passed. That evening,

Ohanian's dad called. His mom had had a seizure and was in the hospital. Magnetic resonance imaging (MRI) detected a malignant brain tumor. By the following morning, Ohanian was in Maryland.

Ohanian's mother's first words when he arrived were "I'm sorry". She was more worried about him than her health. She knew how much he had already been through, not to mention the added weight of running Reddit. However, Ohanian later claimed the force behind his drive to success came from the next several years spent with his mother, who faithfully continued to inspire and encourage him through her battle. "Reddit had to be a success so that I could show them that it was not wasted faith in me". Not only was Condé Nast's acquisition proposal in 2006 a turning point in the company but it was this stamp of approval that Ohanian was able to show to his mother before she passed away two years later.

It is this faith that remains with Ohanian, allowing him to continue on with his life and his entrepreneurial work. From the company's start-up in 2005, Reddit has amassed nationwide attention. The heavy involvement of Reddit's users has since contributed to several newsworthy events. In 2007, users made viral a Greenpeace campaign involving the naming of a humpback whale, which aimed to halt a Japanese whaling expedition. Redditors' (as the site users are called) favorite name, Mr Splashy Pants, ultimately won. Greenpeace's campaign succeeded in stopping Japan's whaling expedition. In 2013, Redditors "upvoted" a picture of a sign hanging from a pediatric cancer patient's window that said "Send Pizza". Soon after, hoards of pizzas were sent to the two-year-old girl's room. Ohanian remains on the board of Reddit's advisors. While Reddit is struggled to turn over positive revenue for 2013, the company has continued to chug along, surpassing a monthly average of 1.5 billion users nationwide. Ohanian has since expanded his entrepreneurial prowess to other social network start-ups, including Breakpig and Hipmunk (co-founded with Steve Huffman). Ohanian also continues to advise other entrepreneurs on the joys and challenges of start-ups. There is no doubt that his mom would be very proud of him (see Online sources).

Introduction

What was the secret of Reddit's success for the past years? Was it just the passion and drive of one of its founders, Alexis Ohanian, who overcame many obstacles during that period of time? This final chapter focuses on that topic as well as ways to end the venture or at least your participation in it. First, the three aspects of building a sustainable venture are presented: identifying and protecting core values; developing goals and strategies; and developing long-lasting operating mechanisms. This is followed by a discussion of valuing the venture and managing the downside. The chapter concludes with several ways to end the venture: mergers; selling the business; closing down; and bankruptcy.

Building a sustainable venture

While at the start every venture is thought to be sustainable and achieve appropriate sales and profits, this occurs for only a few. What makes one venture last far beyond others? While of course the product/ service, the skills of the management team, the economic conditions of the market, and consumer tastes and buying behavior all impact this, three general things have a significant impact on a venture being able to grow and reinvent itself when needed and achieve sustainability.

The first is that it is necessary to identify and preserve the core values of the venture.[1] Even though a venture can change its products/ services, its management team and its organizational form and structure, it should make sure that its core values as reflected in its mission statement, discussed in Chapter 7 – the business plan, are well known throughout the venture and serve as guidelines for the way the venture operates and what it stands for. Procter & Gamble, established in 1837, has gone through many different product/service lines and decisions including totally exiting the food business (Duncan Hines Cake Mix, Folgers Coffee, Crisco Oil and Jif Peanut Butter). The core values developed at its incipiency still serve as the guiding principles of the company. And, as in the case of Procter & Gamble, the core values should not include things that need to change as company and market conditions change. IBM did not follow this principle and added mainframe computers, believing they would be around forever, to the company's core values of customer service, respect for the individual and world-class innovations. By not treating it as a product that should be regularly evaluated and changed, the company was late developing personal and small business computers and floundered. Finally realizing the problem, it was quickly corrected and the company got back on track. Not only must the core values be identified, they need to be continually shared throughout the organization at meetings and on a card that employees can easily carry with them or have on their desk.

The next principle for establishing core values in the venture is setting action goals and objectives to be achieved and also one over-achieving goal to strive for. The regular goals (objectives) of the venture need to be quantifiable, measureable and reachable. A goal of increasing sales in the near future is not a goal that can have action items for achievement but one that needs to increase sales by 1000 units and the number of distributors by ten in the next 90 days is a goal that can motivate the development of plans and strategies for achievement. The specific numbers are quantifiable and measurable and performance-based incentives can be tied to their achievement. These goals need to be reachable with effort otherwise they will lose their motivation aspect if everyone knows that it is not possible.

The one big over-achieving goal needs to be one that the venture constantly strives to meet. Some examples would be the goal of Citibank when it was founded in 1915 to be one of the largest banks in the world or Pepsi/Frito-Lay that no store will be out of stock of Fritos for more than 24 hours. Thunderbird's Walker Center for Global Entrepreneurship established the goal when it was founded to have the number one program and be the number one center in global entrepreneurship in the world. These and other goals should cause a radical change in behavior in order to reach them. Which goal would cause more of a change in your lifestyle: a goal of losing 10 pounds of weight or a goal of training to make the Olympic team?

Sometimes the best way goals are established is by asking the right question(s). Winston Churchill changed the direction of the way the people in the United Kingdom were viewing their actions to World War II. He indicated in September 1940 that the question was not how do we (the people of the United Kingdom) survive but how do we prevail. The answer to the latter question caused plans of action to be implemented that changed the outcome of the war.

The final principle of building a sustainable venture is to develop the basic processes that will allow the venture to continue on even after you are gone. This principle ensures that everything possible is being done to create value in the venture. This means that the CEO and every person in the organization should be developing their succession and recording a history of the operations and important aspects of their position. Sales people should record personal information on each individual they call on so that this can be passed on to the next person taking over their territory.

Building a succession was not carried out by the head of Pan American World Airlines who declared that the company could not survive without him and indeed it did not survive at all. Even a most creative CEO, Walt Disney, caused problems in the company upon his death by leaving videos covering various strategic issues to be played regularly. The company floundered for 10 to 15 years and was almost acquired as managers, instead of addressing the problem and creating the strategy in light of the circumstances occurring, would instead ask "What would Disney do?" All the operating mediums of the venture need to be developed and recorded and all managers need to build their succession for a sustainable venture to be created that will last forever.

Valuing the venture

Valuing a privately held venture is both an art and a science and has two parts of the valuation process – the quantitative part establishes the base and the qualitative part determines the final valuation.[2]

There are several general valuation approaches that can be used in quantitatively valuing the venture. A list of these and their methodologies are given in Table 14.1. One of the most widely used approaches assesses comparable publicly held companies and the prices of these companies' securities. This search for a similar company is both an art and a science. First, the company must be classified in a certain industry, since companies in the same industry share similar markets, problems, economies and potential sales and earnings. The review of all publicly traded companies in this industry classification should evaluate size, amount of diversity, dividends, leverage and growth potential until the most similar company is identified. This method is inaccurate when a truly comparable company is not found.

The second widely used quantitative valuation approach is the present value of future cash flow. This method adjusts the value of the cash flow of the business for the time value of money and the business and economic risks. Since only cash (or cash equivalents) can be used in reinvestment, this valuation approach generally gives more accurate results than profits. With this method, the sales and earnings are

Table 14.1   Quantitative methods for valuing a private venture

Method	Description/Explanation
Fixed price	<ul><li>Two or more owners set initial value</li><li>Based upon what owners "think" the business is worth</li><li>Uses figures from any one or combination of methods</li><li>Common for buy/sell agreements</li></ul>
Book value (known as balance sheet method) 1. Tangible 2. Adjusted tangible	1. Tangible book value: set by the business's balance sheet. Reflects net worth of the firm. Total assets less total liabilities (adjusted for intangible assets). 2. Adjusted tangible book value: uses book value approach. Reflects fair market value for certain assets. Upward/downward adjustments in plant and equipment, inventory and bad debt reserves.
Multiple of earnings	<ul><li>Net income is capitalized using a price/earnings ratio (net income multiplied by P/E number)</li><li>15 percent capitalization rate is often used (equivalent to a P/E multiple of 6.7, which is 1 divided by 0.15)</li><li>High-growth businesses use lower capitalization rate (for example, 5 percent, which is a multiple of 20)</li><li>Stable businesses use higher capitalization rate (for example, 10 percent, which is a multiple of 10)</li><li>Derived value is divided by number of outstanding shares to obtain per share value</li></ul>
Price/earnings ratio (P/E)	<ul><li>Similar to return on investment approach</li><li>Determined by price of common stock divided by after-tax earnings</li><li>Closely held firms must multiply net income by an appropriate multiple, usually derived from similar publicly traded corporations</li><li>Sensitive to market conditions (prices of stocks)</li></ul>
Discounted future earnings (discounted cash flow)	<ul><li>Attempts to establish future earning power in current dollars</li><li>Projects future earnings (five years), then calculates present value using a discounted rate</li><li>Based on "timing" of future income that is projected</li></ul>
Return on investment (ROI)	<ul><li>Net profit divided by investment</li><li>Provides an earnings ratio</li></ul>

Table 14.1 (continued)

Method	Description/Explanation
	• Need to calculate probabilities of future earnings
	• Combination of return ratio, present value tables and weighted probabilities
Replacement value	• Based on value of each asset if it had to be replaced at current cost
	• Firm's worth calculated as if building from "scratch"
	• Inflation and annual depreciation of assets are considered in raising the value above the reported book value
	• Does not reflect earning power or intangible assets
Liquidation value	• Assumes business ceases operation
	• Sells assets and pays off liabilities
	• Net amount after payment of all liabilities is distributed to shareholders
	• Reflects "bottom value" of a firm
	• Indicates amount of money that could be borrowed on a secured basis
	• Tends to favor seller since all assets are valued as if converted to cash
Excess earnings	• Developed by the US Treasury to determine a firm's intangible assets (for income tax purposes)
	• Intent is for use only when there is no better method available
	• Internal Revenue Service refers to this method as a last resort
	• Method does not include tangibles with estimated useful lives (in other words, patents, copyrights)
Market value	• Needs a "known" price paid for a similar business
	• Difficult to find recent comparisons
	• Methods of sales may differ – installment versus cash
	• Should be used only as a reference point

projected back to the time of the valuation decision when shares of the company are offered for sale. The period between the valuation decision and sale dates is determined, and the potential dividend payout and expected price/earnings ratio or liquidation value at the end of the period are calculated. Finally, a rate of return desired by investors is established, less a discount rate for failure to meet those expectations.

Another quantitative valuation method, used only for insurance purposes or in very unique circumstances, is known as replacement value. This method is used when, for example, there is a unique asset involved that the buyer really wants. The valuation of the venture is based on the amount of money it would take to replace (or reproduce) that asset or another important asset or system of the venture.

The book value approach uses the adjusted book value, or net tangible asset value, to determine the firm's worth. Adjusted book value is obtained by making the necessary adjustments to the stated book value by taking into account any depreciation (or appreciation) of plant and equipment and real estate, as well as necessary inventory adjustments that result from the accounting methods employed.

Since the book valuation approach involves simple calculations, its use is particularly good in relatively new businesses, in businesses where the sole owner has died or is disabled and in businesses with speculative or highly unstable earnings.

The earnings approach is the most widely used method of quantitatively valuing a company since it provides the potential investor with the best estimate of the probable return on investment. The potential earnings are calculated by weighting the most recent operating year's earnings after they have been adjusted for any extraordinary expenses that would not have normally occurred in the operations of a publicly traded company. An appropriate price/earnings multiple is then selected based on the norms of the industry and the investment risk. A higher multiple will be used for a high-risk business and a lower multiple for a low-risk business. For example, a low-risk business in an industry with a seven-time-earnings multiple would be valued at $4.2 million if the weighted average earnings over the past three years were $0.6 million (7 x $0.6 million).

An extension of this method is the factor approach, wherein the following three major factors are used to determine value: earnings; dividend-paying capacity; and book value. Appropriate weights for the particular company being valued are developed and multiplied by the capitalized value, resulting in an overall weighted valuation.

A final valuation approach that gives the lowest value of the business is liquidation value. Liquidation value is often difficult to obtain, particularly when costs and losses must be estimated for selling the inventory, terminating employees, collecting accounts receivable, selling assets and performing other closing down activities. Nevertheless, it is also good for an investor to obtain a downside risk value in appraising a company.

One approach that can be used to determine how much of the company an investor will want for a given amount of investment is indicated below:

1. Estimate the earnings after taxes based on sales in the fifth year.
2. Determine an appropriate earnings multiple based on what similar companies are selling for in terms of their current earnings.
3. Determine the required rate of return.
4. Determine the funding needed.
5. Calculate using the following formulas:

$$\text{Present value} = \frac{\text{Future valuation}}{(1 + i)^n}$$

Where:

Future valuation = Total estimated value of company in five years

i = Required rate of return

n = Number of years

$$\text{Investors' share} = \frac{\text{Initial funding}}{\text{Present value}}$$

The step-by-step approach takes into account the time value of money in determining the appropriate investor's share. The following hypothetical example uses this step-by-step procedure.

Arnolite Pallet Company, a start-up manufacturing company, estimates it will earn $1 million after taxes on sales of $10 million. The company needs $800 000 now to reach that goal in five years. A similar company in the same industry is selling at 15 times earnings. An investor from Davis Venture Partners is interested in investing in the deal and requires a 50 percent compound rate of return on investment. What percentage of the company will have to be given up to obtain the needed capital?

$$Present\ value = \frac{\$1\,000\,000 \times 15\ times\ earning\ multiple}{(1 + 0.50)^5}$$

$$= \$1\,975\,000$$

$$\frac{\$800\,000}{\$1\,975\,000} = 41\%\ will\ have\ to\ be\ given\ up$$

The number obtained from using two to three of these evaluation methods then needs modification (usually upward). These qualitative factors are best measured on a subject 1 to 5 rating scale with 5 being the highest. They include such things as: the product/service and its unique selling propositions and replicability; the market size, growth rate and ease of access; and the management team's skills, expertise and capabilities. This then determines a number that becomes the basis for the negotiation.

In addition to valuing the company and determining the percentage of the company that may have to be given up to obtain funding, a critical concern is the deal structure, or the terms of the transaction, between the entrepreneur and the funding source. To make the venture look as attractive as possible to potential sources of funds, the entrepreneur must understand the needs of the investors as well as his or her own needs. The needs of the funding sources include the rate of return required, the timing and form of return, the amount of control desired and the perception of the risks involved in the particular funding opportunity. While some investors are willing to bear a significant amount of risk to obtain a significant rate of return, others want less risk and less return. Other investors are more concerned about their amount of influence and control once the investment has been made.

The entrepreneur's needs revolve around similar concerns, such as the degree and mechanisms of control, the amount of financing needed and the goals for the particular firm. Before negotiating the terms and the structure of the deal with the venture capitalist, the entrepreneur should assess the relative importance of these concerns to negotiate most strategically. Both the investor and the entrepreneur should feel comfortable with the final deal structure, and a good working relationship needs to be established to deal with any future problems that may arise.

Managing the downside

Sometimes during the life cycle of a venture, discussed in Chapter 13, there frequently is a downside, which can be for a short period of time or fatal to the venture's sustainability. This is often due to poisoning of the vision/direction of the venture frequently caused by the idea and the venture at that time being based on anything but a realistic, interactive appraisal of the market. This occurred with Facebook after it went public at $38 per share, watching its stock fall to a low $19 per share with some feeling the company would fail due to the lack of focus on revenue. The goal for every venture is to reach convergence between the market and the idea and to survive and grow. Some problems causing this poisoning and lack of convergence include truly believing without a basis that enough market will be obtained in time before the money runs out due in part to low or inadequate market research. Most frequently the market acceptance rate falls short of the expectations of the entrepreneur for the venture. Some signs indicating that the convergence is not occurring include: when customers continually analyze all the options available; when there are very long gaps between sales with customers; when the big deal is also about to happen; when the order is much less than the forecasted one; when customers are still doing proof of concept testing; and when all the sales reports are happy and optimistic about the future but there are no present sales to report. When these occur, you cannot bury your head in the sand but need to take one of the actions described in the next section of this chapter as the CEO must drive the process by focusing on milestones to extract value, keeping the technology and venture alive and protecting the employees and investors as much as possible.

Mergers

A merger – or a transaction involving two, or possible more, companies in which only one company survives – is another method of expanding a venture. Acquisitions are so similar to mergers that at times the two terms are used interchangeably. A key concern in any merger (acquisition) is the legality of the purchase. The Department of Justice in the United States frequently issues guidelines for horizontal, vertical and conglomerate mergers that further define the interpretation that will be made in enforcing the Sherman Act and Clayton Act. Since the guidelines are extensive and technical, the entrepreneur should secure adequate legal advice when any issues arise.

Why should an entrepreneur merge? There are both defensive and offensive strategies for a merger. Merger motivations range from survival to protection to diversification to growth. When some technical obsolescence, market or raw material loss or deterioration of the capital structure has occurred in the entrepreneur's venture, a merger may be the only means for survival. The merger can also protect against market encroachment, product innovation or an unwarranted takeover. A merger can provide a great deal of diversification as well as growth in market, technology, financial and managerial strength.

How does a merger take place? It requires sound planning by the entrepreneur. The merger objectives, particularly those dealing with earnings, must be spelled out with the resulting gains for the owners of both companies delineated. Also, the entrepreneur must carefully evaluate the other company's management to ensure that, if retained, it would be competent in developing the growth and future of the combined entity. The value and appropriateness of the existing resources should also be determined. In essence, this involves a careful analysis of both companies to ensure that the weaknesses of one do not compound those of the other. Finally, the entrepreneur should work toward establishing a climate of mutual trust to help minimize any possible management threat or turbulence.

The same methods for valuing an acquisition candidate can be used to determine the value of a merger candidate. The process involves looking at the synergistic product/market position, the new domestic or international market position and any undervalued financial strength, whether or not the company is skilled in a related industry and any underexploited company asset.[3]

Selling the business

There are a number of alternatives available for selling the venture. Some are straightforward and others more complex. Each of these methods – direct sale, management buyout and leverage buyout – should be carefully considered.

A direct sale is the most common way for the entrepreneur and investors to exit the venture. The sale can be to a private equity firm or a larger company that can infuse capital and management expertise as well as provide opportunities enabling the company to grow and obtain greater value.

Some important considerations of any business sale are the amount and form of payment the buyer will use. A business is purchased using notes based on future profits. If the new owners fail, the seller may receive little or no payment and possibly may have to take back a company struggling to survive.

Business brokers, though rarely helpful, are an option since selling a business takes time away from running it. Brokers can be discreet about a sale and may have an established network to get the word around. Brokers can earn a commission from the sale of a business based on a sliding scale starting at about 10 percent for the first $200 000. Essential to selling a business is its historical profit and loss statements and a business plan (discussed in Chapter 7).

As indicated earlier, an entrepreneur may find that selling out to a larger company can provide much-needed resources to achieve important market goals. It has also become a more common exit strategy given that initial public offerings (IPOs), the more traditional growth funding option, have become more rare given the current economic environment.

Gurbaksh Chahal, a very successful serial entrepreneur, has started and sold two businesses to larger companies. Each time he was able to use resources from the sale to start a new venture. His first endeavor at the age of 16 was ClickAgents, an advertising network that focused on performance-based advertising. At the age of 18, he sold this business to ValueClick for $40 million, an all-stock merger. Chahal had a three-year non-compete agreement with ValueClick. After the three years, he started Blue Lithium that specialized in behavioral targeting of banner advertising. It tracked web users' online response habits. In 2007, he sold this company to Yahoo for $300 million in cash and remained as CEO during the transition period. In 2009, Chahal started his third venture, gWallet, an advertising company that focused on bringing brands into social media. After raising $12.5 million in venture financing and after his non-compete agreement expired, he rebranded the company as RadiumOne and launched an advertising network that focused on overlaying social and intent data together. In 2011, his company raised another $21 million after investors valued this company at $200 million.[4]

In addition to a large company, private equity firms also acquire entire companies, sometimes for building greater value in them and reselling or going public and sometimes to continue with other synergistic firms to create greater value. Kohlberg Kravis Roberts (KKR), a large private equity firm, purchased Miller Brewing Company as well as Chrysler Corporation. The intention was to increase value in both companies so that exit may be made at a higher value than the payment. Jameson Inns, a chain of 120 40–80-room hotels, was purchased by a private equity firm to combine with an already acquired extended stay company in putting together a package that will have higher value than the purchase price upon their exit.

Sometimes the entrepreneur only wants to sell or transfer the venture to loyal, key employees. This form of sale – management buyout – usually involves a sale of the venture for some predetermined negotiated price. To establish a price, all the assets are appraised as well as the goodwill value established from past revenue.

Sale of a venture to key employees can be for cash or it can be financed in any number of ways. A cash sale is unlikely if the value of the business is substantial. Financing the sale of the venture can be accomplished through a bank or the entrepreneur. This may be more desirable to the entrepreneur in that the stream of income from the sale would be spread out over a determined period of time, enhancing the cash flow of the firm and lessening the tax impact. Another method of selling the venture would be to use stock as the method of transfer. The managers buying the business may sell non-voting or voting stock to other investors. These funds would then be used as a full or partial payment for the venture. The reason that other investors are interested in buying stock or that a bank would lend the managers money is that the business is continuing with the same management team and with its established track record.

Closing the doors

Sometimes when there is no company or private equity firm or employees interested in buying the company, the venture just closes down. This occurs particularly when a venture is in a market that is shrinking or the venture cannot get the traction and sales needed to sustain itself and grow. Also, sometimes the entrepreneur just tires of the business and sees much more opportunity in a new idea/market. This occurred in the case of Dumas Markt H.K. who closed down their business of exporting Hungarian wines to the United States when the entrepreneurs got tired of trying to grow and sustain the company and found something new they both really liked and that had an opportunity to be a unique, solid venture.

Six Flags Entertainment Corporation began as "Six Flags over Texas" in 1961 as a Western-styled Texas theme park. The firm has since grown to own the largest number of properties of any amusement park. However, it has not always been a profitable business. Six Flags filed for Chapter 11 bankruptcy in June 2009, unable to service its $2.4 billion debt due to the decreased ticket sales during the recession. It emerged from bankruptcy in May 2010 with some of its larger creditors taking control of the company, leaving a 15 percent stake for the management. The company filed an IPO the following month. The stock price almost tripled in less than two years due to both increased sales and reorganization to a more sound capital structure. Today, Six Flags Entertainment Corporation is again the largest regional theme park in the world with 18 properties and over $1 billion in revenue.

Bankruptcy

Ending the venture through bankruptcy depends to a significant extent on the bankruptcy laws of the country. Some countries do not even have bankruptcy laws. Other countries have bankruptcy laws that are so difficult that the venture should not have been located there in the first place. In this situation, many owners just exit the country, leaving the company and its assets there.

Since failure is common to many ventures, the bankruptcy laws of a country are important to an entrepreneur. The Small Business Administration estimates that about half of the companies started in the United States fail within the first five years.[5] Given this, it is important to understand the issues involved in bankruptcy and bankruptcy may provide the opportunity to use the bankruptcy options to get the company back on solid financial ground.

The most common type of business bankruptcy is Chapter 7, or liquidation, which accounted for about 70 percent of the total in 2011. Chapter 11 bankruptcy provides an opportunity for a business to reorganize, prepare a new business plan (acceptable to the courts) and then, with time and achievement of new goals, to return to normal business operation. These bankruptcies represented about 21 percent of all business filings in 2011. The remaining business bankruptcies (about 9 percent) are Chapter 13 filings, which allow creditors to be repaid in an agreed-upon installment plan.[6]

Bankruptcy may not always mean the end of a business since it can offer an opportunity to reorganize under Chapter 11 or merge with another company. The results of each bankruptcy filing can be quite different because of the nature of the business or the uniqueness of an industry.

A Chapter 11 filing is designed to allow a company to reorganize and then emerge with its operations again, such as occurred in the case of Continental Airlines and Delta Air Lines in their history. In the case of The Sharper Image, it filed for Chapter 11 bankruptcy in February 2008. Its intent was to close 90 of its 184 stores to save significant operating costs. Under Chapter 11, firms can remain under court control for a certain period of time. The management of The Sharper Image felt that there was not enough time to finance the restocking of the remaining stores, so the company instead chose liquidation to retain some value in the assets. Other retailers such as Wickes Furniture, Whitehall Jewelers, Levitz and Bombay Company acted similarly. American Airlines merged with US Airways to come out of bankruptcy.

In 2011, Think Global AS, a leading manufacturer of pure electric cars, was purchased by Boris Zingarevich, a successful international technology entrepreneur. The Norwegian carmaker declared Chapter 11 bankruptcy after failing to raise much-needed capital. Unable to resolve its financial issues, the company was offered for sale. Zingarevich, whose investment operations are based in Russia, was the winning bidder.

After winning the bid, Zingarevich signed a partnership agreement with a leading US automotive battery maker. He believed that with this partnership and with Europe's top automobile engineering, the new company would be very competitive in the global market.[7]

In February 2004, disaster struck for 72 franchise stores when Ground Round Grill & Bar announced that it was filing for bankruptcy. The franchise stores were owned by local proprietors under a license from the chain. The company also owned 59 restaurants. Founded in 1969, the restaurant had been a pioneer in the casual dining industry but now was faced with debt to unsecured creditors of between $10 million and $50 million. Sell-offs of a number of the restaurants had provided some funds, but any ability to survive the bankruptcy hit a snag when financing was delayed and the company defaulted on its loan payments. The franchisees, however, made some quick and innovative decisions and decided to organize themselves into a cooperative. With this new organization, the Independent Owners Cooperative, LLC, they were able to raise some internal and external funds to buy the brand from the bankruptcy court. In early 2011, the cooperative announced that it had become debt free after making its final bank payment. The cooperative operates about 30 restaurants located in 12 states. The new business model of a cooperative seems to be working as a number of the original franchise owners have now opened new restaurants.[8]

As the preceding examples indicate, bankruptcy is serious business and requires some important understanding of its applications. The Bankruptcy Act of 1978 (with amendments added in 1984 and 2005) was designed to ensure a fair distribution of assets to creditors, to protect debtors from unfair depletion of assets and to protect debtors from unfair demands by creditors. The Bankruptcy Act provides three alternative provisions for a firm near or at a position of insolvency: (1) reorganization, or Chapter 11 bankruptcy; (2) extended time payment, or Chapter 13 bankruptcy; and (3) liquidation, or Chapter 7 bankruptcy. All attempt to protect the troubled venture and managers as well as provide a reasonable way to organize payments to debtors or to end the venture.

Chapter 11 – reorganization – is the least severe alternative to bankruptcy. In this situation, the venture is given time to pay its debts. Usually this situation results when a venture has cash flow problems and creditors begin to pressure the firm with lawsuits. The entrepreneur feels that, with some time, the business can become more solvent and liquid to meet its debt requirements. Even though the time period is fixed and sometimes too short for effective reorganization, this is still in the best interests of a company that has a chance to become solvent to seek protection under this option.

A major creditor, any party who has an interest or a group of creditors will usually present the case to the court. Then a plan for reorganization will be prepared to indicate how the business will be turned around. The plan will divide the debt and ownership interests into two groups: those who will be affected by the plan and those who will not. It will then specify whose interests will be affected and how payments will be made.

Once the plan is completed, it must be approved by the court. All bankruptcies in the United States are handled by the US Bankruptcy Court, whose powers were restructured under the Bankruptcy Amendments and Federal Judgeship Act of 1984. Approval of the plan also requires that all creditors and owners agree to comply with the reorganization plan as presented to the courts. The decisions made in the reorganization plan generally are one or a combination of the following:

• Extension. This occurs when two or more of the largest creditors agree to postpone any claims. This acts as a stimulus for smaller creditors to also agree to the plan.
• Substitution. If the future potential of the venture looks promising enough, it may be possible to exchange stock or something else for the existing debt.
• Composition settlement. The debt is pro-rated to the creditors as a settlement for any debt.

Under Chapter 13 bankruptcy, the individual creates a five-year repayment plan under court supervision. In each case, a court-appointed trustee receives money from the debtor and then is responsible for making scheduled payments to all creditors. According to the Bankruptcy Institute, about two of every three Chapter 13 filers ultimately fail to meet their planned obligations, thus resulting in a Chapter 7 filing.

Chapter 7 – liquidation – the most extreme case of bankruptcy, requires the entrepreneur to liquidate, either voluntarily or involuntarily, all non-exempt assets of the business.

If the entrepreneur files a voluntary bankruptcy petition under Chapter 7, it constitutes a determination that his or her venture is bankrupt. Usually the courts will also require a current income and expense statement.

Some of the key issues and requirements under the involuntary bankruptcy focus on debts not being paid as they become due. An involuntary bankruptcy can be very complicated and take a long time to resolve. However, liquidation is in the best interests of the entrepreneur if there is no hope of recovering from the situation.

Entrepreneurs want to avoid bankruptcy if at all possible. Yet, some often ignore these warning signs and in effect put their head in the sand.[9] These warning signs include: lax financial management until no explanation of how the money is being spent; no documentation or explanation of major transactions; increasing the amount and time of cash discounts; accepting unprofitable business; not paying payroll or other taxes; suppliers demanding payment in cash and sometimes upfront before shipping; banks requesting subordination of debt; and losing customers and employees. When these warning signs are seen, actions can be taken in most cases to turn the venture around without filing for bankruptcy. This is usually accomplished through aggressive hands-on management, communicating with employees and getting employees energized and focused on bringing the venture back to a position of market and financial stability and then growth. This requires open, honest communication and all the issues identified. A realistic plan must be formulated and executed, implementing strategies to increase sales and reduce costs.

Summary

This chapter has focused on building a lasting sustainable company and ending the venture. First, the three issues in building a lasting sustainable company were discussed: identifying and protecting core values, developing goals and strategies and developing sustainable operating mechanisms. Then, the valuation techniques for quantitatively valuing the company along with the qualitative valuation factors were presented. Following a discussion of managing the downside of the venture, several ways to exit the company were discussed – merger and direct sale to a company, private equity firm or employees. The chapter closed by discussing closing down and the three forms of bankruptcy in the United States – Chapter 11, Chapter 13 and Chapter 7.

NOTES

1 Michael Barnett, "Ben & Jerry's says start-ups must begin with values", *Marketing Week (Online Edition)* (24 May 2012), available at http://www.marketingweek.co.uk/news/ben-and-jerrys-say-start-ups-must-begin-with-values/4001864.article (accessed 24 February 2014).

2 Tarek Miloud, Arild Aspelund and Mathieu Cabrol, "Start-up valuation by venture capitalists: an empirical study", *Venture Capital* (2012), **14** (2/3), 151–74.

3 Akbar Zaheer, Xavier Castañer and David Souder, "Synergy sources, target autonomy, and integration in acquisitions", *Journal of Management* (2013), **39** (3), 604–32.

4 See Arik Hesseldahl, Olga Kharif, Douglas MacMillan and Rachael King, "Best young tech entrepreneurs 2010: the finalists" (20 April 2010), available at http://www.bloombergbusinessweek.com (accessed 18 February 2014); Ari Levy and Cory Johnson, "RadiumOne raises $21 million backers led by Crosslink" (10 March 2011), available at http://www.gloombergbusinessweek.com (accessed 18 February 2014).

5 http://www.sba.gov/sites/default/files/sbfaq.pdf (accessed 30 March 2013).

6 See American Bankruptcy Institute's website at http://www.abiworld.org; http://www.uscourts.gov/bankruptcystats (accessed 30 March 2013).

7 Steve Barclay, "Electric car maker THINK resets for a new start", *Automotive Industries* (July 2011), 9.

8 Carlye Adler, "The grand rebound", *Fortune Small Business* (February 2005), 56–60; "Ground Round franchise group to become debt free later this month", *Associated Press Newswire* (16 April 2011); Ground Round website at http://www.groundround.com (accessed 18 February 2014).

9 Sean Wengel, "How to recognise the 10 warning signs of insolvency", *Charter* (2012), **83** (11), 38–9.

Online sources

http://alexisohanian.com/keep-calm-carry-on-what-you-didnt-know-about.

http://techland.time.com/2013/10/01/the-six-most-important-moments-in-reddit-history/.

http://thenextweb.com/socialmedia/2011/10/14/a-rundown-of-reddits-history-and-community-infographic/.

http://www.inc.com/chris-beier-and-daniel-wolfman/alexis-ohanian-reddit-founder-emotional-back-story-start-and-sale.html.

Index